O'Neil Ford Monograph 6:
Narkomfin

Moscow 1928–1930

Moisej J. Ginzburg,
Ignatij F. Milinis

The O'Neil Ford Monograph Series, Volume 6
—Narkomfin
Moisej J. Ginzburg, Ignatij F. Milinis

The University of Texas at Austin
School of Architecture
Ščusev State Museum of Architecture (MuAr)
Center for American Architecture and Design
O'Neil Ford Chair in Architecture

Editor
Danilo Udovički-Selb

Essays
Danilo Udovički-Selb, Wilfried Wang
Dmitry Khmelnitsky, Alla G. Vronskaya
Vladimir Paperny, Tijana Vujošević
Yury Volchok

Series Editors
Kevin Alter
Michael Benedikt
Barbara Hoidn
Wilfried Wang

Assistant Editor
Barbara Terrell

Production Editor
Leora Visotzky
Susan McNally

Typographic Design
Guangji Liu, Cheng Jia

Cover Design
Cheng Jia

Printed and bound in South Korea

Sole Distributor in Europe:
Ernst Wasmuth Verlag GmbH & Co.
D-72072 Tübingen, Germany
www.wasmuth-verlag.de
info@wasmuth-verlag.de

Wasmuth

ISBN 978-3-8030-0788-9

Sole Distributor in the United States of America and Canada
D.A.P. / Distributed Art Publishers
155 Sixth Avenue, 2nd Floor
New York, New York 10013, U.S.A.
Tel. (212) 627-1999, Fax. (212) 627-9484

Contents

5	Introduction	Danilo Udovički-Selb
10	The Political Context: 1928–1930, A Turning Point Between Revolution and Counter-Revolution	Danilo Udovički-Selb
18	Narkomfin Narratives: Dreams and Realities	Vladimir Papemy
30	Double-height Spaces: From Ateliers to "Cathedrals"	Wilried Wang
40	The Communist Egosphere: The Single Room Abode in the Russian 1920s	Tijana Vujošević
48	Sources of the Narkomfin: The New Byt and the Collectivization of Everyday Life	Danilo Udovički-Selb
76	Moisej Ginzburg and Soviet Residential Architecture	Dmitry Khmelnitsky
94	Invisible Colors: The Narkomfin House-Painting Experiment	Alla G. Vronskaya
100	Ginzburg: Architect, Architectural Theoretician, Methodologist, Experimenter, Design Practice Organizer	Yury Volchok
109	The Narkomfin's Building Experiment: A Dialogue Between Culture and Civilization	Yury Volchok
116	Survey Drawings and Models	
130	Historical Photographs	
156	Photographs 2002–2011	
166	Decaying of the Building	
178	Epilogue	
184	Selected Bibliography	
189	Biographies	
191	Photos and Drawings Credits	

Acknowledgments

This book could not have been realized without the generosity of the Ščusev Architecture Museum in Moscow and its collaborators, in particular the exceptional dedication and expertise of its Deputy Director Pavel Kuznetsov. My conversations with the architect Aleksej Ginzburg, Moisej's grandson, and especially interviews that Vladimir Paperny conducted with him, contributed significantly to the understanding of the past and present realities surrounding the Narkomfin and its tragic destiny.

I am deeply grateful to Ekaterina Miljutina Rappaport for the invaluable insights regarding her life and the life of the people who inhabited the Narkomfin; for the visual material she generously provided, and her precious reminiscences about her father—the People's Commissar of Finances Nikolaj Miljutin, patron of the Narkomfin; and for a memorable day spent with her, filled with the warmth and glow of the unique Russian hospitality.

I owe special thanks to the RGASPI (Russian State Archive of Socio-Political History) and RGALI archives (Russian State Archive of Literature and Art) personnel and in particular to Elena Tchugunova, who spent incalculable hours processing needed microfilm documents.

Finally, and above all, I am expressing my gratitude to the wonderful collaborators and contributors to the present monograph, in the first place to my colleague Wilfried Wang, without whose extensive expertise as publisher and editor this manuscript would not have been possible; to Alla Vronskaya, who discussed with me every essay, and shared her scholarly suggestions and insights; and Dmitry Khmelnizky, who pointed out valuable sources, while being permanently available for questions and expert opinion.

This brief, too brief page of recognition could not go without mentioning Guangji Liu's typography and drawings and Cheng Jia's cover design and infinite patience in furthering the typography. We are also grateful to our two translators, John Nicolson and Marian Schwartz, the latter recommended to us by Joan Neuberger, professor in the History Department of the University of Texas; our thanks go to the copy editor Barbara Terrell, who valiantly plowed through various kinds of idiosyncratic English; and last but not least, we are especially indebted to Susan McNally and Glenna Collett for their generous help with the final preparation of the book.

D.U.

Introduction

Danilo Udovički-Selb

The Narkomfin is more than a housing building. It is the converging point of the history of Constructivism. It is the most sophisticated expression of a "social condenser," in Moisej Ginzburg's words, where purposefully reassembled functional spaces are given an active role in transforming social behavior. Echoing the Russian Formalist method of analytic editing— like the cinematic "montage of attractions," to use Eisenstein's expression—it represents a reconfigured semantic series of the notion of dwelling. These new associations, in turn, contribute to the transformation of everyday life—the *byt*. In this sense, the Narkomfin is more than a symbol; it is, in a nutshell, the program of Constructivism. It is also the highest point the construction of House Communes ever reached, the vast experimental field of numerous architects, and architectural workshops conducted in its most prolific time between 1926 and 1930. The work was centered on Ginzburg's and Alexandr Vesnin's workshop, the OSA—the Society of Contemporary Architects. This building is also among the most studied structures of the Soviet architectural avant-garde, and for a good reason—its poetic density still pulsates with ineffable force.

As an instrument for dwelling, the Narkomfin was built—that is, "montaged"—more than eighty years ago, obviously under radically different social conditions and needs from those of today. The contributors to this book are trying to accomplish two things: first, to facilitate a deeper understanding of the building's primary intent, by approximating its historical origins and political circumstance, the creative context, and the specific purpose for which the Narkomfin was conceived. While rigorous about facts per se, we cannot pretend, of course, to build a narrative in any neutral, "objective" way. We cannot escape our own historical horizon, nor should we. History is always an interpretation seen through the lens and the wisdom of the time when the narrative is constructed. Second, in a less immediately discernible way, the authors try to raise interest in the reuse of a masterpiece of architecture, that is, the reordering of its semantics, while rigorously respecting its physical integrity, its universal language. The tragic condition of its current state—including cancerous excrescencies that blocked away the pilotis; half of the crystalline façade of its annex immured in bricks and concrete; primitive shacks added to its flanks—calls for an urgent safeguarding campaign. This struggle for the survival of the building has been led for twenty years by a single person, the grandson of the architect, Aleksej Ginzburg, an architect in his own right. For this reason, while selecting its iconography, the book's editors did not shy away from reproducing explicitly the building's painful wounds, which are akin to leprosy in its ultimate stage. The imagery as such is an urgent appeal for help.

Never completed as planned, since its indispensable annexes were only partially realized, the Narkomfin, conceived as a hierarchy of organically arranged units bestowing a precise meaning to the whole, was never given the opportunity to function to its best, that is, as a full-fledged social condenser. The building, however, is not abandoned; some human life still inhabits it, despite inhuman conditions caused by almost a century of neglect. The Narkomfin's present dwellers refuse to abandon it. This fact alone is a source of hope for the battered masterpiece, another tangible proof of its intrinsic universality and of its inalienable beauty. Against all odds, the still impeccably sharp straight lines of its sills and the voluptuous expanse of wall-to-wall glazed surfaces, stretched over two floors of double-height apartments, seem to transcend time. This condition is also a testament to the exceptional technical care with which the building was put together between 1928 and 1930, as Yury Volchok discusses in the last chapter preceding an inspired biography of Ginzburg.

The Communal Housing concept reached its highest point during these two years, when numerous experimental buildings proliferated, from prototypes to actual built projects. Paradoxically, this period also represented a time of deep political and economic changes that opposed the trend. The Soviet Union was moving away from revolutionary experiment to Stalinist establishment. While the various buildings constituting the Narkomfin were still going up, they already appeared as an oddity in a system that was rapidly turning the country into a "police state," as Nikolaj Buharin warned in 1930. This process, as applied to architecture, is the topic of my own first chapter.

The radical social transformations occurring in the country—the revocation of the NEP's market economy and the introduction of centralized planning—were reflected in various ways on the building proper or by the outright omission of some of its organic dependencies. From a prototype addressing mass housing, the Narkomfin, commissioned as its name indicated by the ministry of finances, was built instead for middle and high-ranking bureaucrats. The penthouse on its roof, installed for the Commissar himself, was an afterthought, whereas the dorms for single tenants, as initially conceived, were employed for housekeepers and nannies of the building's dwellers. The omitted, centrally placed day care directly undermined the emphasis on community rather than family child rearing. In other words, the truncated complex neither addressed the plight of the working class nor did it satisfy anymore the expectations of increasingly conservative apparatchiks, nurtured by Stalin. Under such circumstances, the "transitional" character Ginzburg attributed to his dwellings appears highly ambiguous in retrospect. Ginzburg regarded his Narkomfin as "transitional" because both F and K apartments were still dependent on remnants of the past—such as atrophied kitchenettes for both types instead of outright reliance on community restaurants or various sizes of apartments to allow space for couples with children (type K) rather than fully relying on community child rearing. The question regarding the "transitional" character of the building, however, had lost any relevance at the building's completion in 1930, as it now faced an entirely new political reality. With priorities having radically changed and new, quality buildings for the working class being abandoned (as Dmitry Khmelnizky shows), small type F apartments ended up housing even two families with children, further discrediting the experiment.

The two years that lapsed between the design and completion of the building coincided with profound tremors caused by the start of Stalin's "Revolution from Above." The entire Leninist state of governance was abrogated, from the replacement of the NEP's market economy by centrally orchestrated five-year-plans, to gradual reining in of artistic and intellectual freedoms. Even before its completion, the Narkomfin changed radically its meaning, from a building leading a vast movement of experimental social housing aimed at improving the everyday existence of the working class, to a building awkwardly suspended between an unfinished social project and its rejection by a rising conservative *nomenklatura*.

Opening with the last public defense of architectural modernism on the occasion of the 1928 All-Union competition for the Moscow Lenin Library, the first chapter discusses the historical turning point in the country, from revolution to counter-revolution. In the second chapter, intertwining politics and popular culture, Vladimir Paperny evokes simultaneously the effect of "gangster socialism," which led to prison and death a significant number of Narkomfin's first dwellers, and "gangster capitalism," which caused Moisej Ginzburg's own son Vladimir to disappear in 1997, apparently "kidnapped and killed by members of a real estate mafia because of his opposition to some financial plans" targeting the building.

In the third chapter, Wilfried Wang addresses the question of double-height lodging spaces, from studios to "cathedral" apartments, tracing their origin in the nineteenth and twentieth centuries, while situating them typologically between "Bohemian" artist ateliers and mansions of the high bourgeoisie. He traces the history of so-defined typology, arguing that what Ginzburg and his colleagues conceived were "intermediate" solutions between the two. He further argues that these could be better understood if contrasted with the solutions the modernist designers of the last century brought to the genre, both in terms of social and spatial logic. By doing so, he demonstrates the singular importance of Ginzburg's and Ignatij Milinis' design. He resolves the problem of the "transitional" aspect of the Narkomfin Communal Housing by claiming, in hindsight, that the latter "was not just an example of a transitional housing scheme pointing towards a more egalitarian, if not to say communist society, but a transitional building *per se* as any building is by historical necessity." Ultimately, the Narkomfin proves to be vastly superior to the "ubiquitous faceless public housing settlements," which in both the West and the East became "habitats for neglected people."

In her "Communist Egosphere: The Single Room Abode in the Russian 1920s," Tijana Vujošević addresses the idea of the solitary abode, which in some ideological ideations of Communal Housing would be that of the fully collectivized subject, where the last remnants of the family as a bourgeois institution are dissolved. She brazenly finds analogous formations in capitalist society exemplified by the studio apartment. She sees the habitable cell as the architectural and topological analogue of modern society. If one takes the Bolshevik revolution as defined by its stride for modernity and modernization, the two— the Communist ideal of the single abode for the institutionally liberated individual and the Capitalist "egosphere" of the "self-contained" individual isolated in cell apartments (defined achitecturally for the first time in Le Corbusier's theories and projects of the 1920s)—can be considered analogous. Unlike the case of the Narkomfin as a transitional type of dwelling system, Vujošević highlights Mark Meerovič's "worker's communes," which represent the final stage of abodes for fully collectivized living conditions. Vujošević goes on to discuss the Soviet architectural dicourse in the 1920s, about the dynamic, mechanical environment as the habitat of the nomadic working self, developed through the new theories of the Object [*Veshch*]," related to the ethos of the new *byt*. Ultimately, a question can be asked: Granted the analogy between the two mechanized individual abodes in the capitalist and future Communist societies, could the difference between the two individuals be more emphatic? While the individual in post-industrial capitalism is a self-referential isolated being, the communist liberated individual, conceived as the "New Man," can exist only as a full, cooperative, social being.

The fifth essay (my own) looks at some aspects of the origin of Communal Housing in Russia since the beginning of the last century, with an emphasis on post-revolutionary feminism, referring to the role of such figures as Alexandra Kollontaj, a member of the first Lenin government. The chapter traces an aspect of the development of the Communal Housing as a type, culminating, as mentioned above, at the end of the second decade of the century. It highlights the circumstances of the Central Committee's reversal of its position regarding the experiment. The essay ends with a discussion of the Narkomfin itself in terms of a montaged "instrument for dwelling" and its political incidences.

In the sixth chapter Dmitry Khmelnizky looks at Ginzburg's work as a unique case of an architect who went against the grain and resisted to the last the onslaught of Stalin's Cultural Revolution. Khmelnizky then discusses the Soviet housing policy in the 1930s, which he describes as a complete abandonment of any working class mass housing beyond primitive shacks with rudimentary facilities officially called "temporary hostels for people without children." At the same time, the relatively luxurious apartments built for the OGPU, the NKVD, and the nomenklatura are not only presented abroad as socialist achievements of the regime, but are also often built in semi-secrecy away from the general Soviet population. Very detailed statistical data give his argument a highly convincing streak in support of a unique scholarly testimony. While essentially disclaiming any ideological concerns in Ginzburg's thinking, in favor of primarily architectural and technical concerns, Khmelnizky has an arguable take on the F-type apartment. He proposes that they were "evident concessions" to Commissar Miljutin, who reportedly had advocated "communalization" since 1929. Considering the Narkomfin as a building intended for the nomenklatura, Khmelnizky sees it as an anomaly when compared to what would become the general apartment production for the new ruling class, starting in the early 1930s. In this connection, he discusses the orchestrated rites of "creative discussions," intended to re-educate the architects in the new mantra of "Socialist Realism." He limits his discussion primarily to the reintroduction of pre-revolutionary classicist models. Khmelnizky concludes with the return of modernist rationalism after Stalin's death, with Nikita Khrushchev's forceful condemnation of past Socialist Realism, if without ever mentioning it by name.

Alla Vronskaya looks at the Narkomfin's interior color schemes, on which Ginzburg worked in collaboration with a leading Bauhaus pedagogue, Hinnerk Scheper, who was head of the House-Painting Workshop between 1925 and 1933. The school's precedents influenced Ginzburg, who had visited the Bauhaus during a trip to Germany in 1927. Moreover, Ginzburg radicalized the Bauhaus agenda by applying the results of psycho-physiological experiments to architecture. He was especially interested in exploring the effect of color on the working capacity of a person—in other words, he aspired to "turn architecture into a tool of economizing and restoring" the individual's energy. Ginzburg avoided bright colors used at the Bauhaus after concluding that they had an exhausting effect on the dweller, and relied strategically on lighter color schemes. Hues were so light that they appeared almost imperceptible to the eye; they entered the mind of the subject through pre-cognitive strata, unregistered by consciousness, and thereby economized the energy that would otherwise be spent on their perception. Scheper's and Ginzburg's color schemes affected not the aesthetic sensibility, but the working capacity of a person, literally destroying art in the name of productivity.

In the ninth chapter Yury Volchok evokes the conceptual originality of the Narkomfin house as "montage" rather than "construction" while emphasizing the originality and inventiveness of its engineering features.

The book concludes with Volchok's panoramic view of Ginzburg's life, drawing on the influence it had on his adherence to Constructivism and the choices he made throughout his professional life. After a reference to the theoretical dispute between Ginzburg and Le Corbusier regarding urbanism, Volchok engages in a unique discussion of Ginzburg's theoretical work, his *Style and Epoch* in particular. This prepares the ground for a possible new assessment of the historical and cultural value of the "Dom Narkomfin-a."

Essays

THE POLITICAL CONTEXT

1928–1930, A Turning Point Between Revolution and Counter-Revolution

Danilo Udovički-Selb

The Lenin Library Competition: The Last Public Debate on Modernism

Between the year Ignatij Milinis (1899-1974) and Moisej Ginzburg (1892–1946) began designing their Narkomfin in 1928 and 1930, when they completed their experimental housing "montage,"[1] profound transformations were taking place in the Soviet Union. Not the least among them was Stalin's acceding to a dominant position in the ruling apparatus, which he gradually overhauled by replacing "old Bolsheviks" with "professional revolutionaries," devoted cronies who owed him, not the Revolution, their nascent careers. While total power was achieved only by 1934 at the Seventeenth Party Congress (which Stalin called, not by accident, "The Congress of the Victors"), the NEP (New Economic Policy) was replaced by a centrally planned economy aimed at achieving "Socialism in a single country," thus further alienating the new society from its supposed Marxian Weltanschauung.[2] With the introduction of the First Five-Year Plan, Stalin also embarked on an effort to control the modernist art movements that had flourished in the previous decade.[3] The long view was not so much to impose a particular style, as to replace spontaneous architectural expression with effective control within the Plan. What mattered was to adapt "reality" to a perceived transcendental goal, "historically" entrusted to the Bolshevik leadership. Existing, independent movements were to be gradually infiltrated and reined in. By 1930, without ever renouncing modernity and modernization per se—a declared ideological premise of the Revolution—Stalin's ruling Politburo took into its own hands what until then belonged primarily to professionals. By supplanting independent initiative, direct and indirect dictates from the power centers were to define everyday action, ultimately draining intellectual discourse of all substance.[4]

Toward the end of the 1920s, the nouveaux riches of the NEP (the so-called "Nepmen") were apparently gaining influence on architecture in proportion to their growing economic power. A telling example was the 1927 Italianate Gosbank by the classicist Ivan Žoltovskij (1867–1959), a well-established architect of the Tsarist era. By the early 1930s, the place of the nouveaux riche was taken over by a new type of parvenu, the "apparatchiks," meritorious acolytes and decorated citizens who populated the heights of Stalin's meritocratic world. Not surprisingly, they opted for conservative architecture, analogous to the one the parvenu Nepmen had favored. As a result, at the turn of the decade, Soviet progressive architects found themselves squeezed between the nouveau riche NEP elite, whom they had resisted since the mid-1920s, and a rising class that also favored conservatism. That seemed to leave little space for innovative architecture.

The effort to sustain the Russian modernist cause in the 1930s was launched in the dramatic events that surrounded the 1928 competition for the Lenin Library, when the modernists appealed to the party to help them defend modern architecture. The apparent response was the Politburo's creation of an architectural organization composed exclusively of party members, the VOPRA (the All-Union Society of Proletarian Architects). At the start of the Cultural Revolution, VOPRA was secretly sponsored by the party leadership. More than endorsing a principled position, VOPRA, an essential tool of Stalin's Perestroika of cultural and economic policies, sought to monopolize the terms of the debate.

In the spring of 1928, coinciding with the national competition for the Lenin Library in Moscow, *SA* (*Sovremenaja Arhitektura*) the official journal of the OSA (Society of Contemporary Architects) that Ginzburg founded in 1926, published a letter by a group of young architects from the Ukrainian city of Harkov calling for help and support from the Moscow modernists.[5] The group was fervently devoted to avant-garde architecture and was distressed at what they perceived as mounting conservatism in their town, which was increasingly dominated by pre-revolutionary architects who kept the younger ones at bay. In a desperate attempt to break the grip of academic architecture, which threatened to monopolize the profession, they formed the Iniciativnaja Gruppa to resist the trend. Their appeal fell on fertile ground. Their concerns were shared by the leaders of Soviet modern architecture, and the same issues were dramatically exposed by the turbulent competition for the Lenin Library, one of the decade's most prestigious projects, to be located in the heart of Moscow across from the Kremlin walls.

The competition was juried by the Moskovskoe Arhitekturnoe Obščestvo (MAO), a pre-revolutionary Moscow architectural society reinstated in 1923. It was organized in two parts. One was open to the entire profession, the other only to invited architects. Because of its conservative jury, the open contest for the library attracted fewer than ten entries. In addition to the four invited architectural teams, including the Vesnin brothers Aleksandr (1883–1959), Viktor (1882–1950), and Leonid (1880–1933), who introduced Constructivism in architecture with their 1923 Palace of Labor, the entrants included several well-established academic figures from Tsarist times. Out of four invitees, only the Vesnin team had radically renounced their conservative pre-1914 architecture. The other invited participants were the engineer Il'ja Rerberg, active in the previous century, whose post office on Tverskaja Street (a historicist building awkwardly stripped of its ornament) Ginzburg derided in SA—under the title "Kak ne nado stroit" ("How one should not build"); the Ukrainian Vladimir Ščuko (1879–1939); and the designer of the permanent Lenin mausoleum, Aleksej Ščusev (1873–1949), an architectural chameleon who was accused later in the decade by the Secretary of the Union of architects, the Communist Karo Alabjan (1897–1959), of having "an anti-Soviet way of looking at you."[6]

The new generation of architects that grew out of the 1917 upheavals was trained at the Moscow VHUTEMAS (later VHUTEIN), one of the most innovative schools of art and architecture in Europe. The school offered the students the possibility of choosing between masterskie [master workshops] directed by artists and architects adhering to different modernist orientations, and a traditional academic curriculum run by established classicists.[7] The young Harkov architects, most probably trained through these new programs, were outraged that the list of invited architects for the library failed to reflect the new forces in the field. To resist countrywide reactionary trends of this sort, the VHUTEIN's Scientific and Technical Architectural Club called for a public debate at its premises on Mjasnitckaja Street, in the vicinity of the designated building site for Le Corbusier's Centrosojuz.[8] Ironically, this was also the street where the Vesnin brothers had built Moscow's Central Post Office in 1912 in a fashionable Byzantine style.

The public response to the call was overwhelming. Huge crowds of Moscow students, professors, and architects attended the meeting, turning it, according to the press, into a plebiscite against "architects who were active before the Revolution and who belonged to aristocratic and bourgeois circles."[9] One speaker pointed out sardonically that Soviet architecture seemed to be undergoing its own "Renaissance," with new projects and buildings boasting Palladian façades.

The debate ended with a unanimous resolution emphasizing the need for a "systematic and relentless struggle" against what the assembly regarded as "the indifference of the profession" to the country's actual conditions and against the rejection of contemporary materials and innovative constructive systems.[10] The declaration stated emphatically:

[We are] AGAINST ignoring the new social and existential phenomena in architecture,
AGAINST ignoring contemporary materials and constructive systems,
AGAINST going back to old forms of "national" architecture
AGAINST building in the "styles"
AGAINST an orientation toward "reactionary artistic old formulae"
AGAINST the hegemony of the most reactionary architects in the provincial cities and the republics of the union, i.e., where a struggle against the danger from the right in architecture is indispensable.[11]

What most worried the document's signatories was a "tendency, increasingly evident in the whole country, toward a revival of the old forms of 'national' architecture, and toward the reintroduction of the 'styles.'" Most strikingly, the resolution of the assembly "[called] on the party and other organizations leading the Cultural Revolution to take an interest in the problems of architecture, and to organize discussions on the contentious issue with a broad participation of the party membership and the Soviet public opinion." The resolution concluded that only one thing could solve the crisis: to attract "young architectural forces that have grown and learned their trade in a new revolutionary society."[12]

The call for party intervention indicates how unaware many were at that time (and would remain for most of the decade) of the actual nature of the "revolution from above." The Bolshevik party, especially its Moscow branch—a center of resistance to Stalin—was still perceived in 1928 as inherently progressive, ready to support the avant-garde. However, the revolutionary disguise of Stalin's pronouncements electrified many, and even brought a sense of vindication after years of perceived corruption by the despised Nepmen.

The resolution was published in the general press. New protests flooded the editorial board of the *SA*. "The immense majority of the architectural community had already decried earlier the erection of the Central Telegraph" by the engineer I. I. Rerberg—just two blocks from the Kremlin, the journal reported. Other critics chastised Žoltovskij's Gosbank in Moscow and his obsolete Palace of Friendship in Mahač-Kala.

Also attacked were the Palace of the People, built in a Byzantine style in Erevan, Armenia, as well as the Moresque style of the Baku train station in Azerbaijan.

Deaf to these protests, the jury published its final verdict after the second round of the library contest. The scandal was now complete. Not only had the jury turned down the previous round's prizewinners—the architectural team of Daniil Fridman, Vladimir Fidman, and Dmitrij Markov, with their elegant modernist solution rendered in a graphically innovative blue monochrome[13] —but, as the protesters saw it, they had rewarded the worst, by Ukrainian Vladimir Ščuko (1878–1939). Ščuko was a pre-revolutionary academic architect who belonged to the oldest of the three generations competing for commissions at the end of the 1920s. His building's entry consisted of a peristyle of fourteen square columns with diminutive capitals, all veneered with black granite. The columns supported a massive attic of white marble sculpted like a Roman sarcophagus and bearing, without irony, the name of Lenin. Beyond the entrance hall, visitors were faced with monumental stairs framed by columns and classical sculptures.

In contrast to Ščuko's pompous and intimidating building, Fridman, Markov, and Fidman's winning design from the first round comprised three inviting, transparent library units, clearly conveying the message that they were repositories of knowledge open to all. While forming small plazas and groves, the three buildings of the library were deployed in an ascending hierarchical sequence, away from the noisy boulevard that separated them from the Kremlin walls. With a touch of classicism, such as discreet cornices, the library aptly combined mainstream European modernism with some typical De Stijl devices that were inspired by J. J. P. Oud's or Walter Gropius's early work. Frozen in dynamic balance, the volumes were veneered with dark blue ceramic tiles and huge glass curtain walls. Alternating awnings and balconies along the building's edges gave the third, tallest structure—containing the book stacks—a sense of refined elegance. Irregularly distributed balconies, recesses, and strip windows articulated its massive glass volume. A slender, elongated glass tower, streamlined in the Mendelsohnian fashion, dramatically marked the main, ceremonial entrance, acting like a lit billboard at night.

The smallest building, directly related to the street with an independent entrance, contained daily reading rooms for periodicals. The central library structure, intended for research, projected a huge three-story prismatic bay window. Resembling a giant glass bookcase, the bay allowed optimal lighting to the main reading room, while offering readers a commanding view of the Kremlin palaces and churches. From the street, the bay allowed passersby an inviting view of its internal activity. The library's contrasting permeable and reflective abstract forms acted as a neutral urban link between eighteenth-century Moscow and the medieval Kremlin. Unlike Ščuko's artificially inflated verticality, accented by aimless giant orders, the first-place design in the initial round had offered the simplicity and directness of large horizontal volumes. The one spoke with provincial tiredness, the other with cosmopolitan modernity.

Joining the controversy that filled the pages of the professional magazines, the Party daily *Pravda*,[14] the government daily *Izvestija*, and the communist youth paper *Komsomolskaja Pravda* (none yet fully under Stalin's control) assailed the jury for selecting Ščuko. The criticism directed against the jury became ever bolder. Obviously reflecting the Moscow Party Committee's anti-Stalinist orientation, *Stroitel'stvo Moskvy*, the official city magazine, published a formal protest by the three leading modernist architectural societies, OSA, ASNOVA, and ARU.[15] The temperature rose when the editorial board of *Stroitel'stvo* published an open letter to the competition jury and to its president, the People's Commissar for Enlightenment, Anatolij Lunačarskij, saying: "Lunačarskij has to tell us why Ščuko was selected, and to explain to us why no young architects were invited. We will publish the answer in the next issue of our journal."[16]

Lunačarskij never responded. The failure to answer, uncharacteristic of a man as highly cultivated and open-minded as Lunačarskij, who, by 1919, had invited into his Commissariat the art avant-garde such as Tatlin to lead art education in the country, probably indicates that the jury had retracted its first-round verdict under pressure from Stalin's strongman Lazar Kaganovič (1893–1991). Kaganovič would soon be put in charge of the reconstruction of Moscow and the building of the first Metro line. His predilection for gaudily classicized architecture was to become common knowledge. On his way to the upper echelons of the Politburo (second only to Stalin), Kaganovič, a Georgian of Jewish descent and son of a shoemaker, was one of the new "professional revolutionaries" Stalin was quietly bringing to Moscow from the far-flung republics. Gifted with extraordinary organizational skills, Kaganovič simultaneously held several key positions in the apparatus. Unconditionally devoted to Stalin, he was equally brutal and arbitrary in his decisions.[17]

The call for the party to support innovative modernist architects, the challenge sent to the People's Commissar for Enlightenment, and the media's readiness to support the protesters all speak of the depth of the attachment to modernism among an enlightened public, and of the widespread will to fight for modernism at a time when the country was inexorably sliding toward totalitarianism. Under the circumstances, the Narkomfin, rising from the ground, represented both a beacon of the Modernism the mass rallies called for, and, yet unperceived, a chrysalis already dead in its cocoon.

The VOPRA

The response of Stalin's Politburo to the appeals and protests came two months later, with the launching of a parallel architectural society, the All-Union Society of Proletarian Architects (*Vsesojuznoe Obščestvo Proletarskyh Arhitektorov, VOPRA*). VOPRA is often associated with the RAPP (Revolutionary Association of Proletarian Writers), created spontaneously in 1925. Although both invoke a proletarian ascendancy, the former was an independent movement, while VOPRA, composed exclusively of party members, was an instrument of the "revolution from above," started with the abolition of the NEP in 1928.[18]

The creation of this association reflected the Party's effort to regain preponderance in the debate. The new architectural group, a Trojan horse amidst autonomous architectural associations, had the Party apparatus behind it, something the authentic avant-garde architectural societies did not. Therefore VOPRA, using the Party channels, could spread and consolidate itself almost instantaneously throughout the key republics and centers of the Soviet Union (Armenia, Ukraine, Georgia, Leningrad, and Tomsk). This was a feat that the forty Moscow members could not have achieved on their own in such a short time.

The controversy about the Lenin Library remained inconclusive. Stalin had more immediate political crises to deal with, and was probably not particularly interested in Ščuko's project, leaving it to Kaganovič. Like many other major competition projects, the Lenin Library remained paper architecture for several years. With Kaganovič fully in charge of the reconstruction of Moscow by the mid-1930s, Ščuko's library was finally completed in 1938, probably by political detainees of the Gulag. Across from the Lenin Library, the Kremlin's towers were newly topped with red stars made of gilded ruby glass. Lit at night, their dominance encapsulated symbolically the victorious totalitarian system, as Stalin now explicitly associated his regime with the Kremlin of the tsars. In all likelihood inspired by Kaganovič himself, VOPRA was founded in 1929 by a number of young communist architects from around the country, including the Armenians Karo Alabjan (1997–1959), Gevorg Kočar (1901–1973), and the Russian Arkadij Mordvinov (1896–1964). They later participated as a team in the competition for the 1931 Palace of the Soviets, proposing a forthrightly modernist project. All the first leaders of VOPRA were either former students of Aleksandr Vesnin's or Ginzburg himself at the Vhutemas, and all were practicing modernist architecture. Mordvinov had even been briefly on SA's editorial board, and was later replaced by Ivan Leonidov—something for which Mordvinov never forgave him. He coined the derogatory term "Leonidovščina" to indicate alleged vacuous formalist architecture. The term was adopted as a scarecrow in the lexicon of architectural criticism under Stalin.

In what appeared as a paradox, given its support from the new regime, VOPRA immediately joined the protests against the results of the Lenin Library competition. The reasons were complex.

Between 1929 and 1933, when the second round of competitions for the Palace of the Soviets was held, it was still difficult to assert in public that proletarian architecture could be anything but modern, that is, rational and functional. The opposite would have sounded counter-revolutionary. Therefore, even though it was created as an instrument of the Revolution from Above, at this early stage VOPRA could only affirm the modernist cause, Kaganovič's personal conservative taste notwithstanding.

VOPRA was charged by its covert sponsors not so much with attacking or defending particular architectural positions, but with monopolizing the debate, irrespective of the cause of the day, with the party supporting it. By the time the Lenin Library was built ten years later, VOPRA members, who had vehemently protested Ščuko's classicist winning project in 1929, had been long adorning their own buildings with classical orders. Most VOPRA members had been in the Bolshevik party since 1917. By 1929, however, their party cell was fully mobilized, first for subversive work against independent architectural movements, then against the VHUTEIN, and finally against the journal *SA*.[19] Evidently enacting a strategic plan defined by the party, VOPRA first promoted, in April 1930, the creation of a confederated Union of all architectural societies, the VANO (*Vsesojuznoe Arhitekturnoe Naučnoe Obščestvo*—All-Soviet Architectural Scientific Society), with a Moscow branch called MOVANO. The idea of assembling the various movements into a federation was, in fact, first proposed by the Presidium of Ginzburg's OSA early in 1929, obviously to maintain some control over the inevitable. Since this was not its initiative, however, VOPRA rejected the idea.[20] The procedure exemplified the way VOPRA simultaneously undermined the independent organizations and tried to monopolize the architectural discourse. This did not prevent VOPRA from sponsoring the VANO a year later, with the party's blessing, taking the first step toward creating a single architectural organization that would be easier to infiltrate and control. However, unable to impose themselves on the other federated modernist groups, which were not keen to waste their time in VANO meetings, VOPRA reversed itself and began virulent attacks against it. Another more insidious problem was that VANO members were expected to prepare reports about the activity of each confederated group. However, probably because VOPRA overlapped with the architectural party organization (whose meetings and membership were secret), VOPRA refused to comply.

Their attacks on VANO notwithstanding, VOPRA architects used their VANO membership to claim the right to place some of their own members on *SA*'s editorial board. Probably following a behind-the-scenes top party directive, VOPRA's leader Alabjan managed to have *SA*'s neutral, professional name "Contemporary Architecture "changed into the ideologically charged *Revolucionaja Arhitektura* (*RA*). The new name was consonant with the unfolding "revolution from above." But not a single issue of *RA* ever appeared, although it was announced on the back cover of *SA*'s last issue with a flashy design by Gan calling for subscriptions[21] a fact clearly pointing to the unfolding drama. By the end of the year, the journal had folded. Like a virus implanted into a cell, VOPRA was gradually undermining and destroying the institutions of the avant-garde from within.

Just a few months later, in January 1931, a new journal, *Sovetskaja Arhitektura*, was founded as the bureaucratic "Organ of the Department of Housing at the Institute of Economy of the Communist Academy" under the enlightened editorship of Nikolaj Miljutin, known for his theoretical work on the Linear City, designing and later inhabiting the penthouse on top of the Narkomfin he commissioned from Ginzburg. In the new journal, Alabjan took the position of deputy editor. From the old *SA* editorial board, only Ginzburg survived. Avant-garde artist Varvara Stepanova replaced Gan as the journal's designer, suggesting that, although an increasing number of modernists were being silenced, modernism was not yet attacked frontally. Gan was arrested six years later and is believed to have died in 1942 in the Gulag system. Stalin's grip on power was strengthened, if not completely assured, at the Sixteenth Party Congress in 1930. By 1932, the Central Committee issued a decree replacing VANO with a single monolithic architectural organization, the official SSA (Sojuz Sovetskyh Arhitektorov). The journal *Sovetskaja Arhitektura* was replaced by the single-minded Arhitektura SSSR, the official organ of the SSA, with the former VOPRA leader Alabjan installed as chief editor.

Although architects had been expecting such a party takeover for some time, papers of the RGALI (*Rossijskij Gosudarstvenij Arhiv Literaturi i Iskustv*) show that it nevertheless caused considerable shock, as meeting after meeting was held to discuss how to cope with the situation. The control mechanism established through VOPRA helped the bumpy transition. A compromise was achieved between the Constructivists represented by Viktor Vesnin and the leaders of the former VOPRA, Mordvinov and Alabjan. Vesnin assumed the presidency of the SSA, while Alabjan became its executive secretary, his real power lying in the secret role the union's party cell would play over the coming years. Mordvinov took a position in the Ministry of Enlightenment, once occupied by Tatlin. It is from this position that he coined the term "Leonidovščina" in an internal speech at the commissariat in February 1933. The term would become a key reference in the diatribes against the formalists that followed. None of the former editorial board members of either *SA* or *Sovetskaja Arhitektura* were invited to join the board of the *Arhitektura SSSR*.

This victory of the Cultural Revolution over the architectural profession encouraged the Politburo to turn its subversive actions into a system. Manipulation from behind the scenes in the name of a historic purpose, similar to the Bolsheviks' clandestine activities before they seized power, was a favored method of control throughout the 1930s. From the moment Vesnin became head of the new official All-Union of Soviet Architects (SSA), he was secretly monitored in the name of "revolutionary alertness" by his shadow figure Alabjan, a mere "executive secretary." Alabjan, whose party cell received instructions directly from the top, that is, from Kaganovič, played the role of the *eminence* grise within the Union. His position as chief editor of *Arhitektura SSSR*, rounded up his power.

This manipulation, which Kaganovič practiced with the help of the party members in the union leadership, was facilitated by the secrecy of all party meetings, as well as the secrecy of the party membership lists. In principle, only party members were supposed to know who was in the party and who was not. Although cynicism and raw ambition motivated some, members regarded their Party as a historically mandated vanguard, and genuinely believed the Party was not only implementing a revolutionary plan, but also fulfilling a transcendental historic imperative embodied in the leadership. Perceiving themselves as both agents and accelerators of history, communists claimed that ultimately history was on their side, regardless of possible mistakes or temporary setbacks. This determinist claim reflected a peculiar trans-historic, metaphysical conception of the party. Secrecy added an aura to the imaginary "revived class struggle" against long dismantled social groups that Stalin had called for since 1928. Such fiction opened the door to arbitrary acts. Many modern architects saw themselves as loyal supporters of the cause, and at the same time as defenders of a compelling architectural legacy.

The last defense of Constructivism under Stalin was pronounced in a forceful official speech by Viktor Vesnin—a deputy of the Supreme Soviet since 1936—at the First Congress of the Soviet Union of Architects in 1937. The speech was, surprisingly, reproduced verbatim the next day in *Pravda*, and was received at the Congress with enthusiastic applause and laughter, as Vesnin listed systematically all the turncoats and their projects. Ginzburg himself opened a Sanatorium, the "Ordžonikidze" in the Northern Caucasus, whose main façade was an imaginative take on the Milanese *Novecento*, the architect Caneva's work in particular. The inconspicuous back façade, unlikely to be photographed, appeared as the swan song of a modernist, as he quoted memories of Le Corbusier, Gropius, Mies van der Rohe, and his own Narkomfin in Moscow.

1. Ginzburg considered the concept of "montage," derived from Russian formalism, a more adequate term for the Constructivist concept than "building."

2. Immediately after the October Revolution, Antonio Gramsci published an article where he stated that the Revolution of the Bolsheviks was played "against Marx's Capital." When he visited Lenin in 1921, he went further telling him that socialism would not be possible at the low stage of Russia's means of production, and that the best he could expect was a form of "State Capitalism" whose first accumulation of capital might be less cruel than the one that took place in the West because the country was led by a workers' government. See, among other writings on the subject, Antonio Gramsci "La rivoluzione contro il capitale" in *Avanti!*, 24 December 1917.

3. Lenin introduced the New Economic Policies (NEP) at the end of the Civil War in an effort to revive production and consumption through a limited market economy.

4. Hugh D. Hudson Jr., *Blueprints and Blood: The Stalinization of Soviet Architecture, 1917–1937.*

5. *SA* 1 (1928), 40. The journal *SA* (*Sovremennaja Arhitektura: Contemporary Architecture*) was founded in 1926 by Ginzburg. He brought to *SA*'s editorial board some of the most important figures of the architectural avant-garde, including the young Ivan Leonidov (1904–57). Aleksej Gan, staunchly dedicated to the new society, revolutionized typesetting and book layout with his designs for *SA*.

6. RGALI, Sojuz Sovetskyh Arhitektorov: Union of Soviet Architects, SSA papers, 1930–37.

7. The VHUTEMAS (Vyšie Hudožestveno-Tehničeskie Masterskie—Higher Artistic and Technical Workshops) was founded in 1919 by the People's Commissariat for the Enlightenment (NARKOMPROS) under the Commissar Anatoly Lunacharskij (1875–1933). By 1924 VHUTEMAS trained as many as 1,500 students. The school was renamed VHUTEIN (Vysšij Hudožestveno-Tehničeskij Institut: Higher Artistic and Technical Institute) toward the end of the 1920s.

8. *SA* 2 (1928), 3.

9. "A necessary struggle: protest resolution on the VHUTEIN dispute," SA 3 (1928), 6.

10. Ibid., p.4.

11. Ibid., p.3.

12. See "Protiv neprincipelnogo eklektizma"("Against 'Unprincipled Eclecticism,") *SA* 3 (1928).

13. *Stroitel'stvo Moskvy* 6 (1928), 3.

14. The main editor of *Pravda* at the time was Nikolaj Buharin, the leader of the Central Committee's opposition to Stalin's policies. He was soon to be demoted from the position.

15. ARU (Associacija Arhitektorov-Urbanistov: Association of Architects-Urbanists) was founded by Ladovskij in 1928 after he left ASNOVA in response to the Five-Year Plan's huge program of urbanization.

16. *Stroitel'stvo Moskvy*, July 1929, 6. The Moscow Party organization was known for siding with Nikolaj Buharin and Nadežda Krupskaja (Lenin's widow), as the so called "Right" in the Central Committee, rather than Stalin. Nikita Khrushchev, a closet anti-Stalinist, was the Mayor of Moscow.

17. In the margins of documents he was preparing for the 1930 Sixteenth Party Congress, at the start of the great purges he orchestrated, Kaganovič casually jotted a handwritten note in red pencil saying that about "25 percent" of the party membership would have to be expelled. His brutality earned him the nickname Iron Kaganovič. RGASPI archives, Kaganovič papers.

18. Perepiska s CK. Sekretny del Sojuza Arhitekrorov SSSR (Correspondence of the Secret Section of the Union of Soviet Architects with the Central Committee). Fond 674, Papka No. 5, Opis 1 Delo (ed Hran.) SSA papers. Alabjan, the powerful leader of VOPRA, carried an intense secret correspondence with Central Committee members and politburo strongmen such as Kaganovič and Sergo Ordžornikidze—as documents I have consulted so far show—at least one year prior to the dissolution of VOPRA and the mandated merging of all architectural groups into one single official Union of Soviet Architects.

In this correspondence, as well as in secret meetings with VOPRA members, Kaganovič was explicit about how the role of architecture should be understood, and what would be the significance of style in the "intensified class struggle," launched by the Cultural Revolution in 1928. All the themes Kaganovič articulated in secret, VOPRA elaborated in its public utterances. After the creation of a unique union of architects in May 1932, Kaganovič acknowledged to the now dissolved VOPRA members, that maintaining multiple architectural groups had been a mistake. Alabjan continued this correspondence in later years, occasionally reporting on the activity of the party group (previously VOPRA) directly to Stalin (May 1935), and to the other "secretaries of the Central Committee" such as Andreev, Kaganovič, Ždanov (main watchman for the implementation of Socialist Realism in the arts), Iežov (the NKVD chief), and Molotov (the president of the government). Kaganovič later admonished the party members of the Union not to attack the Constructivists too harshly in public because they were still building all over the country (Hudson, Blueprints and Blood, 168). Conversely, they could conduct a merciless struggle against the "formalists,"a phantom term.

19. *SA* 4 (1928), 109–10. The official Soviet history about the demise of the modernists at the VHUTEIN, and of the School itself—uncritically accepted to this day by many Russian scholars—is that at the end of the 1920s the young generation of students allegedly rejected the modernists' "lack of experience." According to this official Soviet myth, the young were fed up with box-like architecture, and demanded what they considered a serious education, that is, a change in favor of classicism and the learning of the classical orders. What was erased from collective memory is that the school did provide that curriculum to the students who chose it.

20. See "Tvorym Federaciju" ("Let's Create a Federation") *SA* 3 (1929), 89. The documents also belie the accepted notion that VOPRA had refused to join VANO as Anatole Kopp claims in his *L'Architecture de la période stalinienne* (Grenoble: Presses Universitaires de Grenoble, 1978). Quite to the contrary, it was the first to join it as the RGALI, SSA papers show.

21. *SA* 6 (1930), back cover.

North East end after completion of the building

Narkomfin Narratives: Dreams and Realities[1]

Vladimir Paperny

Our culture develops by short dashes under fire.
Zinovy Paperny

A Cultural Shift

In the late 1920s the development of Soviet culture started moving on two separate tracks—and in opposite directions. On the one hand, there was a renewed push to realize some of the Marxist ideals, such as reduction of the role of the traditional family, transformation of private housekeeping into a social industry, transformation of the care and education of children into a public affair, emancipation of women, solidarity of international workers, and elimination of the distinction between town and country, as well as between mental and physical labor. This push was coming from both the remaining idealistically minded government officials and the avant-garde architects who finally, at the peak of the New Economic Policy (NEP, introduced by Lenin), had a chance to realize their theories. On the other hand, there were signs—obvious from today's perspective but often vague for the participants—of attempts by a small group of people, who were actually running the country, to prepare for war.[2] Their efforts were aimed in exactly the opposite direction, at strengthening of the traditional family[3] in order to increase birthrate and to strengthen the control over the population; sealing the state borders to prevent people from leaving the country[4] and to curtail contacts with foreigners; strengthening of labor discipline[5] by adopting stiff penalties for minor violations and by creating labor camps;[6] and generating hard currency to finance industrialization, mainly by selling nationalized royal jewelry, masterpieces of art,[7] and grain.

In 1928, when Moisej Ginzburg and Ignatij Milinis were about to start construction of the Narkomfin building, this clash between the two opposing trends was already present. On some level, internationalism, collectivism, and Lenin's NEP were still operating principles. The First Exhibition of Contemporary Architecture organized by Ginzburg's OSA, with many foreign participants, took place in July-August 1927. In October 1928 Le Corbusier won the commission for the Centrosojuz (Central Union of Consumer Societies) building in Moscow, while the Centrožilsojuz (Central Union of Housing Cooperatives) published guidelines for a typical dom-kommuna (*house-commune*), which prohibited "drunks, hooligans and icons."[8] These guidelines were ambiguous—they endorsed a collectivist lifestyle and, at the same time, enforced strict discipline.

In 1928, measures were still taken to "maximize use of private capital in housing construction,"[9] but on the other hand, the 15th Congress of VKP(b) explicitly wanted "to reduce and eliminate capitalist elements from the economy."[10] In 1928, contacts with foreigners were sharply curtailed. This could be seen, for example, in the abolition of the Committee for organizing exhibitions of foreign technology.[11] A little later, letters and books sent by Le Corbusier to his Soviet friends started being returned to the sender.[12]

The 15th Congress of VKP(b), which took place in December 1927 (later called the Collectivization Congress), marked an important watershed in Soviet history. A resolution was adopted to develop the first 5-year plan (perhaps influencing the Nazi 4-year plan nine years later). Leon Trotsky and Grigory Zinoviev were expelled from the party following their anti-Stalin demonstrations in Moscow and Leningrad on November 7. At the Congress, for the first time in the fight with the opposition, "incriminating evidence" regarding arrested opposition leaders, obtained by the secret police, was used. "One of the opposition leaders arrested by the GPU," said delegate Leonov, "confessed that he had discussed the preparation of terrorist acts."[13]

Doors to former Moisei Ginzburg's (left) and Aleksandr Dejeka's (right) apartments on the second floor. Photo: 2013 © Vladimir Paperny

Various approaches to collectivization of agriculture were debated throughout the 1920s, but it was not until December 27, 1929, that Stalin came up with the formula "liquidation of the kulaks as a class on the basis of total collectivization."[14]

The word "collectivization" bears some overtones of the previous epoch—of spontaneously emerging house-communes of the early 1920s, of Konstantin Mel'nikov's collective bedrooms, and even of the Narkomfin communal house itself. But the reality behind the word was quite different. In fact, this "liquidation of the *kulaks* as a class" meant the *physical elimination* of a certain class of the population. As a result of this policy, which included forced collectivization, between 1929 and 1941 more than 2 million peasants were deported, and 6 million died from starvation. Despite an unprecedented famine, a large part of the expropriated grain was sold abroad to finance industrialization. The large cities were surrounded by armed soldiers to prevent dying peasants from entering, yet the highest rate of urbanization in Russian history occurred during this period (1929–1931).[15]

When one reads architectural journals of that period, *Sovremennaja Arhitektura* (*Contemporary Architecture*, 1926–1930) or *Sovetskaja Arhitektura* (*Soviet Architecture,* 1931–1934), one finds it hard to believe that architects of the Russian Avant-garde lived in the same country as the rest of the population. Events, which some historians called "Stalin's revolution" or "Stalin's counter-revolution" and which as easily could be called "the Second Russian Civil War," left no traces on the pages of these magazines. Very talented architects continued to present their brilliant ideas and to discuss technical innovation and ways of eliminating the distinction between town and country—as if they lived in an ivory tower, oblivious to the horrors outside. But soon the bombs started falling closer. In 1934, Aleksandr Smirnov, to whom Nikolaj Miljutin (Ginzburg's client and collaborator) had dedicated his book *Socgorod*, was expelled from the party and later executed. In 1935, Mihail Ohitovič, Ginzburg's close associate, was arrested and eventually executed. In 1936, another of Ginzburg's close collaborators, Solomon Lisagor, disappeared in a similar fashion.

"What was Moisej Ginzburg's relationship to Marxist ideology?" I asked his grandson Aleksej, also an architect.

"His book *Style and Epoch*," Aleksej replied, "was not about some bright communist future. It was about the modern world and the new challenges, which needed to be answered. There is a big difference between a house-commune and a communal house like Narkomfin. Ginzburg proposed a way of living, which now seems natural, because we all live like that. Ginzburg added large public spaces to small apartments, plus all the necessary functions—a kindergarten, a gym, a cafe, a laundry room.

He managed to formulate and answer a question: what should be a human dwelling in the modern era?" "So," I asked, "all his Marxist phraseology was just mimicry, desperate attempts to survive?" "Your guess is as good as mine," he answered.[16]

My guess is that, as an astute observer and a logical thinker, which he was, Moisej Ginzburg understood perfectly well what was going on in the country. At some point, he made a conscious decision to concentrate on strictly professional tasks in order to stay alive, and he succeeded. But even in the professional sphere, he had to make sacrifices. His sanatorium in Kislovodsk and his proposal for a young pioneer camp (*Artek*) show a noticeable retreat from his earlier ideas. Luckily, the Narkomfin building was finished before stiff control over the USSR construction industry was established. The transitional period between two dramatically different historical and cultural periods made the "transitional type" of building possible. Moisej Ginzburg was able to leave a lasting legacy, where his theoretical and practical insights came together in a single architectural complex. After this unique building was completed, its fate was beyond Ginzburg's control.

The Narkomfin's Dwellers

The building was intended for the employees of the People's Commissariat for Finances. It was considered a prestigious place to live. "The house was for the elite," says Aleksej Ginzburg, "although today the word 'elite' makes everybody cringe. This included, besides the Ministry's employees, writers, artists, Ginzburg himself and other architects."[17]

As Miljutin's daughter Ekaterina remembers, "First there were people working for the Ministry and then people working *with* the Ministry.[18] This was the case among others of Rabinovič, a sergeant with the Red Army, or Nikolaj Semaško,[19] a physician. A lot of bohemians were happy to move there. Aleksandr Dejneka[20] was on the second floor. His wife Šima, a very fancy lady, had a wonderful convertible car, like those we see today. It was just incredible."[21]

A plausible story about the origin of the penthouse Miljutin built on the roof of the Narkomfin, as Ginzburg's grandson reports, is that Ginzburg and Milinis wanted to come up with the most modern ventilation system, but in the end, there was not enough money to buy the equipment. Since the ventilation room on the roof had already been built, Miljutin decided to convert it into an apartment for his family and actually constructed a type K cell there. Ginzburg and Miljutin quarreled terribly about it because the drawings had already been published in many magazines. They later reconciled.[22] For his own family, Moisej Ginzburg selected the most spacious type K apartment with two levels and five rooms. There were eight apartments like this in the building, two on the second floor—Ginzburg's and Dejneka's. Within the whole social strategy of the project, these apartments implied the most traditional way of life. Still, certain democratic principles were maintained. Miljutina continues:

Actually we did not have any [social] barriers. Cleaning ladies of the Narkomfin had their apartments here, as did ministers, and all the children played together, we did not make any difference. When we prepared for exams, everybody was in our apartment, and it was 20, 30 kids maybe, studying for the exams. There was no sense of privacy like we have it here [in the US]. It was private in a sense, but at the same time we lived . . . collectively![23]

By the time Miljutin had his penthouse, his political standing had become shaky. "He was in conflict with Stalin," says Ekaterina Miljutina, "he left Stalin's cabinet slamming the door but, strangely enough, he was never arrested. Most often people who were very friendly to Stalin but spoke badly behind his back, they were arrested, but he was never arrested, though he was very, very nervous and maybe that caused some of his illness."[24] Elsewhere, she elaborated: "He slept with a gun under his pillow, saying 'they are not going to get me alive.'"[25]

Ekaterina Miljutina was born in 1936. Her rather idyllic memories of her childhood do not include the period between 1937 and 1938 when most of the residents of the building suddenly disappeared. The Memorial society[26] has a list of 19 residents executed as people's enemies (see Appendix) who had lived in the Narkomfin. Among them:

17 members of VKP(b);
3 People's Commissars;
2 deputy People's Commissars;
9 people with the title "head," "director," "chairman,' or "manager."

The Memorial society does not have a list of residents who were arrested but not executed and sent to labor camps instead. It is safe to assume that there were at least as many. In short, more than half of the residents of the communal house disappeared between 1937 and 1938. A large number of them ended up in the barracks of labor camps, experiencing the terror of total "collectivization." During and after World War II, the empty space under the building was enclosed and turned into ground-floor apartments, thus destroying the house's original character. The same thing happened with Le Corbusier's *Centrosojuz* building in Moscow—the look of a building floating in air contradicted the traditional vision of a building "growing from the ground." Le Corbusier's *Centrosojuz* building in Moscow was restored to its original shape in the 1980s. The Narkomfin never was.

Attempts at Restoring the Building

The very first attempt to save the building, which had never undergone any substantial repairs, was made in the mid-1980s by Moisej Ginzburg's son Vladimir and grandson Aleksej—without the help of any client, sponsor, or government. Vladimir's fate was rather tragic. He became an orphan at the age of 16 and decided to become an architect as a tribute to his father. Vladimir Ginzburg and his friend Kogan entered the Moscow Architectural Institute (MAI)[27] in 1952. That was the time of the infamous "killer-doctors" trial. Kogan's father was one of the doctors arrested in connection with the "Zionist conspiracy,"[28] and Kogan was expelled from MAI as a son of a people's enemy. Vladimir Ginzburg was also expelled for not reporting Kogan to the authorities. After Stalin's death, when all doctors were released and acquitted, the younger Kogan was readmitted to MAI, his guilt no longer existing. However, Ginzburg was not. His guilt was still considered valid: he did not report Kogan. Instead, Vladimir graduated as an architect from the Institute of Land Management.

Vladimir Ginzburg disappeared in 1997, under mysterious circumstances. It was suspected that he had been kidnapped and killed by members of a real estate mafia because of his opposition to some of their plans, possibly related to the Narkomfin. The body was never found. Some tragic irony exists in the fact that Moisej Ginzburg had managed to survive the "gangster socialism" of the 1930s, whereas the "gangster capitalism" of the 1990s turned out to be deadly for his son.

In the second half of the 1990s various commercial organizations showed interest in restoring the building. The majority of them had no appreciation for the building's architectural value. They regarded it merely as a piece of real estate or even a piece of land for new construction. "In such cases," wrote Aleksej Ginzburg in 2006, "my father tried to explain that the only option here was restoration. He used his moral authority to prevent changing the building's layout and structure. In 1995, we found what seemed to be an ideal solution: my father began negotiations with an American company, one of whose presidents was himself a professional architect."[29] This project, like many others before and after, failed. "The American company," continued Aleksej, "in spite of its experience in working with real estate in Moscow, suddenly got bogged down in a bureaucratic tangle with Moscow's Land Committee. Finding themselves up against strong resistance, they abandoned the project after several months of efforts."[30]

Around 2006, the developer Aleksandr Senatorov, the owner of real estate behemoth *MIAN*,[31] an "oligarch" and a yoga and martial arts aficionado, became interested in the building. "There were rumors," says Lorenzo Tripodi in his documentary *Dom Novogo Byta*, "that a developer decided to invest in the Narkomfin as a pledge of love, asked by his beloved to save the Constructivist masterpiece in exchange for the trip to the altar"[32] Aleksandr Evangeli, an art critic and professor at the *Rodčenko School*,[33] currently lives in apartment No. 39 of the Narkomfin, the same apartment where the Deputy People's Commissar Vasilij Hronin used to live until he was arrested and shot in 1937 (see Appendix). He put the Senatorov story in historical context. Says Evangeli:

View from Dejneka's (later IMAGO's, now vacant) balcony. Photo: © 2013 Vladimir Paperny.

In the mid 2000s, Russian art and Russian businesses were on a rise. The "oligarchs" found it useful to equip themselves with girlfriends, who were able to solve the problems of laundering fast money, the dirty initial capital. A perfect tool for that was art. First galleries, then art foundations began to sprout everywhere. Senatorov's girlfriend, and later wife, Alexandrina Markvo, was not interested in galleries and foundations—they already were becoming commonplace. Instead, she was given these outstanding ruins as a toy. The idea of a boutique hotel emerged. Unfortunately, we know too well what building a hotel in Moscow means; just look at the hotel Moskva.[34]

Evangeli refers to the system, which initially developed under the former mayor of Moscow, Jurij Lužkov, and did not seem to change much under the new mayor, Sergej Sobjanin. Architectural critic Grigorij Revzin described the system this way: "If you look at who owns the buildings, for example, the hotel 'Moscow,' you will see that the owners are joint stock companies, with names like 'Corporation Hotel Moscow,' for example, where 51 percent of stock belongs to the Moscow government, or some businessmen close to Jurij Lužkov."[35] Obviously, any transformation of the Narkomfin building into a business asset of the Moscow government would automatically preclude it from being on the list of the UNESCO cultural heritage sites.

Senatorov's first choice for the restoration was Pavel Andreev, the architect who had been criticized for participating in projects that resulted in destruction of monuments and demolition of historic buildings in Moscow.[36] When activists of the architectural preservation movement learned about Andreev's involvement in the Narkomfin building, they panicked. Fortunately, Senatorov decided to rely on experts. Bart Goldhoorn and Elena Gonsales (*Project Russia* magazine), as well as Clementine Cecil and Marina Hrustaleva (MAPS),[37] attended the first brainstorming sessions. As a result of these sessions, Senatorov created the "Narkomfin Foundation" to explore the building and to interact with experts. He finally selected Aleksej Ginzburg as the restoration architect.

"My attitude towards the project went through several stages," says Alexandr Senatorov. "Our understanding of financial options changed significantly over time—in terms of what we wanted out of this project and what kind of reuse was possible. In the early stages, we thought of converting it into a boutique hotel. Before the crisis, there was a lot of money, and you could work with the most expensive materials. We hoped that some crazy investor would buy it."[38]

At that stage, selling individual apartments seemed unacceptable. The Senatorov-Ginzburg design proposal of 2008 was very specific: "It is important that the exploitation of the house be designed and implemented as a single system, thus prohibiting commercial sale of apartments. This becomes possible with the creation of an art hotel."[39]

After the financial crisis, the idea of a boutique hotel did not seem attractive anymore. "Yield is determined by the rental market, amounting to 3–4%," Senatorov claimed. "You cannot borrow money in Russia at this rate, so it becomes an unprofitable operation. Selling condos gives a radically different return."[40]

Looking for ways to convert apartments into condominiums, Senatorov decided to try something radical. He asked himself, what would it take him to want to live there? Everything about the building seemed perfect—manageable apartments, great location. For the yoga and martial arts enthusiast there was only one thing missing: sports.

Therefore, Senatorov's latest project involves building a swimming pool in the narrow strip between the building and the fence of the expanded territory of the American Embassy.[41] The ground there is sloped towards the fence. In the proposal, the sloping lawn abruptly goes up, becoming the roof of the pool. In essence, Senatorov wants to create something similar to the grass-roofed Hypar Pavilion in the Lincoln Center in New York, although he admits that he has not seen it.

Senatorov's chances for success seem to be low. First, the Narkomfin building has the official status of an "architectural monument,"[42] and getting permission for digging next to it, even from the notoriously corrupt Moscow bureaucracy, is close to impossible (not to mention any ethical considerations). Second, building anything within a few meters of the Embassy may be problematic for both the Russian and the American security organizations. Senatorov is, nevertheless, optimistic: "Maybe the Americans would buy a few apartments, for them it is an ideal place — small

Aleksandr Rodčenko's photo (left) and Aleksandr Senatorov doing a handstand on the Narkomfin roof. Photo courtesy Aleksandr Senatorov.

apartments, hotel service, and could not be closer to work. We'll talk to McFaul."[43]

There is a dim ray of hope in the fact that "saving masterpieces of the Russian Avant-garde architecture" appears more and more often on agendas not only of grass-root organizations like *MAPS* and *Arhnadzor* but of the government institutions, such as the Moscow City Hall and the Moscow Urban Forum.[44]

Current Residents and Lifestyles

Current living conditions in the building violate every imaginable building code and sanitary

This amazing crumbling structure is still affirming the power of creative thinking over unfair, cruel, and at times violent circumstances.

norm. "Narkomfin is being exploited like a natural resource," says one resident. "Whoever owns the apartments is just collecting rent, but doing nothing for the building. No repairs, nothing."[45] The rents in the Narkomfin are steadily rising. Currently, most of the residents pay 40,000 rubles a month ($1,257) for a rundown place.

In the late 1980s, Soviet housing authorities found the Narkomfin house "unsafe" and started offering residents comparable apartments elsewhere. Many accepted and moved out. Some kept bargaining for a better deal, but negotiations collapsed with the collapse of the Soviet Union in 1991. Since 1998, residents have been allowed to legally privatize their apartments. Some Narkomfin residents did, some decided against it. By 2006, when Senatorov became interested in the building, only about 12 apartments were occupied, some of them privatized. The rest were abandoned, all pipes and cables literally cut off by the authorities to prevent squatting. Nevertheless, some of the abandoned apartments were used by the remaining residents as storage, with illegally installed locks.

In 2006, Senatorov started acquiring apartments, negotiating with owners of the privatized ones and with the City Hall about the abandoned ones, eventually purchasing 30 out of 46 lodgings. In 2010, Nikolaj Palažčenko, an art dealer and curator of the art center Vinzavod[46] approached Senatorov, saying: "You have empty apartments and I have talented artists with no place to work." With the help of Senatorov's management company, Palažčenko started renting out vacant apartments to his creative friends—artists, designers, photographers.

On the "creative" side, there are people like Donatas Grudovič, actor, producer, and a performance artist. He used to live in Dejneka's former apartment (No. 18) but recently was kicked out by some residents, with the help of the police, for his noisy performances. He described his living conditions with sneering humor: "Every

Anton and Polina (IMAGO) show their unisex uniforms. Photo: © 2013 Vladimir Paperny.

morning I have to shit in a plastic bag and throw it over the fence to the US embassy. I already gave all my booze to the plumber . . . but to no avail." But this, to him, is a fair price for living in a Constructivist masterpiece. He loves Futurism and would want to recreate some of the communal ideals of the 1920s: "I wish we could have a real commune here. So that everyone could live here, work on one common project and wear some kind of uniform."[47] He is fascinated with the ideas and symbols of the early Soviet past. Before the opening of one of his performances, "The Morning of the Useful Time," he requested that all involved swear that they would willingly embrace whatever might happen, even if they didn't like it; that they would carry on and not leave the group. This is where his fascination with the Soviet past borders on parody. Still, he seems quite serious. "Repeat after me," he goes on, "I renounce my name and solemnly swear to be loyal to the common purpose. I renounce all names and titles."[48]

Today, residents comprise a very diverse group of people. Some stay simply because they are stuck, having missed out on both the offers from the Soviet authorities in the 1980s and privatization opportunities of the *perestrojka* era. In general they don't like the building and don't care about its avant-garde pedigree. One of them, Viktor Suvorov, grumbles in a documentary: "They call it 'Constructivism'—bloody Jewish Constructivism."[49] Inevitably, there is an ongoing conflict between these people and the "creative" group initially recruited by Palažčenko.

Another resident, Aleksandr Evangeli, tries to explain what makes him stay in the building:

Constructivist architecture was a utopian humanitarian project, designed to improve consciousness through architecture. This "orthopedic" impulse existed in this architecture from the very beginning, and it was quite repressive. As somebody who lived here for three years, I understand that this architecture is incompatible with certain habits, especially some of the late-Soviet habits, such as hoarding stuff for example. The building has no windowsills. After the revolution through the late 1920s, a windowsill was a symbol of middle-class comfort. There was always a samovar sitting on it and potted plants, usually geraniums. When I moved here, I found several generations fighting this oppressive space. People built sills; all this open constructivist space was boarded up, creating cozy little rooms. People built second and third floors, mezzanines, etc. There was nothing left from the original space flooded with light. Even the top row of windows was usually boarded up. What amazed me was the amount of absurdity. These windows are easily manipulated, leaving gaps for air. However, people who lived here would cut small fortočki *(glass vents) into the big window panes. These vents obviously were more difficult to control, but the tradition required to have a small frame within a large one. I have no explanation, other than it's the architecture and the desire to make my space . . . accurate.*

Senatorov and Ginzburg's proposal to convert the building into a boutique hotel, 2007. Courtesy Aleksandr Senatorov.

To clarify his point, Aleksandr turns on his computer to show a 20-minute film *Farewell to the Fireplace* shot in his apartment by his students from the Rodčenko school. The film has a certain similarity with Grudovi's *The Morning of the Useful Time*. Both play with the themes of the 1920s—collectivism, feminism, and the equality of men and women.

Farewell to the Fireplace is a silent film, accompanied by atonal piano improvisations. It imitates Constructivist graphics and montage but is shot in color and high definition. The plot echoes that of Vladimir Majakovskij's (Mayakovsky's) play of 1929 *The Bedbug*, in which a young man dies and is revived in the utopian collectivist future, where all contradictions are resolved; Majakovskij is even listed as the screenwriter. Here, too, we find a fascination with the Soviet past bordering on parody.

Apparently, what Aleksandr Evangeli is trying to tell us with this film is that Ginzburg's architecture carries a certain aura. People who find themselves in this architecture are forced to think and act in a certain way, which points out—and in that sense only—the "repressive" character of the architecture.

Almost every resident of the building I talked to was ready to admit that the building possessed a magical ability to influence creativity. Anton and Polina, who now live in the Dejneka apartment, formed a clothing company, IMAGO, and their unisex uniforms have some similarities to the works of Liubov Popova and Varvara Stepanova of the 1920s. Artist and stage designer Vitalij Burikin first walked into the building in 2011. To him the space looked like a set for a horror film. He immediately wanted to live and work there. "Crazy?" asked the doorman. "Yes!" replied Vitalij cheerfully. He finds many "different energies" here. "You can meditate here. The spirit of creativity always lived here and always will, even if everybody's gone."[50] When "oligarch" Aleksandr Senatorov does a handstand on the Narkomfin roof, he looks like one of the characters in Rodčenko's famous photographs. At times he wonders: "How did I get into this mess?" But he is hooked on the project and is not likely to abandon it, even if he loses money on it, which is almost guaranteed.

In short, this amazing crumbling structure is still affirming the power of creative thinking over unfair, cruel, and at times violent circumstances.

Interior of Miljutin's penthouse

Hallway of second floor

Appendix

Residents of The Narkofin building executed between 1937 and 1940.

Source: the Memorial society, http://mos.memo.ru/shot-39.htm#s6

Apt. 8. Gurovič Eduard Jakovlevič, b. 1896, a member of the CPSU, the head of the central administration of the Eastern River Transport of the USSR People's Commissariat of Water Transport. Executed 08.01.1938.

Apt. 12. Kopylov, Nikolaj Vasil'evič, b. 1889, member of the CPSU, the head of the trust "Orgenergo" of Commissariat of Heavy Industry. Executed 20.06.1938.

Apt. 13. Kriučkov, Peter Petrovič, b. 1889, director of the Museum of Maxim Gorkij (Gorky). Executed 15.03.1938.

Apt. 13. Kriučkova, Elizaveta Zanohar'evna, b. 1902. executive secretary of the magazine "*The collective farmer.*" Executed 17.09.1938.

Apt. 26. Poluian, Ian Vasil'evič., b. 1891, member of the CPSU, head of Main Energy Department of the RSFSR People's Commissariat of Public Utilities. Executed 8.10.1937.

Apt. 29. Bunokharcev, Dmitrij Pavlovič, b. 1898 member of the CPSU, PhD, a correspondent of the newspaper "Izvestja" in Germany. Executed 3.06.1937.

Apt. 39. Nočhronin, Vasilij Nikiforovitč, b. 1889, member of the CPSU, Deputy People's Commissar of Internal Trade of the RSFSR. Executed 26.11.1937.

Apt. 41. Gurevič, Moisej Grigor'evič, b. 1891, member of the CPSU, Deputy. People's Commissar of Health of the RSFSR. Executed 26.10.1937.

Apt. 42. Sokolov, Nikolaj Konstantinovič, b. 1896, member of the CPSU, Chairman of the Board of the State Bank of the USSR. Executed 30.07.1941.

Apt. 42a. Ivanov, Boris Aleksandrovič, b. 1893, member of the CPSU, Head of the Secretariat of the President of the CPC of the RSFSR. Executed 15.03.1938.

Apt. 43. Lebed', Dmitrij Zaharevič., b. 1893, member of the CPSU, Deputy Chairman of People's Commissars of the RSFSR, a member of the Central Committee of the CPSU. Executed 30.10.1937.

Apt. 44. Strievskij, Konstantin Konstantinovič, b. 1885, member of the CPSU, chairman of the Central Committee of the Union of Workers of heavy machinery. Executed 21.04.1938.

Apt. 45. Sulimov, Danila (Daniil) Egorovič, b.1890, member of the CPSU, chairman of the CPC of the RSFSR. Executed 27.11.1937.

Apt. 46. Krylenko, Nikolaj Vasil'evič, b. 1885, member of the CPSU, People's Commissar of Justice of the USSR. Executed 29.07.1938.

Apt. 47. Karp Sergej Benediktovič, b. 1892, member of the CPSU, chairman of the State Planning Committee of the RSFSR. Executed 30.10.1937.

Apt. 49. Antonov-Ovseenko, Vladimir Aleksandrovič, b. 1883, member of the CPSU, People's Commissar of Justice of the Russian Federation. Executed 10.02.1938.

Apt. 49. Antonova-Ovseenko, Sofia Ivanovna, b. 1898, homemaker. Executed 08.02.1938.

Apt. 50. Nikolaj Lisicyn, b. 1891, member of the CPSU, the People's Commissar of Agriculture of the RSFSR. Executed 22.08.1938.

Apt. 51. Gerasimov, Ivan Semenovič., b. 1894, member of the CPSU, managing director of SHK RSFSR. Executed 26.10.1937.

1. I am grateful to Marina Khrustaleva and Danilo Udovički-Selb for their help and valuable suggestions.

2. The anticipation of war could be seen in Soviet publications on city planning. See, for example, "Stroitel'stvo i oborona SSSR," *Stroitel'naja promyšlennost'*, no. 9 (1927), 620-621; L. Segal, "Zaščita gorodov ot aero-himičeskih napadenij," *Stroitel'naja promyšlennost'*, no. 2 (1929), 161-163; L. Skliar, "Planirovka gorodov s točki zrenija maskirovki." *Promyšlennoe stroitel'stvo*, no. 1 (1930), 77–78; D. B. Bronevskij, "Stroitel'stvo gorodov i zaščita graždanskogo naselenija ot napadenija s vozduha", *Stroitel'naja promyšlennost'*, no. 3 (1932), pp 61–62.

3. Culminating in the 1930s with the criminalization of homosexuality—*Sobranie zakonov i rasporia□enij rabo□e-krest'ianskogo pravitel'stva SSSR* (SZ, 1934, 1, 5) —and abortions (SZ, 1936, 34, 309). All translations are mine unless otherwise indicated.

4. Introducing the death penalty for "escaping abroad" (SZ, 1934, 33, 255).

5. Measures are taken to fight "fluidity of the work force" (SZ, 1930, 60, 641), gambling is banned (ÑÇ, 1928, 27, 249), sale of narcotic substances is restricted (SZ, 1928, 33, 290).

6. SZ, 1930, 22, 248.

7. See Nikolaj Iljine and Natalia Semenova, *Prodannye Sokrovišca Rossii* [Sold Russian Treasures], Moscow: Trilistnik, 2000.

8. *Iz Istorii Sovetskoj Arhitektury 1928–1932*, Moscow, 1973, p. 9.

9. SZ, 1928, 26, 231. Emphasis added.

10. *XV S'ezd* Vsesoiuznoj Kommunističeskoj partii (b). Stenografičeskij otčet. Moscow-Leningrad, 1928, p. 59. Emphasis added.

11. SZ, 1929, 2, 13.

12. In the Foundation Le Corbusier archive, there is Nikolaj Kolli's letter to Le Corbusier, sent in 1934 from Rome, saying that the day he was flying to Italy with the Soviet delegation, almost at the moment of boarding the airplane, the authorities gave him all the materials and books Le Corbusier had been sending him for two or three years. Thanks to Danilo Udovički-Selb for sharing this information.

13. *XV S'ezd*, p. 296.

14. I. V. Stalin, "K Voprosam Agrarnoj Politiki v SSSR". Reč na konferentcii agrarnikov-marksistov, 27 December 1929. *Voprosy leninizma*. Moscow: 1952. p. 325.

15. The most authoritative source on collectivization is still the 1986 classic, Robert Conquest: *The Harvest of Sorrow: Soviet Collectivization and the Terror-Famine* (New York: Oxford University Press), 1986.

16. Author's interview with Aleksej Ginzburg, August 24, 2013. Editor's interview with Miljutina, June 2012.

17. Ibid.

18. People's Commissariat for Finance.

19. Nikolaj Aleksandrovič Semaško, People's Commissar of Public Health.

20. Aleksandr Aleksandrovič Dejneka (Deyneka), modernist figurative painter.

21. *Dom Novogo Byta* (A House for the New Lifestyle), a film by Ogino Knaus, 2013. Directed by Manuela Conti and Lorenzo Tripodi. In the film, Miljutina speaks in fluent but broken English, which is corrected in the subtitles. I am quoting the subtitles, with minor edits for clarity.

22. Ibid. This story contradicts Miljutina's version. She describes a more serene relationship between the client and the architect. See Ekaterina Miljutina, "*My naš, my novyj mir postroim,*" In: *Arhitektor Nikolaj Miljutin* (Moscow, NLO, 2013), p. 412.

Editor's note: The title of the book is taken from a verse of the *Internationale: "We will build a new World . . ."*

23. Ibid. *Dom Novogo Byta*

24. Ibid.

Editor's note: Miljutina also tells the story of the secret police actually coming to arrest her father, but he managed to confuse them by calling the Kremlin and claiming that it was a case of mistaken identity. Another Miljutin lived in the area. He had also prepared an escape route.

25. Ekaterina Miljutina, "*My naš, my novyj mir postroim,*" in: *Arhitektor Nikolaj Miljutin* (Moscow, NLO, 2013), 418.

26. Memorial, a Russian historical and civil rights society, that focuses on recording the Soviet totalitarian past (http://www.memo.ru).

27. MAI later became MARHI.

28. The Doctors' plot ("doctors' affair," "doctors-saboteurs," "doctors-killers")—the anti-Jewish episode in the Soviet Union in 1952–53. Several prominent Moscow doctors, predominantly Jews, were arrested as conspiratorial assassins of Soviet leaders.

29. Aleksej Ginzburg, "The Narkomfin Building: The History of Trying to Save the House." In: *20th Century: Preservation of Cultural Heritage* (Moscow) 2006, p. 125.

30. Ibid., p. 128.

31. Later *MIAN* became a part of the *Kopernik* (Copernicus) Group.

32. *Dom Novogo Byta.*

33. The Rodčenko Moscow School of Photography and Multimedia founded in 2006.

34. Author's interview with Aleksandr Evangeli, August 27, 2013. Editor's note: Following an obvious speculative scheme the hotel was demolished and an identical one was rebuilt in its place.

35. http://www.saltt.ru/node/4725.

36. Andreev was responsible for a crude rebuilding of the Moscow Manež (Manège) after a suspicious fire; he destroyed Rimsky-Korsakov's estate on Tverskoj Boulevard. He is involved in the reconstruction of the "Central" hotel on Tverskaja street, and there are plans for the demolition of Hotel Chevalier in Kamergerskij Lane.

37. The international Moscow Architecture Preservation Society (MAPS) was set up in May 2004 by a group of young historians, journalists, and architects from different countries, living in Moscow, following the demolition of two major Moscow landmarks (the Moskva Hotel, the Voentorg department store), and the highly suspicious fire in the Manež.

38. Author's interview with Aleksandr Senatorov, August 28, 2013.

39. Pre-proposal of restoration and adaptation of a residential building for hotel purposes. (Alexander Senatorov's archive). Moscow: 2007. p. 31.

40. Interview with Senatorov.

41. The territory was expanded in the 1990s, and a portion of it is just a few meters west of the Narkomfin building.

42. In 1987, the residential and public buildings of the Narkomfin acquired the status of "monuments of regional importance" (reference No. 604). In 2002, the historical and architectural value of the laundry building was confirmed, and it acquired the status of an "identified site of cultural heritage," and in 2004, the territory of the whole monument was defined, approaching the limits of land acquisition of 1929. See: http://www.archnadzor.ru/2008/04/07/dom-narkomfina-žiznenny-e-kollizii

43. Ibid. Michael McFaul was the current US Ambassador to Russia till February 2014.

44. MAPS, see footnote 37. Arhnadzor (architectural watchdog), a non-profit association of citizens for the preservation of architectural monuments, established in 2009.

45. Reported by Natalia Melikova, who interviewed residents for her "Constructivist Project" (http://theconstructivistproject.com).

46. "Vinzavod," Center for contemporary art, located in the former brewery (later Wine Factory) "The Moscow Bavaria."

47. Ibid.

48. Ibid. *Away from All Suns*, a documentary flim by director Isabella Willinger, 2013 quoting the English subtitles.

49. Ibid. I am quoting the English subtitles. In the Russian soundtrack, one can hear Suvorov saying "**жидовский конструктивизм**"(kike constructivism).

50. Author's interview with Vitalij Burikin, August 27, 2013.

Marina Khrustaleva (MAPS) and Aleksej Ginzburg (Ginzburg Architects) in Miljutin's penthouse. Photo: © 2013 Vladimir Paperny.

Double-height Spaces: From Ateliers to "Cathedrals"

Wilfried Wang

Double-height spaces in buildings create a sense of generosity and drama. Expressed in simple facts, double-height spaces involve a larger enclosed volume than single-story spaces for a given useable floor area; they come into being only as a result of a special effort. Double-height spaces not only feel more generous, they also require a generous and understanding client who is willing to invest in such a display of space.

Double-height spaces in the context of domestic architecture have their origins in the Bohemian world of artists' studios, as well as in mansions of the *haute bourgeoisie*. During the early twentieth century, double-height spaces were applied in mass housing schemes to provide that sense of generosity and spatial identity otherwise lacking in the standard single-floor apartments. In the late twentieth and early twenty-first century, double-height spaces have returned to the fold of bourgeois domestic culture, thereby closing the circuitous route that this spatial motif has taken since its excursion into social housing design.

If the early socialist Charles Fourier (1772–1836) oriented his collective housing project, the Phalanstère,[1] on the Palace of Versailles, thereby giving the needy access to the grandeur of the feudal classes, then in terms of the spatial quality of the residential unit it comes as little surprise if subsequent architects of collective housing schemes oriented their spatial typologies on similar feudal and bourgeois models. Most notable in this context are the heights of palatial and bourgeois rooms. On the one hand, the use of double-height spaces can be regarded as a vestige of such references, and, on the other hand, as a three-dimensional, sectional inflexion.

In their mature, abstracted form of the late 1920s, the double-height spaces used by Moisej J. Ginzburg (1892–1946) and Ignatij F. Milinis (1888–1974) in the Narkomfin (1928–30) for the staff of the People's Commissariat of Finances (Narodnyj Kommissariat Financov) in Moscow were ideally ambiguous, suiting the traditional "nuclear" families, still in search of a conventional "home," as well as the modern Soviet dwellers who were ready to engage in the then-collectivized mode of living. It is in this sense that one can understand Ginzburg's characterization of the Narkomfin Communal Building as an experimental dwelling of a "transitional type,"[2] for the real communist state had not yet been reached by everyone and concessions had to be made in the interim.

The fierce political debate during the interwar period in the Soviet Union about the new communist way of life—*byt*—and therefore the professional discourse on the ideologically "correct" direction of collective housing reveal the volatile conception of architecture and society.[3] The modernist belief that the environment is able to form the individual and the collective only if the correct design is properly realized—new buildings for a new society—led to the architects' view that an intermediate communal design would be needed to reach the ultimate state of a communist society. The architects of the Narkomfin thus merely regarded their own design as a stepping-stone in the grand plan toward a new *byt.* Collective housing of the ideal communist state of the early 1930s, in the Soviet Union and other countries, would separate the act of sleeping (together with hygiene) from eating, child care, and sociocultural formation. The principle of functional segregation would be equally operative at the settlement and building level.

The various double-height units in the Narkomfin, the so-called type K on levels 1 and 2 (double-height units in the normal sense), as well as the types F on levels 3 to 5 (the one-and-a-half high units), offered a spatial variety that did not conform to the ideals of the new *byt*, but were clearly understood by Ginzburg to be vestigial typologies. In hindsight, with the reception of modernist housing design of the last century, the reasons Ginzburg and his colleagues, including the critics of the Narkomfin Communal Building, thought of these typologies in these "intermediate" terms can be better understood if one reviews some of the origins of the double-height motif.

Sources of the Double-height Motif

A wide range of double-height types has been pursued over the last two centuries. In relation to twentieth century housing schemes, the selection process of a specific type has followed a distinct *sociospatial* logic. In its social logic, the desire and search for spatial generosity as expressed in the height of a room can be understood in relation to other known spaces (bohemian, bourgeois, feudal, and others). In terms of its spatial logic, a double-height compartment is a volumetric entity in relation to two other inhabitable units of space. While as a motif the double-height space has been applied to different building types—from ateliers to "cathedrals"[4]—the origins of the gallery section as applied in the Narkomfin can be traced to a number of sources. In the course of this architectural search for the appropriate double-height type for public housing, certain spatial types have been transformed to such an extent that their vestiges can just about be recognized in later iterations, while reinterpretations of subsequently transformed types might in turn lead to new directions.[5] The skill of architectural composition can be seen in those instances in which both the patterns of use and the spatial morphology are synthesized to form a proportioned, appropriate organic whole.

An Architectural Office

One early usage of the double-height motif in a "modern" building can be found in Sir John Soane's house on Lincoln's Inn Fields in London. There are, in fact, two instances of this section being applied in the creation of such grand spaces, though differently proportioned (strictly speaking, both spatial compositions extend in their dimensions to three levels; however, conceptually, both involve the perception of two levels). First, there is the floors of the architectural office to the north of No. 13 Lincoln's Inn Fields, stacked on top of the ground floor by means of four pairs of freestanding columns (this section constructed between ca. 1810 to 1837). The upper floor is treated like an independent plane, not connected to the surrounding walls. Together with the roof vault the office feels like a freestanding ædicule, reminiscent of Antonello da Messina's depiction of Saint Jerome in his *Study* (ca. 1475, National Gallery, London). This double-height motif can be described as the table-in-a-room type, whereby the uninterrupted singularity of the room is counterpointed by the freestanding, inhabitable "table" structure. The outer enclosure provides the sense of grandeur, whereas the inset frame structure creates a sense of protection and human scale.

Second, there is the narrow double-height space connecting the so-called "Monk's Parlor" at the basement with the "Picture Room," one level higher up (completed before 1837). This vertical slot of space provides moments of surprise as the triple set of foldable wall panels of the "Picture Room" are opened to reveal the densely hung sets of watercolors of Soane's projects on these panels. The view is set free to the opposite windows and the "Monk's Yard" as well as to the gloomy "Monk's Parlor" beneath. Soane's mastery of filtered zenithal light is without parallel in overcast England. The principal of the vertical light slots, not to be confused with the aforementioned uninterrupted double-height spaces, can be seen applied elsewhere in the gaps between the floor and the wall within the area of the "Dome." Here the gaps are bridged with iron grilles that allow visitors to freely walk around otherwise narrow passages. Light from the sky thus illuminates almost shadow-free the three levels of space beneath the large "Dome." Soane found his historical references in Roman architecture, particularly in Pompeii with its *trompe l'œil* wall paintings of miniaturized ædicules. In these Roman images, the phenomenological framework is the dome of the sky under which simple edifices are placed. Thus, in the modern transposed and abstracted version of this framework one sees the gallery as an ædicule in relation to the ceiling of the uppermost floor, quasi the sky.

Victorian Hallways

Some three decades later in mid-Victorian Britain, with industrialization having given rise to a visible number of self-made gentry, nouveau riche manor owners would imagine a baronial lifestyle using another variant of the double-height spatial motif. The halls of these manors became the calling card of those who thought they could suggest a medieval lineage. Dark wooden walls and ceiling panels with Elizabethan ornament, nooks and crannies complete with a recessed fireplace, indirect and diffused light falling onto a creaking staircase that would lead up to a gallery from which the double-height would be enjoyed as a

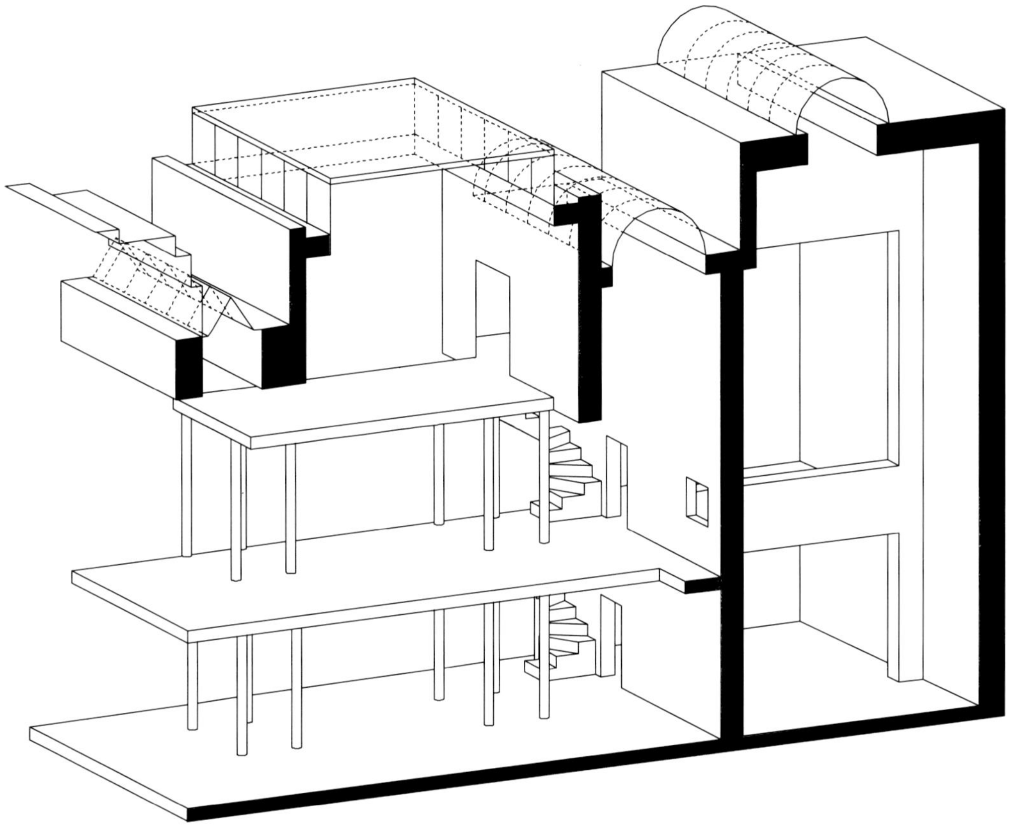

Sir John Soane's office (left), Monk's Parlour (right) and Picture Gallery (back), London, 1827, sectional axonometric (by Cheng Jia)

reward for scaling the height—these concerted elements impressed visitors with a conspicuous display of uninhabitable airspace while providing comfort in the personalized niches and the glow of the fireplace.[6] Typologically, a Victorian hallway, as a development of the double-height motif, would consist of a singular space with a stairway and gallery or landing appended to it, or in some cases, with the stairway and gallery treated as a quasi-solid volume within the hall, thereby creating a more substantive relation between space and promenade.

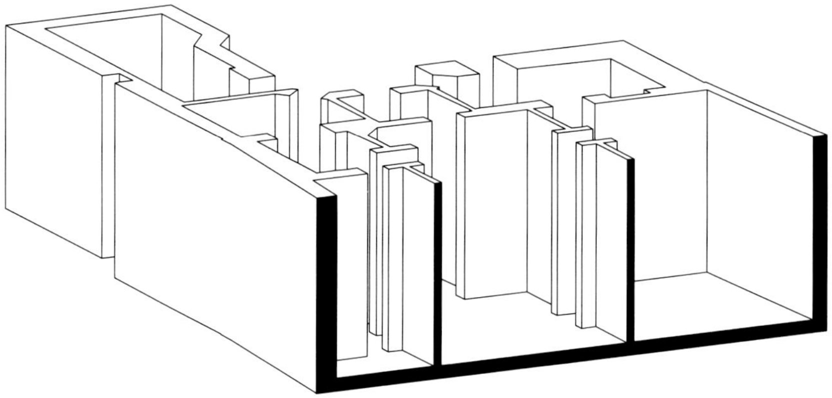

Upper floor, Kniže shop, Graben 13, Vienna, before alteration, sectional axonometric (by Cheng Jia)

Viennese vestiges of hallways and a tailor's atelier

Again some three decades later, Adolf Loos, as an unapologetic Anglophile, imported key aspects of these Victorian mansions to Austria. In his alterations to grand Viennese houses and apartments, in which the ceiling heights were such that either a full gallery or half-gallery could be introduced in order to produce a greater sense of space, the English hallway is transformed into a miniaturized version (for example, the Strasser Villa, Vienna 1918–19; the Rufer Villa, Vienna 1922; and even in the designs for the Viennese "*Siedlungshäuser*" (Settler's Houses) of 1921,

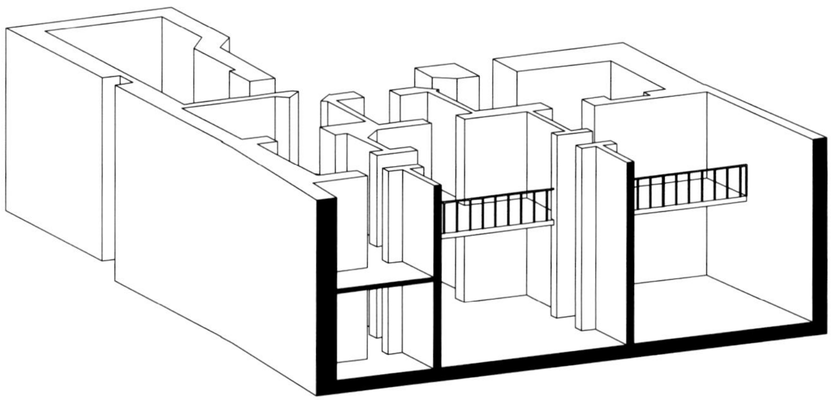

Adolf Loos, Kniže shop, Vienna, 1910–1913
Upper floor and new gallery, sectional axonometric (by Cheng Jia)

the precursor for the Viennese *Werkbundsiedlung* houses of 1930-32). Most significant in this spatial research is the transformation of the mezzanine floor for the shop of the bespoke tailor Kniže in Vienna (1910–1913). In fact, Loos introduces a gallery into the mezzanine, whereby the usable floor space is almost doubled. In this instance, the continuous ceiling spanning the front rooms and covering both the now "double-height" spaces and the gallery becomes the unifying reference plane; in this case, the plane is merely articulated by a false beam. Contrary then to the Victorian hallway, in which space is seemingly conspicuously wasted, Loos' introduction of a mezzanine gallery is an inventive spatial trick to increase the useable space while at the same time producing a dramatic double-height volume.

The galleries in the Kniže Store take up about one third of the original volume of the room, creating intimately scaled spaces underneath while providing a longer distance view of the exterior from the gallery level. Here the dialectic between the larger room and the smaller subdivisions appears synthesized into a spatial and tectonic organism, whereby the transformative nature of the design has been superseded by the galleries' beams and fitted furniture; all of this reads like an English country mansion. The "Siedlungshäuser" of 1921 with the different widths (especially the 5 and 6 meter types) are in their essence the origin of Loos' subsequent Werkbund houses. Whereas the "Siedlungshäuser" are conceived as two-story houses, the Werkbund houses are effectively three stories, including a double-height space; the volumetric relation between Loos' Werkbund houses and Ginzburg and Milinis' Narkomfin Type K is strong.

Loos' spatial conception is one of carving out spaces from a given volume. It is a geometric and dimensional game that does not involve integers of space or complete units of floors. Rather, as his more well-known villa designs according to the *Raumplan* (spatial plan) demonstrate and as the project for Twenty Villas for the Côte d'Azure shows, Loos delighted in the interlocking of finely resolved volumes to create intermediate zones of occupation, thereby permitting a graded relationship between smaller and larger spaces, as in the relation between a theatre box to its auditorium. Loos' use of the double-height type in his house designs owes more to his refined sense of spatial calibration than to any adherence to a systematic aggregation of unitary spaces, the latter being a compositional principle that is followed by most architects who were involved in public housing in the late 1920s and 1930s.

Double-height Modules

Le Corbusier knew of the Kniže Store in Vienna; he sketched the shop front twice while visiting Vienna in 1911. Given the fact that the shop's interior was not completed until 1913, he may not have seen any of the tailor's ateliers at the mezzanine gallery level. Regardless of this possibility, it is significant to understand Le Corbusier's use of the double-height motif as one less to do with the increase of useable floor area through the addition of an intermediate floor than as the omission of part of a floor plane in order to create a more generous sense of space in an otherwise rather conventional or even disproportionate room.

From 1916 onward, Le Corbusier pursued a number of domestic projects that included double-height spaces, principally living rooms. These include the Villa Paul Poiret (project of 1916) and the Maisons Citrohän 1 and 2 (1920, 1922). At the same time, there are the realizations for the Atelier Ozenfant in Paris (1922)—more a tall artist's studio than a double-height space, even though a small gallery was built at the rear of the top floor—and the *Pavillon de l'Esprit Nouveau* for the Paris *Exposition des Arts Décoratifs* (1925); the latter as the precursor to the post-World War II *Unité d'Habitation* housing schemes.

The Villa in Auteuil (1922), as a precursor to the subsequent Maison La Roche (1923) with its triple-height gallery space; the Maison Cook (1926); the Villa Stein (1927), and the Citrohän version of the Weissenhof houses (1927) all express the double-height motif as instances of the subtraction of a floor section in order to achieve a double-height volume. This fact is more clearly understood in relation to the contemporaneous housing scheme for Pessac (1925), where the stringent geometry is the clearest characteristic of an otherwise regularly stacked set of floor slabs.

Significantly, Le Corbusier's research in these villas and houses with double-height spaces is carried out on behalf of clients from the petite to the grande bourgeoisie, only to be applied after World War II in the *Unité d'Habitation* mass housing schemes. Pessac is Le Corbusier's only realized interwar mass housing scheme for petit bourgeois users—significantly harking back in parts to the free-standing villa typology, some four years after Loos designed his post–World War I "Siedlungshäuser" for returning soldiers, designed as row houses.

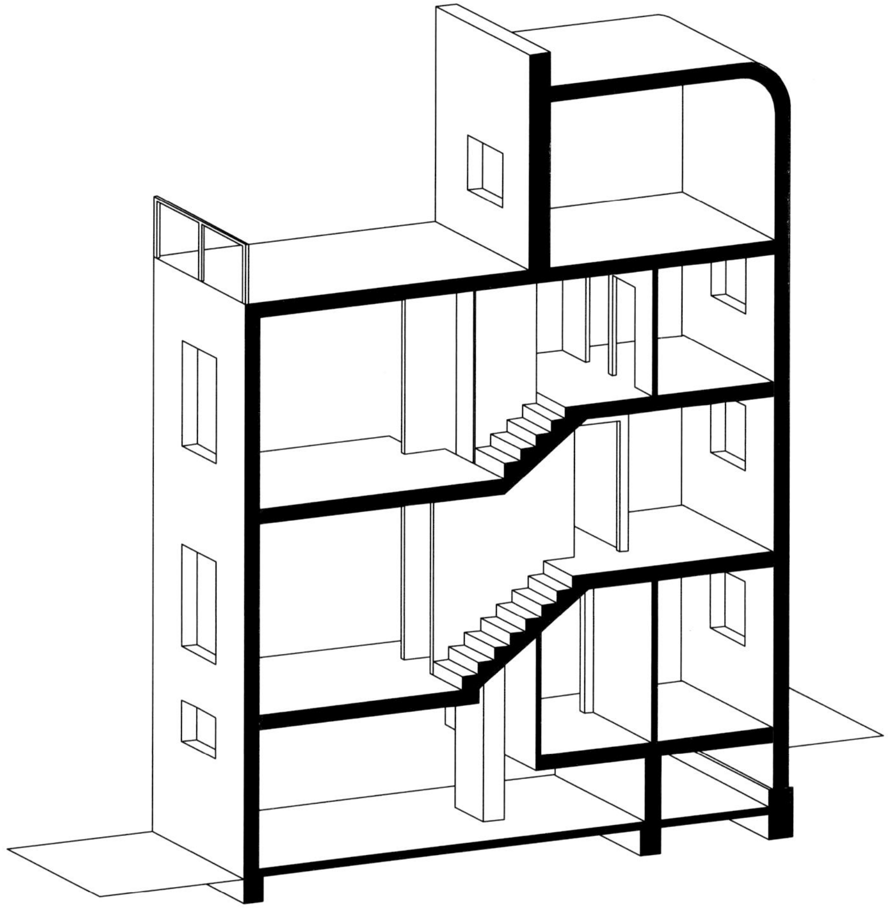

Hans Scharoun, Apartment Building for Singles, Breslau, 1925-1932, sectional axonometric (by Cheng Jia)

Split Level Access: Scharoun's "Wohnheim" in Breslau (Wrocław)

A different approach to the configurational treatment was taken by Hans Scharoun in his apartment building for singles and young couples as part of the Breslau Werkbund Exhibition of 1929 (design started in 1927), the so-called "Wohnheim" (residential home). While not including any double-height spaces in the design, Scharoun used the split-level section in the two residential wings that was also applied in the Narkomfin Communal Building for the unit type F on levels 3 to 5.

In the overall configuration of the "Wohnheim," Scharoun sought to balance the wings with the tight and minimal space standards of the single and double bed units with the generous communal spaces at the building's center (and the restaurant beneath the shorter wing with the two bedrooms). The external beer garden and the interior restaurant thus form the heart of the overall balanced but asymmetric scheme. The naval styling provides a sense of grandeur: analogous to the transatlantic steamers, in which small cabins give onto access galleries, the "Wohnheim" is held together by generous communal areas, terraces, the building's views, and outreach into the immediate surroundings and the curving and embracing details.

Unity and Variety

Compared to the Breslau "Wohnheim," the Narkomfin is treated as an overall rectangular parallelepiped configuration underscored by the almost identical repetition of projecting strip windows on the east and the repetitive windows on the west, that in the end, due to their indeterminate number, have the effect of unifying the overall planar façade (the staircase on the west façade was a later addition). There is little of the naval styling elements visible at the Narkomfin as compared to Scharoun's "Wohnheim." The configuration of the Narkomfin was a concentrated block, placed on relatively thin columns and thus opening much of the ground floor to free circulation and ventilation. The resultant "floating" box underscores the unity of the building as such.

The relationship between the circulation elements (staircases and corridors) and the four different unit types (B, F, 2F, K, plus the communal unit and the penthouse) was such that there was a high degree of efficiency. Thus, what is invested over and above the normal floor-to-volume ratio in the split sections and the double-height units was gained in terms of a more concentrated circulation system. This too led to an increase in the potential of encounters in the two corridors. By avoiding a dark, double-loaded corridor on each floor, thus also precluding cross-ventilation in the dwellings, Ginzburg and Milinis' Narkomfin strikes a balance in favor of increased awareness of neighbors, and although it offers a smaller range of unit types when compared to Le Corbusier's Unité d'Habitation buildings, the Narkomfin Communal Building avoids the problems of deep sections and internal corridors.

Given the scale of the Narkomfin and the knowledge of public housing schemes that have been completed since 1930, the significance of Ginzburg and Milinis' design gains a new dimension. The housing question has since been answered with endless variations, leading to ever larger, ever less proportionate, ever less humane complexes. In the late twentieth century, the economies-of-scale argument had become intellectually and architecturally exhausted. The ubiquitous faceless public housing settlements in the East and in the West became the habitats for neglected people. Their occasional demolition was frequently celebrated, even being stylized as marking the end of the modernist period of architecture.[7]

In hindsight then, the Narkomfin was not just an example of a transitional housing scheme pointing toward a more egalitarian, if not to say communist society, but a transitional building per se as any building was by historical necessity. It was built for and inhabited by privileged public servants; the head of its department even lived in the penthouse unit, and Ginzburg lived in a special type with a circular balcony on the south side. Its spatial typology has not lost any of its appropriateness even for the differentiated society of the early twenty-first century.

With the advances in technology, the industrialization of food production, the use of microwaves, the loss of importance of the kitchen as a social space, and the greater demands placed on every adult member of a family to earn her and his own way, the bourgeois characteristics that each unit of the Narkomfin offers principally as a result of the application of the double-height motif removes this building from the cold mechanical nature of much late twentieth century public housing design. From this point of view, the Narkomfin was not transitional, and it was the double-height motif that helped it to retain its continued relevance.

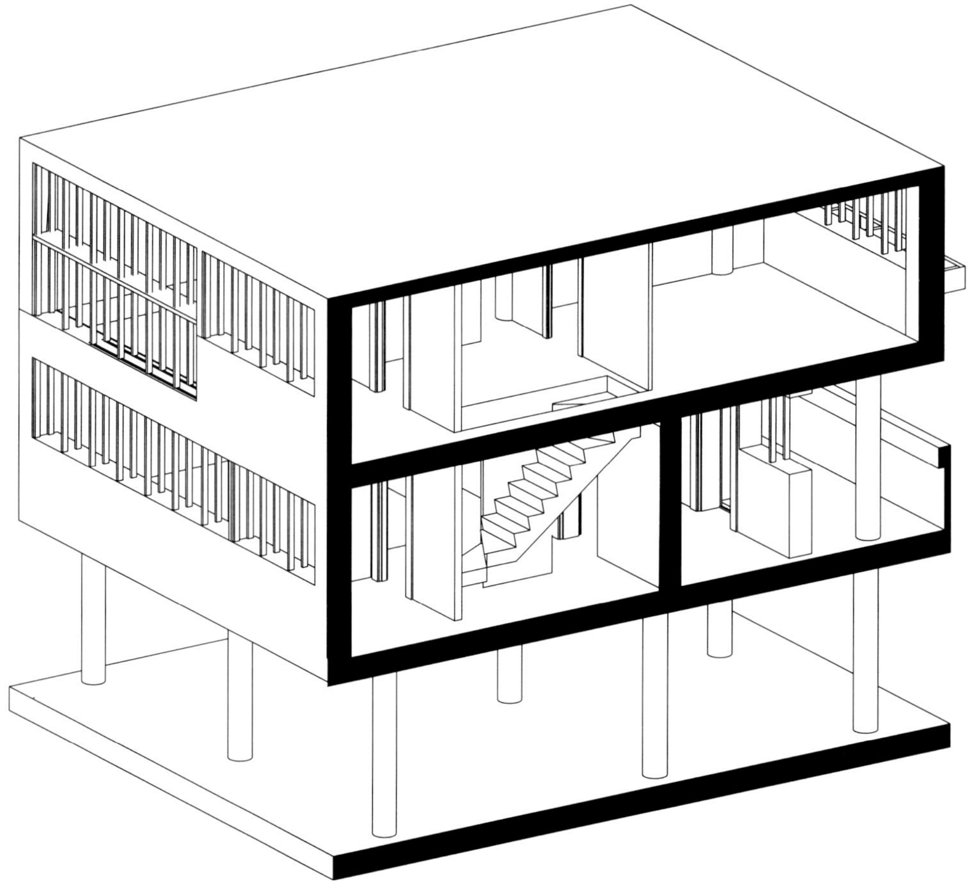

K Type, Idealized Axonometric (Cheng Jia)

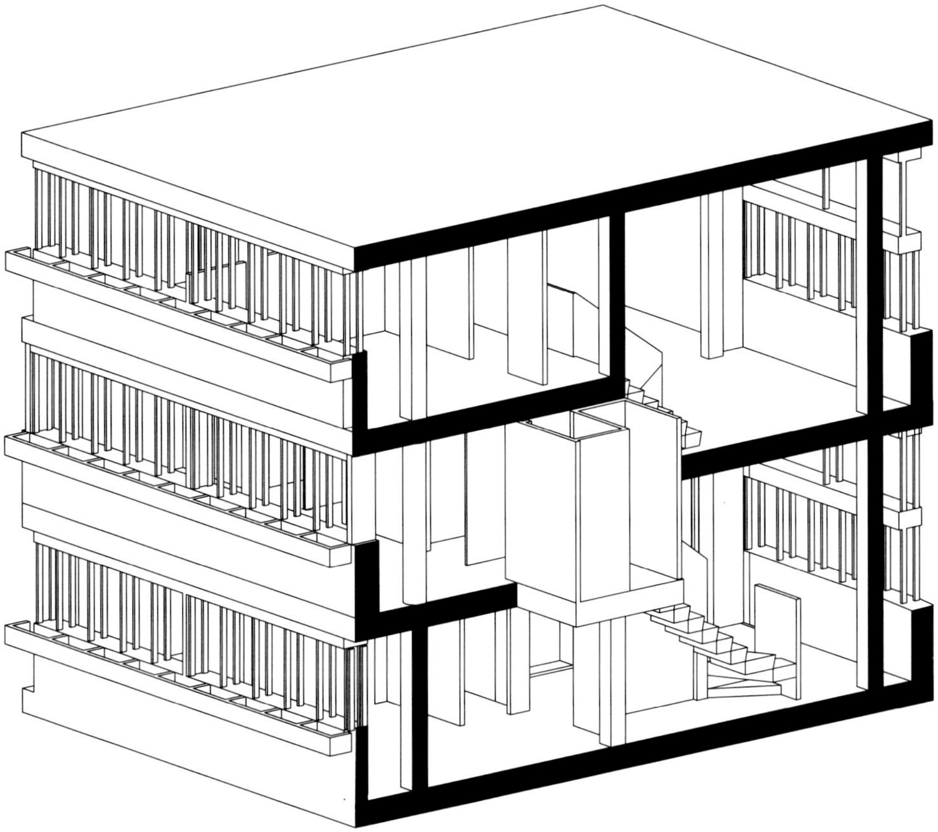

F-Type, Idealized Axonometric (Cheng Jia)

1. In this connection see the building configuration of the "1st Zamoskvorečje" Cooperative Communal House 1926. Architect Ajzikovi, Engineers G. Volfenzon, A. Barulin, S. Leontovi, on ulica Lesteva 18, Moscow, which displays an axially symmetric, quasi-telescopic layout; *Stroitel'stvo moskvy*, No. 2, Moscow 1928, p. 16.

2. Moisej J. Ginzburg, *Žilišče. Die Wohnung. L'Habitation. Opyt pjatiletnej nad problemoj žilišča. Ein Beitrag zu den Wohnungs- problemen.* Problème d'Habitation. Moscow 1934, pp. 82–87. The head of the national finance committee, Nikolaj Alexandrovič Miljutin, in fact was to reside in the penthouse unit on levels 6 and 7 of the Narkomfin Communal Building.

3. Victor Buchli, "Moisej Ginzburg's Narkomfin Communal House in Moscow: Contesting the Social and Material World," in *Journal of the Society of Architectural Historians*, vol. 57, no. 2, Jun 1998, pp. 160–181.

4. In this context, the word "cathedrals" has been appropriated by US-American real estate agents, whereby the description of "cathedral ceilings" is meant to appeal as much to the classical connoisseurs of architecture as to the religiously-minded purchasers and to conjure up historical legitimacy in the best possible post-modern practice and late-bourgeois generosity.

5. Since 1928, Ginzburg, head of the research team (brigade) had been part of the section for housing research at the Strojkom RSFSR (Committee for Building of the Russian Socialist Federation of Soviet Republics).

6. Robert Kerr, *The Gentleman's House: Or, How to Plan English Residences, from the Parsonage to the Palace; with Tables of Accommodation and Cost and a Series of Selected Plans*, John Murray, London 1864, pp. 160–3.

7. See Charles Jencks, *The Language of Post-Modern Architecture*, London 1977, pp. 9–10.

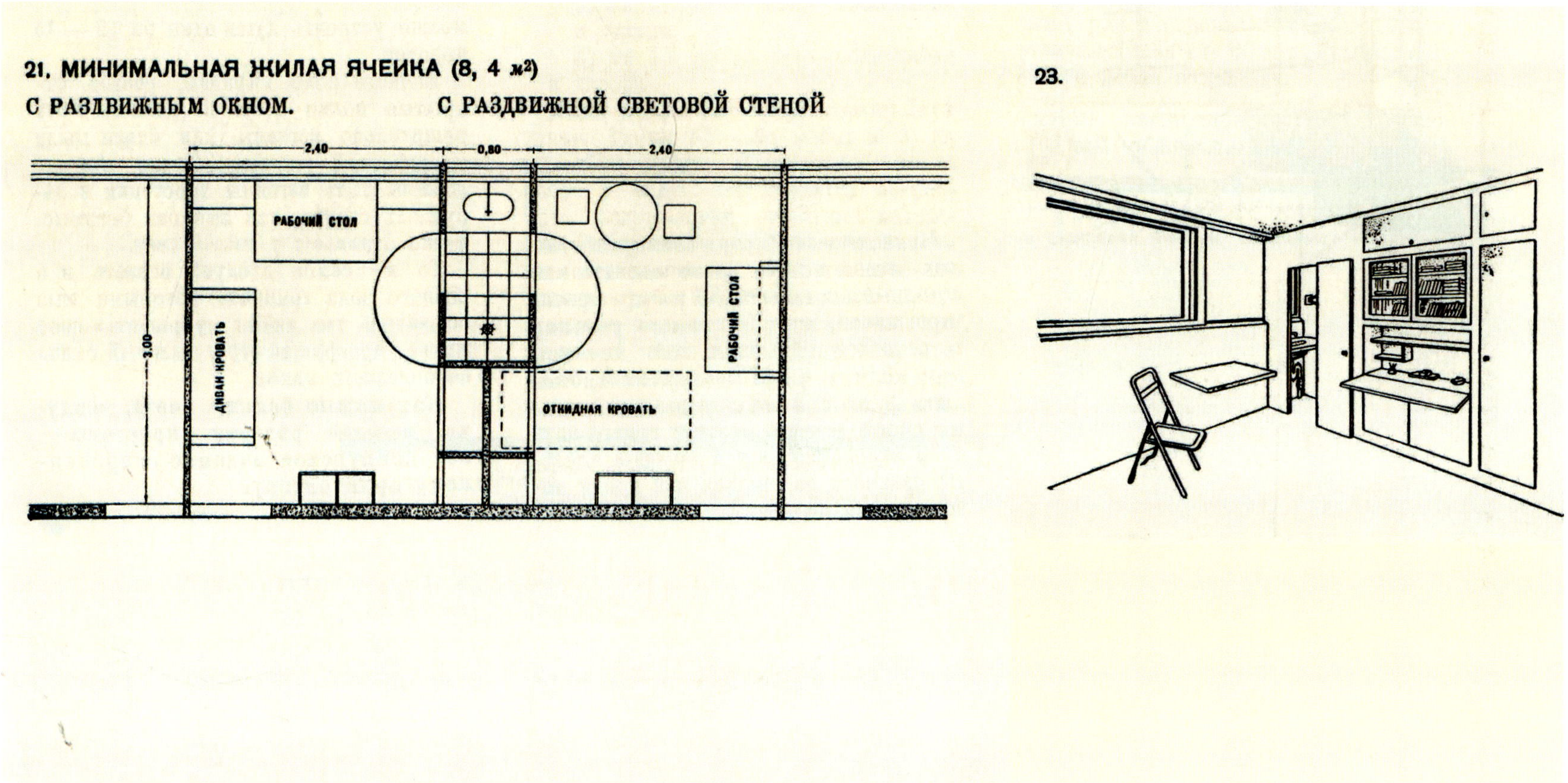

Fig.1 Nikolaj Miljutin, Minimal Living Cell in Socgorod, 1930 (Nikolaj Miljutin, Problema stroitel'stva socialističeskih gorodov. Moscow: Gosudarstvennoe Izdatel'stvo, 1930)

The Communist Egosphere: The Single Room Abode in the Russian 1920s

Tijana Vujoševič

The cultural logic and the political order of Western capitalist society are materialized in the studio apartment. This is what Sloterdijk proposes in "Cell Block, Egospheres, Self-Container: The Apartment as Co-Isolated Existence," addressing the role of architecture in the creation of the modern self.[1] "The tendency towards cell-formation," according to Sloterdijk, "is the architectural and topological analogue of the modern society."[2] Sloterdijk's "cell" is the spatial envelope enclosing the self-indulgent, self-reflective, autoerotic capitalist individual. In a small space, the "egosphere" contains a vast array of "ego-technologies," means of exploring and crafting one's image, such as mirrors, books, diaries, and devices for self-grooming. All in all, the studio is devoted to what Sloterdijk calls "pairing with oneself."[3] The one-room cell is serially produced and complements the architecture and culture of the stadium as a site of mass existence.

Sloterdijk traces the development of the "cell-block" to the monastic and to the work of Le Corbusier, his theories and projects of the 1920s, and his Unité d'Habitation as the first built modern cellular formation. He claims that the egosphere is an invention of the West, and claims that the dominant Communist mode of habitation, the house-commune (dom-Kommuna), precluded the formation of spaces for individual habitation and self-pairing. What immediately comes to mind is that such a sharp division cannot really hold water. For one, the organization of Sloterdijk's Western paradigm, Unité d'Habitation, mirrors that of the much earlier Narkomfin building, and that Le Corbusier's influence on the Russian avant-garde, as well as the other way around, was immense. There is a larger issue at stake, that is, whether it was at all possible, in the East like in the West, to articulate a culture of orchestrated collectivity without also designing "self-containers." I hope to show that the egosphere was as important for Communism as it is for modern capitalist culture. I will also explore its peculiarities, namely, which ideas about the socialist self it articulated and how it defined the citizen of the Communist future.

Before discussing radical modernist design, I want to stress that the distribution of single-room abodes rather than the construction of communes was the most important tool used by the Soviet government in the late 1920s as a means of disciplining and governing the population. Mark Me'erovič provides a detailed study of this situation.[4] According to him, there were attempts in the first half of the 1920s to create "workers' communes" around the factories, which would prevent mass migration and moving from one factory to another by fostering a community similar to that found in village communes. But because of the different values and habits of the working class, for which marriage and family were not sacred, this did not work. The main means of controlling the population became the distribution of individual units, and the housing deficit actually benefited the government. One would have the right to inhabit a government procured unit only if one were employed. And, since 1927, a time when the NKVD took control of the issue, one's documents, and thus official identity, were tied to the place of domicile. Without work one would be without housing, and, consequently, without civil rights. Only workers and classes affiliated with the working class were eligible for housing. "Socially alien" (*social'no čužie*) elements, including the sick and the insane, merchants, and hired laborers, were excluded. And everyone's housing situation was precarious: only a couple of weeks after abandoning work, or being absent from the housing unit, a citizen could lose it, and it could be assigned to someone else. Housing policies were aimed less toward organizing communal living and more toward sanctioning desirable behaviors and identities of individuals. In this process, the possession of an individual habitat affirmed one's identity as a worker and a useful member of society, an identity that, like the possession of the unit, was always precarious.

The problem of the individual unit and a worker's individual identity was very prominent in avant-garde projects for house-communes, which did not address the main concerns of the government, but which remain a paradigm for the Soviet architectural experiment, which Sloterdijk also has in mind when discussing Communist legacy. They are mostly studied in terms of the communal spaces and modes of communal co-habitation for which they provided.[5] But in these designs, the articulation of the individual cellular unit was equally important.

One of the best-known projects in the area of town-planning and collective living is Nikolaj Miljutin's *Socgorod*, designed in 1930 (Fig. 1). It is a "disurbanist" work, which proposed eliminating differences between city and country and organizing collective living blocks surrounded by nature, in which there would be collective studies, sitting rooms, and dining rooms. Miljutin pays extraordinary attention to the development of the single unit, the "living cell" of 8.4 m^2. The living cell is a site where his program, the elimination

Fig.2/3 Aleksander Toporkov, Furniture Designs, 1920s (VHUTEMAS Collection, Getty Research Institute) (above and right)

of the family, would be put into practice. Reading Marx, Miljutin calls for the abolition of "official and unofficial prostitution," i.e., marriage, and celebrates alliances made according to people's preferences, independent of property and economic reason. The symbol of marriage is the double bed, which Miljutin eliminates from his project. The Communist is essentially single. And he or she has only a single bed. The unit is porous and allows for inter-cellular alliances. Two neighbors share, instead of a bed, a sink and a

shower. What unites Communist citizens, instead of sex, is the love of hygiene, and they can ostensibly socialize by sharing the ritual of ablution. But Miljutin stresses that he does not want to reduce the dwelling "to a mere toilet."[6]

He tries to articulate what the individual sphere is, what the personal needs of a solitary inhabitant are. He defines them as the following: book use, relaxation, safekeeping of things, and grooming. How does the worker go about satisfying these needs? Miljutin wages a war against decoration, the "various rags which our inhabitants so love to 'prettify' their dwelling, turning it into such a dusty accumulation of useless trash."[7] Instead, he provides built-in furniture: a working table, a divan-bed or a collapsible bed, storage, a medical cabinet. He describes it as "the minimum necessary equipment that is indispensable for man's living quarters."[8] Everything in the "cell" slides, folds, and unfolds. The bed folds into the wall. The desk folds into a closet or is set parallel to the wall. The chair can be folded or unfolded. The inhabitant is in a constant physical relationship with the interior. He does not only live—he also operates home as a physical laborer by opening, closing, sliding, folding its parts, living in locomotion. In effect, the apartment is not only a space for self-reflection, but also an assemblage of equipment, which is to be physically operated, worked with. Whereas Sloterdijk's capitalist subject was a passive reflective subject, the Communist inhabitant is also a worker, and he is molded as a physical laborer through the way he inhabits his egosphere. By providing built-in furniture, Miljutin wants to "end man's [. . .] enslavement by his possessions."[9] Without possessions and without personal belongings except for clothes and books, one lives in the apartment like a nomad, as a guest, as a subject in transit, free and rootless. Apart from being cast as the laborer, one characteristic of this new proletarian self who inhabits the "cell" is precisely this un-rootedness. This is at the same time a reflection of reality that resulted from government politics of destabilizing housing rights and a vision of subjectivity unencumbered by tradition. Similarly, the demand to "work" with the apartment, which identified the inhabitant as a worker in the most visceral sense, not only corresponded to the official practice of using housing as a means of affirming working class identity, but also presented a design for an active, rather than passive, contemplative self.

The idea of the dynamic mechanical environment as the habitat of the nomadic working self had been developing in Russia since the mid-1920s in new theories of the "Object" [*Vešč*].[10] In his 1925 essay "Everyday Life [*byt*] and the Culture of the Object," noted art critic Boris Arvatov wrote that objects are mechanical anthropomorphic creatures. According to him, "Collapsible furniture, moving sidewalks, revolving doors, escalators, automat restaurants, reversible outfits, and so on constituted a new stage in the evolution of material culture. The object became something functional and active, connected like co-workers in human practice. Mechanization + dynamization led to the mechanization of the Object, its transformation into a working instrument."[11] Similarly, Alexandr Toporkov in his *Technical Everyday Life and Contemporary Art* of 1928 tries to introduce Le Corbusier's theories to the Russian public but goes beyond promoting merely machine aesthetic and principles of economy and utility as he claims that the use of "American furniture" (collapsible armoires, rotating shelves, secretaries, registers, calculators) in Russian offices and in the home will lead to the creation of a new "non-humanist" self who plugs into the mechanized world.[12] This was the case of his own designs for the domestication of "American furniture," such as a closet on wheels, a model of a collapsible bed, and an armoire with flipping shelves (Figs.2, 3). In his words, these were not only experiments with new form, but also experiments in creating the new man, as "these seemingly obedient and mute slaves, which provide us with essential services, also act upon us, force their masters to change, turn them into a different breed of men."[13]

El Lissitzky shared this attitude. In his 1920 "Equipping the Residence with Furniture," he discussed the apartment as an assemblage of equipment. The two basic types of furniture were the "transformable and convertible" and the

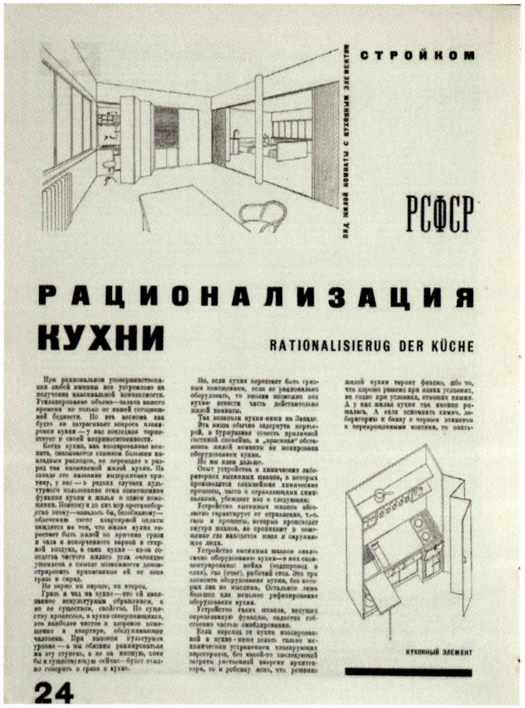
СТРОЙКОМ

РСФСР

РАЦИОНАЛИЗАЦИЯ КУХНИ

RATIONALISIERUG DER KÜCHE

КУХОННЫЙ ЭЛЕМЕНТ

24

Fig.4 Kitchen Element (*Sovremennaja Arhitektura*, no. 1, 1929, courtesy of Getty Research Institute)

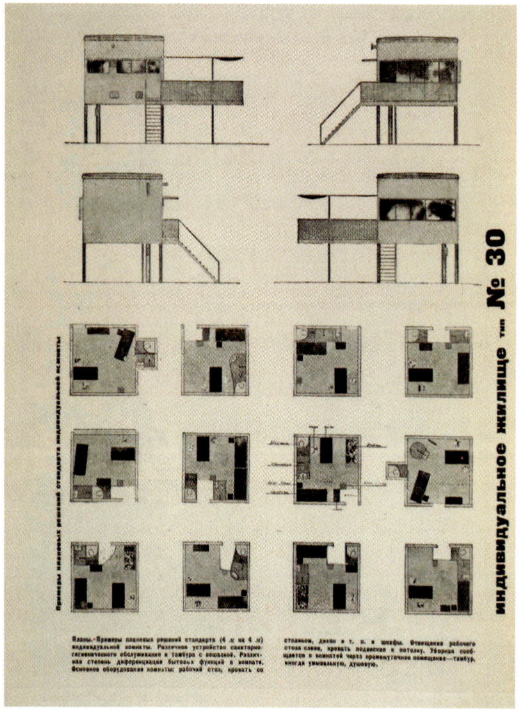

Individual House no. 30, elevations and 12 plans in *Sovremennaja Arhitektura*, 1930

"combinatory."[14] The standard unit to be equipped was the one-room apartment, the "box." According to Lissitzky, the "box" provided for a free, nomadic existence. These basic types moved into the apartment as they do into a steamship cabin or railroad car compartment, bringing with them just linen and items for personal use.[15]

Lissitzky executed this program in his furnishings for Unit F, developed in 1930 for the Housing Committee of the Russian Socialist Federal Republic by architects including Moisej Ginzburg and Mihail Baršč. The Unit F resulted from a "scientific" analysis of what was called "residential boxes" for mass production.

According to the architects, the ideal "box" was Unit F, where two split-level, one-room apartments shared a corridor, like Le Corbusier's "Unité d'habitation" some twenty years later. Each unit would effectively be one room, split into two levels, one with a height of 2.25 m and one with a height of 3.5 m. One level was for sleeping, and the other one for dining. Lissitzky developed a standard with partially built-in furnishings, which included a round table, a shelf, a sofa, and three soft-top stools that could form a second sofa when placed along the wall next to the soft back fastened to the wall. There were two fold-down beds fastened to the wall in the sleeping place. The one-room apartment became a site where theories of "dynamization" and "mechanization" of the workers' environment were tested. Another contraption found its way into Unit F. It was not a piece of furniture, but rather a room, an entire kitchen that was condensed into a piece of workplace equipment. In the quest for efficiency and transformability of the one-room apartment into a site of labor, a room also could be treated as object or mechanical apparatus. Russians drew inspiration from the West. In 1928, an architectural correspondent of the constructivist journal *Sovremennaja Arhitektura* visited the housing exhibition in Stuttgart, where he discovered the Frankfurt kitchen by Margarethe Schütte-Lihotzky, designed from standardized elements. He was impressed by its efficiency as a workplace. "Special care is taken that hands do not cross while washing dishes: the housewife takes the dirty dishes with her left hand, washes and wipes it and puts it with that same left hand to dry on the board," stressed the correspondent. "The principles of the economy of labor and time are brought here to great perfection."[16] The Frankfurt kitchen was soon transformed into a uniquely Soviet contraption. The mutant Soviet offspring of the German architectural invention was the "kitchen element," introduced in the January 1929 issue of *Sovremennaja Arhitektura* (Fig.4). It incorporated all the basic elements of a kitchen reassembled as an oversized armoire.

This was supposed to be a "transitional" kitchen, which would be abandoned when living became communal in the distant future. The kitchen betrayed a fascination with disassembling and reassembling, with condensing space, with the working apparatus as the axis of everyday life and the mechanism for creating a worker's identity. It was meant to be unfolded, folded, opened, closed, and effectively worked on, rather than worked with. It belonged to a subject in action living in a society of impermanence, and it defined domestic space as a space to be refashioned and reconstructed and its inhabitant as a constructor.

The "kitchen element" was not the only appropriation and transformation of a Western domestic model. The most curious example is the transformation of Le Corbusier's Villa Savoye into a one-room "egosphere," the "Individual House no. 30." When the Building Committee set out in 1929 and 1930 to design the ideal workers' dwellings, it applied Corbusian principles. The house had a free façade and strip windows and was raised on pilotis (Fig.5). But it measured 4 by 4 meters. Instead of partitions, there were different combinations of basic objects: bed, desk, table, and sanitary unit, which determined "the everyday functions in the room."[17] In a version developed for the competition for Magnitogorsk, everything was supposed to move and change. At night, the bed is pulled out. In the morning, the bed is folded in and the shower curtain is pulled aside for a morning shower. Then the table and the chair are unfolded. Everything was operable, as in other "equipped" Russian apartments.

Le Corbusier's ideas about the un-rootedness of architecture and its detachment from the site were interpreted in a peculiar manner: as the basis for a new kind of design imagination and as a basis for a new kind of collectivity. The Section for the Redistribution of the Population of the State Planning Committee (the members of which were again Ginzburg and Baršč, and their

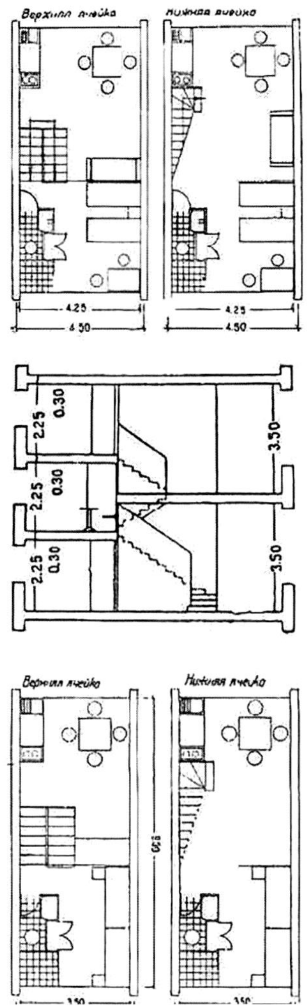

Fig.5 Housing Committee of the RSFSR, Individual House no. 30, 1930 (*Sovremennaja Arhitektura* no. 6, Nov. 1930, courtesy of Getty Research Institute)

spiritual leader, the sociologist Mihail Ohitovič) integrated the Individual Villa into a disurbanist project for a "commune of (single room) houses," which would be an alternative to the "house commune." Villas could move and be placed, according to the user's desires, at different distances and form different connections, so that one day in the future an organic and voluntary collective would be created. But the precondition for creating both the dom-kommuna and the organic collective of moving houses on stilts was the elaborate rethinking of the socialist "egosphere."

We have seen that the design of the individual living cell in the Russian 1920s played a key role in how the proletarian self was imagined and constructed within the context of living conditions, political ideals, and housing policies of the time. Rather than excluding the possibility of individual, cellular existence, the possibilities of designing for a socialist collectivity depended on how the individual unit was conceived. The Russian "egosphere" had its peculiarities, as it defined not a passive, self-indulgent, self-reflective subject, but a subject envisioned as a laborer, constantly in physical interaction with the mechanic cell, and a subject envisioned as a nomad and constructor inhabiting a world in a state of permanent transition. Soviet design for cells and cell-blocks was historically and politically specific, but it was in no way independent from developments in the West. It was influenced by the ethos of efficiency, mechanization that marked the early modern movement, and probably exemplified this ethos to the extreme, as the notion of the "machine for living" acquired a new and more potent meaning when the inhabitant was imagined as a worker literally operating the house, and when the house literally became an assemblage of equipment defining the identity of the inhabitant as that of a physical laborer.

The system of parallels between the Western and the Eastern "egosphere" is even more complex and quite circuitous. In the 1950s, at the time when he was designing the Unité d'Habitation, which in its organization resembles Unit F, Le Corbusier constructed his Cabanon in Roquebrune-Cap Martin in France (Fig.6).The programmatically traditional Villa Savoye inspired the politically radical Individual Villa no. 30, and, uncannily, the eccentric Cabanon had the same dimensions and similar internal organization to the Villa no. 30. In the Cabanon as the ultimate architect's "egosphere," Le Corbusier negotiated the requirements and demands of individual existence in an elementary state, while simultaneously working on the structure of the model cell-block of Western modernity. These two parallel projects reflect the parallel project of the Soviet 1920s: the architectural negotiation of the self and the architectural negotiation of collective existence.

Fig 6. Le Corbusier, Cabanon de vacances, 1951–52, plan (Source: WikiArchitecture)

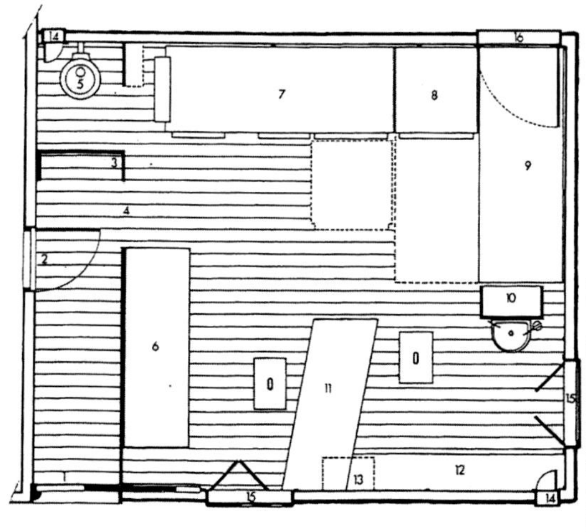

This text is based on my presentation "Living Efficiently," delivered at Open: 33rd Conference of the Society of Architectural Historians of Australia and New Zealand, Gold Coast, Queensland, Australia, 2–5 July 2013."

1. Peter Sloterdijk: "Cell Block, Egospheres, Self-Container: The Apartment as a Co-Isolated Existence," translated from German by Daniela Fabricius, *Log 10* Summer/Fall 2007, pp. 89–108.

2. Ibid, 89.

3. Ibid, 99.

4. Mark Grigor'evič Me'erovič, *Kak Vlast' Narod k Trudu Priučala: Žilišče v SSSR—sredstvo upravlenija ljud'mi 1917–1941 gg.* [How the government taught people to work. Housing in the USSR—means of governing people 1917–1941], Stuttgart: Ibidem-Verlag, 2005.

5. See for example Anatole Kopp, *Town and Revolution: Soviet Architecture and City Planning 1917–1935.* Thomas E. Burton, translator. London: Thames and Hudson, 1970; Selim Omarovich Khan-Magomedov, *Pioneers of Soviet Architecture: The Search for New Solutions in the 1920s and the 1930s,* trans. Alexander Lieven, ed. Catherine Cooke (London: Thames and Hudson, 1987); Andrej Ikonnikov, *Russian Architecture of the Soviet Period,* Lev Ljapin, translator. London: Collets, 1988.

6. Nikolai A. Miljutin. *Socgorod: The Problem of Building Socialist Cities.* Arthur Sprague, translator. Cambridge: MIT Press, 1974, p. 82. Originally *Problema Stroitel'stva Socialističeskih Gorodov.* Moscow: Gosudarstvenoe izdatel'stvo, 1930.

7. Ibid., 84.

8. Ibid., 81.

9. Ibid., 81.

10. Editor's note: In his 1923 international journal *Vešč / Object / Gegenstand* no. 1–2, El Lissitzky explains that "for us, art is nothing other than the creation of new 'objects.'"

11. Ibid., pp. 126–127.

12. Alexander Toporkov, *Tehničeskij Byt i Sovremennoe Isskustvo.* [Technical everyday life and contemporary art], Moscow and Leningrad: Gosudarstvennoe Izdatel'stvo, 1928.

13. Ibid., 92-93.

14. Lazar Lissitzky, "Oborudovanie Žilišča Mebelju" (1929), cited in Selim O. Khan Magomedov, *Heroes of the Avant-Garde: Lazar Lissitzky,* Moscow: S.E. Gordeev, 2011.

15. Ibid., 202.

16. L. Jacobson, "The Frankfurt Kitchen," *Sovremennaja Arkhitektura* No. 5 1928, 166.

17. "Individual House No. 30," *Sovremennaja Arhitektura* no. 6, Nov. 1930, 13.

North-East end of the building following the first intervention: the balconies of the first floor were closed with windows and a room was added on the ground floor to accommodate the habitual 'Lenin Corner

Sources of the Narkomfin: The New Byt and the Collectivization of Everyday Life

Danilo Udovički-Selb

Before us no longer stands the little wife, the shadow of the husband—before us stands the personality, the woman as human being.
Alexandra Kollontaj[1]

In Soviet Russia the workingwoman should be surrounded by the same ease and light, hygiene and beauty that previously only the very rich could afford. Instead of the workingwoman having to struggle with the cooking and spend all of her free hours in the kitchen . . . communist society will organize public restaurants and communal kitchens.
Alexandra Kollontaj[2]

A benchmark of modern architecture, Ginzburg's (1892–1946) and Milinis' Narkomfin (1899-1974)[3] has often been associated with the *Dom-Kommuna* housing typology, a highly experimental concept of collective dwelling, which reached its zenith by 1929.

The *Dom-Kommuny*, or literally the "Home-Communes," were understood as housing institutions that took care of all the daily living needs such as child rearing, meal preparation, entertainment and fitness clubs, libraries and reading rooms, down to laundry services.[4] The most extreme form of such housing facilities implied the dismantling of the traditional concept of the family itself. Although this did not fully apply to the Narkomfin, given its hybrid, even transitional character, Ginzburg's and Milinis' project represented certainly the most notable and most sophisticated housing in the decade following the Bolshevik Revolution (Fig.1). Widely transcending the confines of Soviet architectural practice itself, the Narkomfin anticipated by twenty years Le Corbusier's own experimental housing block in Marseille. The Narkomfin was inspired in part by the revolutionary idea, seductively alive throughout the 1920s, of employing architecture as a means of transforming the bourgeois style of habitation into something radically new. Central to this idea was the concern for the emancipation of the "working woman," in equal measure a housewife and breadwinner. Granted that many other conditions had to be met, what could be the response to such a program in architectural terms? Was it possible to advance woman's emancipation from "household slavery" through the spatial and functional re-conceptualization of the home? And what forces were at work shaping the thinking of the time and the design of the Narkomfin?

Within the paradigm of "modernization," the ambition of the Bolsheviks and anarchists alike was to transform the state and social relations down to the very *byt*, the daily life itself. To this effect, a special women's section of the party, the *Ženotdel*, was created to organize outreach work involving other women. Among the Bolsheviks, Lenin was one of the most dedicated proponents of revolutionary women's emancipation. He promoted it in speeches and articles throughout the Civil War. Not surprisingly, he immediately nominated the flamboyant Alexandra Kollontaj—the "Klara Zetkin" of the Bolshevik revolution[5] —to the post of People's Commissar of Social Affairs,[6] making her the first woman in modern history to hold the title of government minister. Revered among feminists to this day, Kollontaj, the leading advocate of women's struggle for equality in Soviet Russia, was instrumental in fleshing out the ideological foundations concretized in the

Dom-Kommuny. From her government position, in concert with a variety of social and political organizations, especially the *Ženotdel* [Women Section], Kollontaj emphasized what the Soviet State would bring women: children's houses, maternity leaves, literacy programs, cafeterias, and public laundries:[7] in essence, the program of the *Dom-Kommuny*.

The deeper origins of the first Russian collectivist design hypothesis are, however, numerous and complex. Lenin advocated a radical socialization of the common "way of dwelling," which was heralded in the first days of the October Revolution in his seminal "Declaration of the Fundamental Rights of the Working and Exploited People."[8] The Declaration, promulgated in January 1918 and implicitly intended as an extension of the 1789 *Déclaration des droits de l'homme et du citoyen*, led to the nationalization and expropriation of all lands, including the entire real estate realm. City communes acquired the right to confiscate all unoccupied dwellings and distribute them to the indigent and homeless. On December 14, 1918, all urban real estate speculation was forbidden. The Declaration harked back to the principles Engels formulated in his 1872 pamphlet, "The Housing Question."[9] Lenin's Declaration opened vast opportunities for territorial planning and socialization of the human habitat.[10] The pamphlet would be echoed, albeit in a less radical form, in the Austrian Social Democrats' laws of the "Red Vienna," as early as 1919. The intense debate across Russian society on the modalities of the Declaration's implementation was sharpened in 1921, when Aleksandra Kollontaj published in Germany the Manifesto of the Soviet "Worker's Opposition."[11] The Manifesto envisioned social renewal through the reorganization of the physical space on the condition that workers' self-rule was restored. Kollontaj's hopes were high. New architectural and urban typology would usher in a new model of life for the working class. This meant that the traditional bourgeois family was put to the test. Kollontaj's practical and theoretical work remained instrumental in linking the new concept of family relationships to the creation of new spatial models of communal living.

It is significant to note, in addition, that the ongoing discourse about the housing issues was not strictly Marxist. Many other social concepts populated Russia's body politics prior to the October Revolution, and the Bolsheviks themselves were influenced by a range of social theories. The Russian Marxist thought was among the least developed in Europe. As Antonio Gramsci pointed out on various occasions, the Bolshevik Revolution itself occurred in contravention to *Das Kapital*. In this sense, the theories of the pre-Marxian "utopian socialists" played a significant role in shaping the ideological framework of urbanistic and architectural solutions put forward regarding the new *byt*.[12] The Narkomfin has to be considered in the light of such eclectic discourses. Calling for innovative dwelling models, Kollontaj organized teach-ins in "female emancipation,"[13] mostly in Russia. As early as November 1918, she convened a feminist congress, which was attended by 1200 women, including Klara Zetkin.[14] The "reform of the home" (Kollontaj's own expression) was the centerpiece at the congress. Ten years later, at the height of the "new *byt*" movement, socialist *byt* reconstruction theorists adopted a significant part of that assembly's debates.[15]

The literature on the social significance of a new *byt* proliferated rapidly as Bolshevik politics intersected with revolutionary ethics.[16] In the wake of the February and October Revolutions, two distinct tendencies defined the birth of the communitarian ideology. The first stemmed from dreams of a total transformation of society, based on the radical rejection of established community and family norms. Eliminating the family and embracing the social structures that would follow were at the core of a new collective life. As such, it stood closest to Kollontaj's advocacy of a new social morality. The second orientation envisioned a non-ideological architectural discipline—a discipline defined by highly professional, "scientific" dwelling typologies. The latter favored only a gradual transformation of the hitherto prevalent *byt*,[17] while its spatial prototypes were articulated in the *Dom-Kommuna* architectural typology. The apartment itself, a mere "cell for living," would offer only the most intimate, personal living spaces. Primarily focused on architecture, this second view was only mildly responsive to political considerations. The concept of the Narkomfin, as Ginzburg understood it, fell at the intersection of the two.

To understand this seminal building in all its complexity, one must therefore consider it from within such political, urban, and professional realities at a time of dire economic conditions and growing ideological cleavages between the so-called "Left" and "Right" factions in the Central Committee. Lenin's widow Nadežda Krupskaja sided with Buharin and the "Right" as they resisted Stalin's conservative reversal regarding the family and women's emancipation,[18] the way they fiercely opposed forced land collectivization.[19]

Fig. 2 Cover *Sovremennaja Arhitektura* 1930, 1–2 , (left) "On the Reconstruction of the byt"; the Central Committe ordinance (right)

By 1930, while the Narkomfin was still under construction, the Central Committee's sudden indictment of the *byt* experimentation signaled the growing prevalence of Stalin's "centrist" faction, which favored establishment over revolution, but also the need to sidetrack any program that did not contribute most directly to the breakneck pace of industrialization as the Five-Year-Plan stipulated.[20] The very significance of the unfinished building was implicitly reconsidered.[21] The May 1930 Central Committee Directive, published by all the media including, prudently, by Ginzburg's own architectural journal *SA* (Fig.2), stipulated not quite unreasonably that

Along with the growth of the [reconstruction]

of the socialist byt, certain unfounded, semi-fantastic and therefore harmful experiments are conducted by some comrades (Sabsovič,[22] *in part Larin and others) who want to jump "in one stroke" over the obstacles that stand on the road to the socialist reconstruction of the way of life, which are created on the one hand by the economic and cultural backwardness of the country, and on the other by the need at this particular moment to gather all the resources available for the rapid industrialization of the country.*[23]

He added, "Utopian undertakings [such as the abolition of the family and marriage, separating the children from their families for collective rearing] . . . would represent an enormous waste of available resources, and discredit severely the very idea of a socialist reconstruction of the way of life." The accused architects were chastised for their "opportunism" and "radical left phraseology."

The CC recommended to the Government—the *Sovet Narodnyh Komissarov* (SNK)—to establish "in a matter of fifteen days, regulations for the construction of workers' housing (laundry facilities, bathhouses, child-care facilities, factory kitchens, canteens etc.)."[24] In moving the issue into the hands of the Government for expediency and "realism," the initiative in planning of workers' housing was, for all practical purposes, snapped away from the architects' hands. Such a move stood just one step away from the withholding of all resources except the most barren housing necessities of industrial workers.[25] Ginzburg's Housing Institute, established in 1926, was reaching the end of its activity.

After 1930, the growing centralization of power, accelerated industrialization, and forced land collectivization took precedence over the search for alternative living and housing typologies. Severed from its social and political demand, the Narkomfin fell into gradual oblivion. By 1936 its inhabitants themselves became easy prey to Stalin's repression.[26] Amidst forced industrialization, the mass employment of feminine force was instrumentalized by the state for its own purposes. Kollontaj's ideas regarding worker's self-government and feminist ethics had lost all political currency, as she was sidelined as a Soviet diplomat to Scandinavia and Mexico, albeit as the first woman ambassador in history—her second record.[27] Whereas there is no direct evidence that Ginzburg cited Kollontaj in his writings or lectures, this towering figure of early Soviet feminist theory and activism could not have eluded Ginzburg's attention. As a minister of Lenin's first government for social affairs, and the leader of the Workers' Opposition, she was an omnipresent figure in the field like no other. What is certain, at any rate, is that Ginzburg's design approach to the Dom-Kommuny, as well as both his disurbanist housing theory and ten years of experimenting with the subject—all of it summed up in his 1934 *Žilišče* (Dwelling)—clearly pointed to a privileged connection between the two. Central to his Constructivist discourse on the "Social Condenser of the age"[28] was the belief that architecture could influence social behavior.[29] The single building most associated with the idea was the Narkomfin.

Communal Living: An Evolving Concept

The manifestation and formation of an authentically modern workers' way of life, which thus far has changed little, and which we can envisage only to a certain extent, will determine the remaining unknowns as well; only as a result of this process will it be possible to define this still vague ideal.
M. Ginzburg, *Style and Epoch*, 1924[30]

It is only natural that a solution in a modern sense to the problem of human housing will come much later, at the time when the new conception of style would become so pervasive as to fill all the corners of the human existence.
M. Ginzburg, *Style and Epoch*, 1924

Early attempts at building affordable housing in a collectivist mode occurred more than a decade before the October Revolution, in 1904, at the eve of the first uprising against the Tsar Nikolaj II. The first projects, and those that followed, between 1904 and 1917, speak of the relative enlightenment of the burgeoning Russian industrial bourgeoisie, which opposed the Tsar's and the aristocracy's absolute power. Better acquainted with Marx's *Capital* than the proletariat, the nascent industrial bourgeoisie already looked beyond nineteenth century paternalist social models.

As the architect N. V. Markovnikov wrote in his "The House-Commune, Past, Present and Future,"[31] a significant example of such clairvoyance was the case of G. C. Slodovnikov, a merchant who at the turn of the century gave the city of Moscow six million rubles for the construction of affordable housing. This philanthropic donation prompted a debate between the recently created Garden City Association, based on Ebenezer Howard's urban theories, and the Moscow City Hall. The Association advocated the development of workers' suburban settlements, whereas the City Hall favored urban multistory buildings. A competition was called to settle the controversy. The winners were architects Apyskov and Lunickij (Fig. 3), who proposed a kind of collective housing project "*à redents*"—a series of cells in a zigzag deployment, set in the midst of gardens, and connected by a segmented corridor. An incorporated communal space under a glass dome served the entire community (Fig 3). Howardian city projects proliferated from the Garden-City's projects for a series of "Sputnik-Cities" [satellite cities] sprouting around Moscow; to Semenov's 1912 satellite projects along the railroad Moscow-Kazan; to Ivan Fomin's projects of Garden-Cities around Riga, Petrograd, and the Crimea—all the way to an industrial city designed in 1917, just a few months before the Bolshevik takeover. Given such precedents, it is understandable that prerevolutionary progressive ideas contributed significantly to the maturation of the architectural avant-garde's own concepts.[32] In contrast with such overarching Howardian pastoral narratives,[33] however, the Proletarian Revolution brought a new theme of its own into the urbanistic discourse—the burgeoning movement aligned with the futurist "urban poetry" of Mayakovsky (Majakovskij). Its mythology of the machine was best exemplified in Nikolaj Černihov's urban fantasies.

Fig. 3 Apyskov and Lunickij, Workers Housing Project, Competition entry, Moscow, 1904–1905

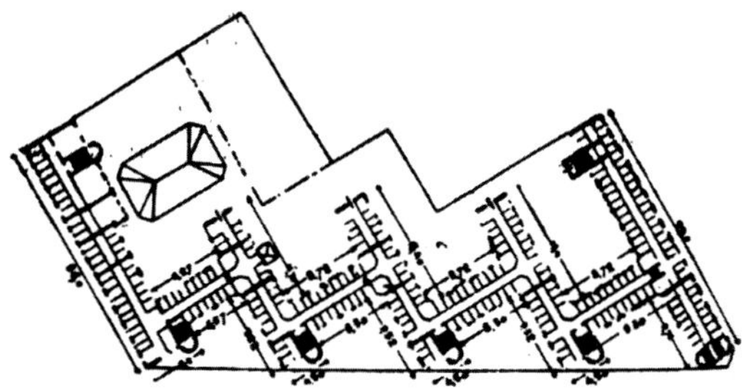

This double orientation, ambiguously playing itself out in the Russian avant-garde, was fed on both nostalgia for the original peasant values (echoed in the "disurbanist" movement) and the mechanistic dreams of dense industrial cities promoted by the "urbanists."[34] It could be said that the Narkomfin's Arcadian setting in a park with broad horizons, combined with its "paquebot" machine aesthetic, conjured up the two.[35]

For Ginzburg, the new social patron of the architectural production was the working class, whose "current fundamental problem [was] the implementation of all the architectural issues connected to the concept of the 'worker's home' and the 'house of labor.'" He therefore considered that the resolution of the workers' housing problem and its extensions would become a fundamental component of the "new style" itself. In other words, the search for housing prototypes would ultimately inform the core of the Constructivist architecture as such. The housing research laboratory he started in 1926 on the request of the STROJKOM (Building Committee of the Russian Soviet Republic) was the culmination of half a decade of the avant-garde's typological distillation.[36]

The first *Dom-Kommuny* designs began to appear in the early 1920s. Such was the 1921 design of D. P. Buryskin and L. M. Tverskoj's "Phalanstère" for Petrograd. It is interesting to note that in section their "Phalanstère" anticipated Ginzburg's own original duplex apartments for the Narkomfin (Fig.4). Predictably, however, the general approach of these projects harked back to eighteenth and nineteenth century models, as had been the case of the very first works of the future leaders of constructivism, still imbued with neo-classicism, a style deemed progressive before the Revolution.[37]

By contrast, Nikolaj Ladovskij, the founder of ASNOVA in 1923 (Association of New Architects) and leader of the so-called Rationalist school,[38] presented already in 1920 an exceptional alternative. His entry for a communal housing competition distinguished itself with provocative formal originality (Fig.5). Introducing daring deconstructive tectonics—the hallmark of his VHUTEMAS teaching—he prefigured the Vesnins' 1923 competition project for the Palace of Labor. Ladovskij's housing project captured brazenly the spirit of both the Russian cubo-futurist language and German architectural Expressionism.[39] On the other hand, echoing Viktor Šklovskij's linguistic Formal Method, his procedure involved the principle of "estrangement" of everyday banality

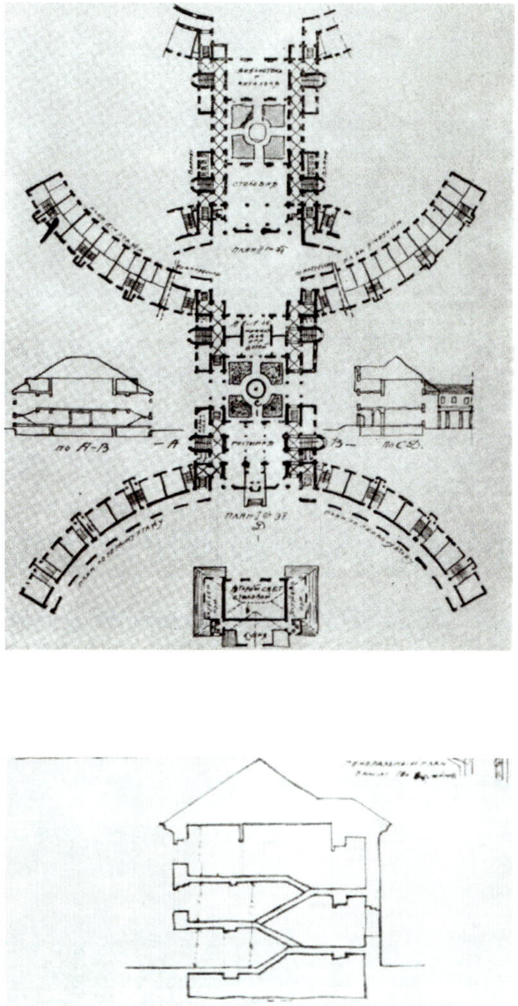

Fig. 4 D. P. Burynskin and L. M. Tverskoj, "Phalanstery" 1921 PLAN & Section of Unit; note the similarity with the Narkomfin's F Type section.

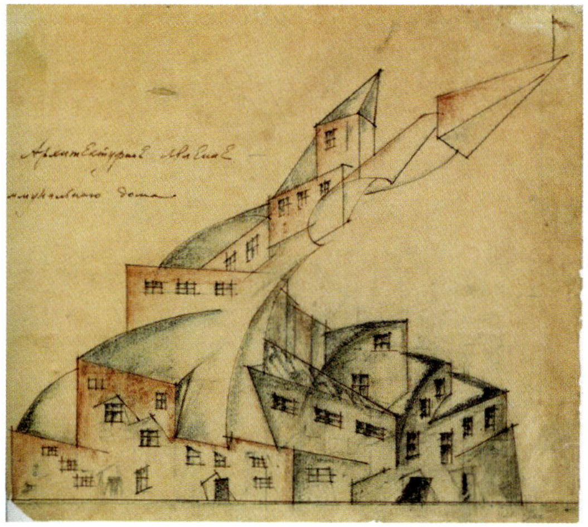

Fig. 5 Nikolaj Ladovskij, Communal Housing, 1920. Courtesy of State Museum of Architecture, Moscow

Fig. 6 Vladimir Krinskij, Communal Housing, 1920. Courtesy of State Museum of Architecture, Moscow

through formal semantic displacements of the given.[40]

In search of a revolutionary renovation of a tired *byt* through form, Ladovskij revolutionized his own art. More interested in the language of form than in any specific social issue, he favored the awakening effect on the psyche architecture could provoke. He indulged in daring cantilevered structures and deconstructed assemblages of functional volumes that conveyed a sense of movement, that is, of the fourth dimension already present in El Lissitzky's Suprematist PROUNs "Seeds" for the "Affirmation of the New." Malevič's (Malevich) trans-rational art ("*Za um*" or "beyond reason") was not foreign to the process either. Equally innovative was Vladimir Krinskij, a fellow "Rationalist" of Ladovskij's. He seems to have gone even further in the architectural exploration of prerevolutionary cubo-futurist compositions, although not much is known about it since only one image survived (with no plan or section) (Fig.6).

In radical counterdistinction to such experiments, in 1922 Leonid Vesnin won a competition for a House Commune (Fig.7). Vesnin's project, in some ways akin to a populist *Heimatstil*, contrasted unfavorably with the competition entry for the *Leningradskaja Pravda* he and his brothers presented together only two years later.[41]

The 1922 competition program for workers' lodgings looked for prototypical projects to be situated on two different sites, one next to the monastery Simonov in the Simonovskij Rajon, and the other along the large avenue Serpuhovskaja in the Zamoskvoreče Rajon. Unlike the ubiquitous Garden-City typology, these projects were the first to address an urban setting, calling for continuity with the city's fabric. The program of the competition,[42] run by the conservative Moscow Architectural Society (MAO),[43] presented three- or four-floor brick buildings, with no effort toward technological or typological innovation. The winner was again Leonid Vesnin along with the brothers Il'ja and Panteleimon Golosov. The Golosov conservative project in no way anticipated either the modernist career the brothers were going to have (in particular Il'ja's famous "Zujev" workers' club in 1926 and Panteleimon's "Pravda" building in 1930). It is possible that both Leonid and the Golosovs were taking into account that the project was situated in an eighteenth century section of the city. Some deference was probably in order to accommodate MAO's conservative position as well. With its high roofs and stretched classicizing verticals, the language of their project could be associated in some ways to Heinrich Tessenow's

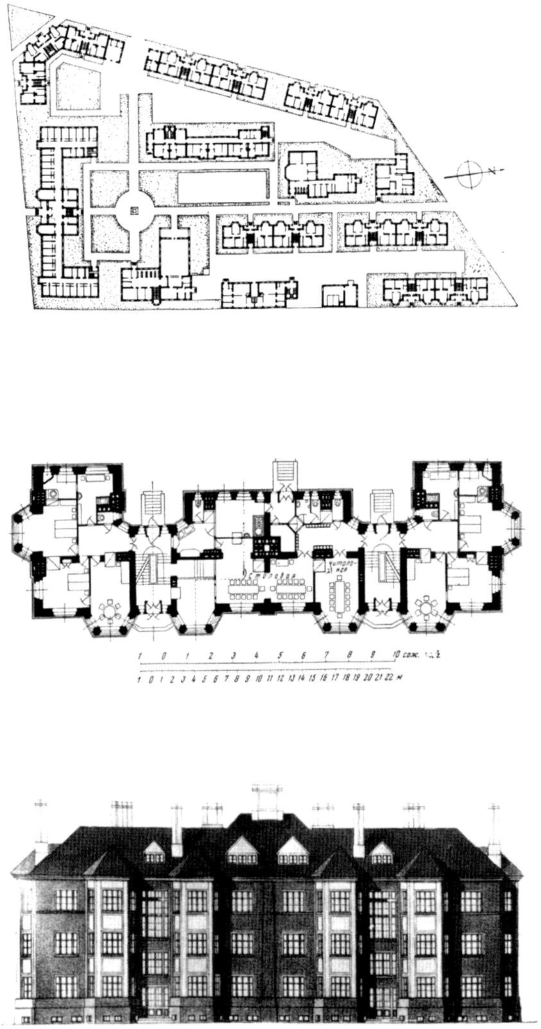

Fig. 7 Leonid Vesnin, Workers Housing, Simonovskij Rajon, Moscow, 1922

architecture. What distinguished the project of the brothers Golosov, however, was its urbanistic setting with the dynamic diagonal disposition of the buildings that slashed an otherwise inert trapezoidal site. A double curve on the site's northwest and southeast ends softened, and visually enriched the rigidity of the general spatial setting (Fig.8). Ginzburg referred to these competitions in his 1924 *Style and Epoch*, saying that:

The latest competitions sponsored by the Moscow Architectural Society have produced a series of projects that compare favorably with those of Europe. However, the essence of these numerous solutions, both those which have been implemented and those which have not, naturally reflects not a feeling for a new form, but an absolute dependence on past cultures. . . . What we unquestionably have here is not workers' housing as such, but ordinary housing for an economically disadvantaged segment of the population.[44]

With the New Economic Policies (NEP) now in full swing, and the focus gradually shifting from workers' housing to the needs of a rising middle class, Markovnikov resumed building a Garden-City, "*Sokol,*" in Moscow's Krasnopresenskij Rajon under the auspices of the Moscow Building Cooperative. "Residential auto-sufficiency," as Manfredo Tafuri suggested, "[was] used as the definition of an independent economic initiative"[45] (Fig. 9). The community consisted of one-family houses with gardens, or of multi-family blocks built in various materials: solid bricks, wood, light cinderblocks, cement, or scoria. Although somewhat rough in execution compared to its English precedents, this kind of settlement targeted a rising well-to-do class. With the reviving of a market economy, the workers' housing question was inevitably pushed to the back burner, against the wish of the Bolshevik left and of the trade unions.

This unexceptional production was interrupted by Melnikov's entry to another 1923 competition (won by Nikolaj Kolli's project for the Zamoskvoreče in Moscow) (Fig. 10). Melnikov infused the project with a sense of deliberate collage-like flexibility and random testing of transormable typologies. Formed as an open-ended double fan, it displayed, not unlike the Narkomfin (but here spread horizontally over the site), apartments of two main sizes: four buildings fanning in a semi-circle contained large apartments; beyond them were a series of smaller "à redent" units with a variety of typical plans exploded in linear paterns from an imaginary center. The communal facilities were reached by a covered hallway attached to the large units.[46]

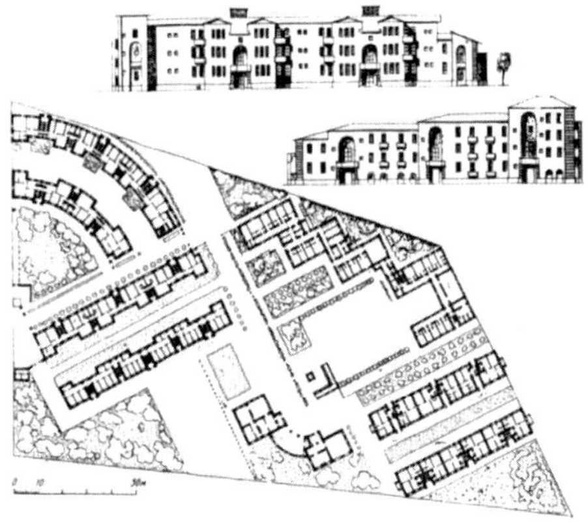

Fig. 8 Brothers Golosov, Communal Housing, Zamoskvoreče, Moscow 1923

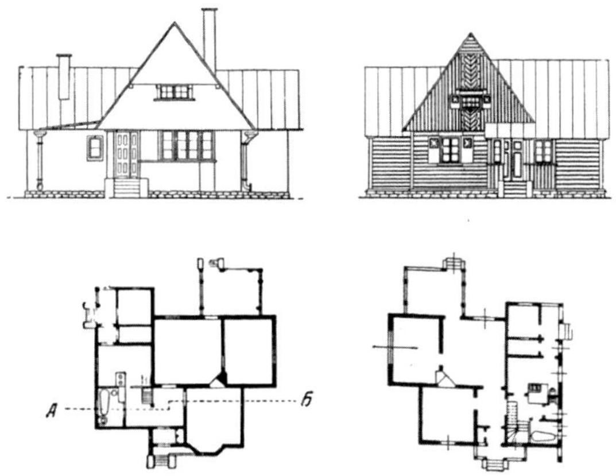

Fig. 9 N. V. Markovnikov, Garden City "Sokol,', near Moscow, 1923

The Heyday of the Dom-Kommuna Concept

Following the 1928 revocation of the NEP, the *Dom-Kommuna* concept regained momentum. It reached its highest point between the end of 1929 and early 1930, mobilizing the entire spectrum of the specialized publications in response to the Five-Year-Plan. The *Dom-Kommuna* was no longer an isolated laboratory experiment on the margins of Ginzburg's architectural production, which he started in 1926, after he founded the OSA (Society of Contemporary Architects).[47] By the early 1930s it had acquired a central place in the discourse regarding Soviet housing policies in general.

The breakthrough in the popular reception of the *Dom-Kommuna* concept occurred when *Dom-Stroitel'stvo Moskvy* (a publication of the Moscow City Council) dedicated an entire issue to the question of communal living.[48]

The idea of the *Dom-Kommuna* had reached a point of maturity both theoretically and practically. It was now ready for full-speed dissemination across the country in built form. Having radically changed its graphic design in 1928, along constructivist aesthetics, *Stroitel'stvo Moskvy* itself reached its top distinction in 1929–30, when El Lissitzky started designing some of its covers (Fig. 11). The journal's editorial highlighted a few important points. It was necessary " . . . to avoid [at this juncture of social evolution] any effort that would consider the *Dom-Kommuna* as a self-sufficient instance. It is essential that the architects tackle the problem, with gradual experimentation in programmatic terms [i.e.] moving step by step in order to awaken an active interest of a large segment of the proletarian public opinion."[49] In the critical years preceding the 1930 16th Party Congress, *Stroitel'stvo Moskvy* (with Nikita Khrushchev as City Mayor) unself-consciously followed the Moscow Party's implicit resistance to Stalin's "revolution from above,"[50] the curtailment of the NEP in the first place. What characterized this new phase for the *Dom-Kommuny* most explicitly were the absence of ideological dogmatism and a dedication to conceptual flexibility. Three significant unbuilt, or partially built complexes, illustrate the point: Nikolaj Miljutin's Socgorod, Ginzburg's Narkomfin, and especially Ivan Leonidov's famous proposal for the city of Magnitogorsk (Magnetic Mountain). All three seemed to operate along the lines of *Stroitel'stvo Moskvy*, where flexibility in planning was defined by a limited durability of the projected structures, that is, well under sixty years. The justification of such a short lifespan was the belief that each successive five-year-plan would bring increased economic wealth, allowing radical renovations

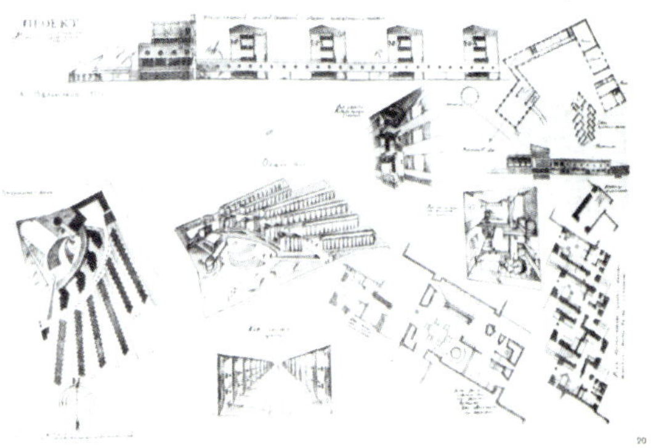

Fig. 10 Kontsantin Melnikov, Communal Housing, Zamoskvoreče, Moscow, 1923

Fig. 11 *Stroitel'stvo Moskvy*, front cover by El Lissitzky

and innovations of the habitat in the future, that is, "constantly moving ahead of the demands of the socialist man." This would amount to a kind of "permanent revolution" in the housing realm—to paraphrase Trotsky's social theory. In a typically "disurbanist" approach, Miljutin postulated a variety of aggregated dwelling cells composed and recomposed along a linear city, modeled on the idea of the assembly line. This echoed Ginzburg's own "disurbanist" city where the Narkomfin and its community services were conceived as a flexible unit of a larger "green city," a position Ginzburg had recently adopted under the influence of the young sociologist and his OSA collaborator, Mihail Ohitovič.[51] The city was to be made of clusters of various dwelling types connected to community services.

Leonidov's concept for the new city of Magnitogorsk, an industrial metallurgic settlement developed under his direction out of the OSA workshops, carried the idea of communal living the farthest (Fig.12). Leonidov belonged to the youngest generation of Constructivists as the student of Aleksandr Vesnin at the VHUTEMAS, the highly experimental school, run as a large students' commune.[52] His direct experience of community life possibly informed the collectivized city he was to conceive for Magnitogorsk.[53] He varied the scale between predominantly low-rise clusters of dwellings and outdoor amenities encouraging close community interaction and play. Occasional high-rises balanced the composition. Bound to maintain a human scale, Leonidov was strongly opposed to giant communitarian edifices so common in the 1929–30 projects with their anonymous ghetto crowdedness. Avoiding total collectivization of life, Leonidov paid careful attention to eye level design and landscaping, distinguishing his approach from those limited to global air-views, common in the modernist practice. The orthogonal grid of the general layout allowed for a variety of urban settings. Selim Han-Magomedov observed that Leonidov "elaborated a theory of 'small-scale collectivization' where the *Dom-Kommuna* model [was] defined by a linear distribution of the city. It referred to a singular moment of fusion between the disintegration of a 'disurbanized city,' and the mediation of a rigid collectivist universe increasingly dominant in the field."[54]

Unlike the small-scale collectivization, the large-scale 1929-30 projects appeared to claim opposing principles. Despite taking, in many cases, the Narkomfin as a point of departure, their overblown scale invited alienation rather than shared life. Most of all, like the nineteenth century socialist utopias, they boasted a rigid determination of every aspect of collective existence. Such were S. Ajzicovič's large communal house (financed by the building cooperative of the Proletarskij Rajon)[55] (Fig. 13) and the "Mosblisojuz" project of Čildišev and Rozenfel'd (Fig.14). They championed an oversized, eight-floor Narkomfin with more than one thousand inhabitants each.[56]

Fig. 12 Ivan Leonidov, project for the City of Magnitogorsk, 1930

Fig.13 S Ajzicovič, Communal House, Proletarskij Rajon, 1929

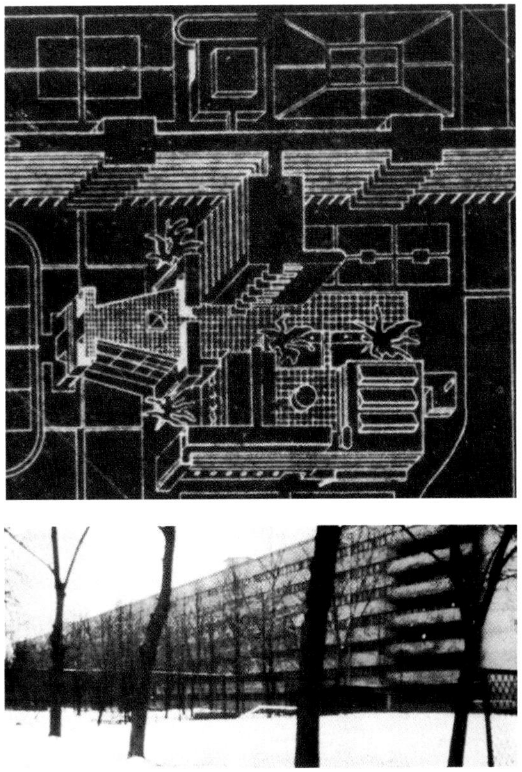

Fig. 14 Čildišev and Rozenfel'd, Mosblisojuz, Moscow, 1929

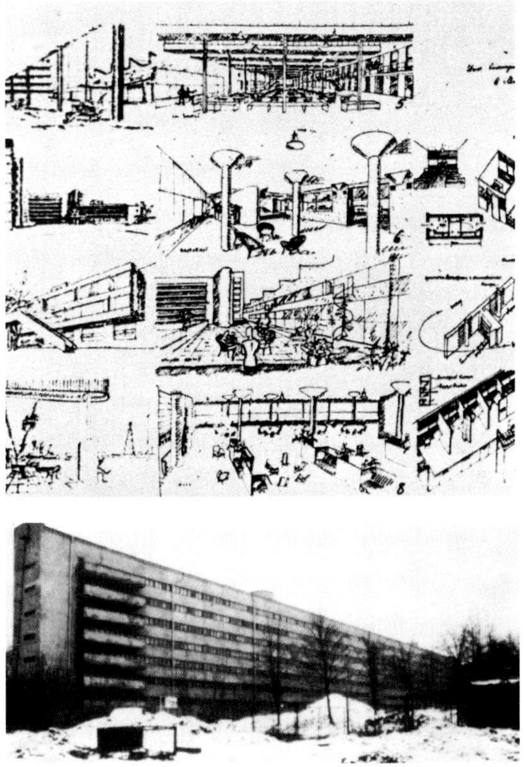

Another example of high social determinism (even if markedly superior in quality to the two previous ones) was I. Nikolajev's 200-student housing.[57] According to the architect's own description, his "total machine" for a socialized mode of living and learning led to a highly rationalized life dictated by a careful agenda. "The typical cell," as Nikolajev described it, "includes a series of spaces used in common [study room, reading room, library]. The division of the facilities is derived from the "specialization" of vital problems such as night sleep, eating, exercising, studying, and resting. Each inhabitant of the communal house is addressed from the point of view of the common needs study and work impose.[58]

Completed in record time (in the first half of the 1930s), the building presented yet another distinction: the service facilities, which included a theater, assumed a central, dominant position.

By their deployment over the site, the facilities also defined outdoor spaces such as a plaza with a fountain, gardens, and sports activities—all very similar to the 1930 House-Commune the brothers Vesnin designed for the city of Kuznetsk[59] (Fig. 15). While the 200-m-long flat dormitory building defined the scale, the diversity of the communal facilities gave the ensemble a rich plastic articulation. Together, the buildings resulted in some sort of autarchic, highly programmed phalanstery, where collective facilities dominated even the most minimal "accessorial" activities such as personal night cubicles—the only niches of privacy, even though two students shared the cell itself.[60]

The evolution and progressive refinement of the communitarian concept found a significant conclusion in the project of a typical *Dom-Kommuna* by V. Vladimirov and M. Baršč(1904–76)[61]—the latter, a brilliant graduate under Ginzburg from the VHUTEIN[62] and member of the OSA (Fig.16). The project got the full attention of the journal *SA*[63] as one of the first full-fledged large scale

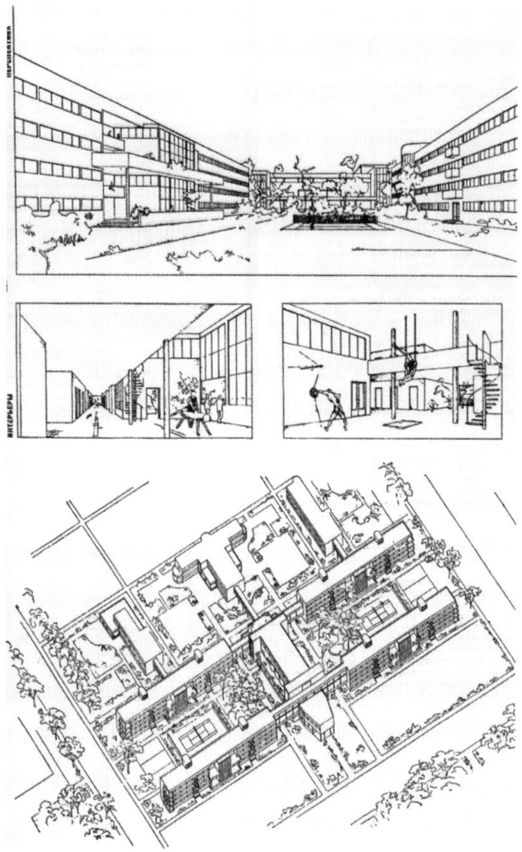

Fig. 15 Brothers Vesnin, House-Commune, Kuznetsk, 1930. I. Nikolajev, Student Hostel for two hundred students

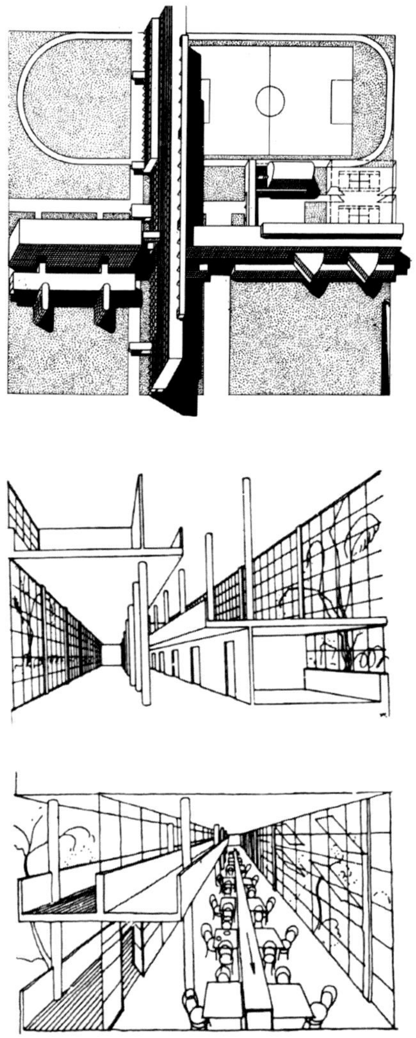

Fig.16 V. Vladimirov and Mihail Baršč, competition entry 1927

buildings of this type.[64] The design was elaborated as part of Ginzburg's, that is, OSA's housing workshop for the STROJKOM, concluding four years of search for new dwelling types. Compositionally very rich, the main concept was a cross-like north-south, east-west distribution of the two main volumes of the building. The first contained primarily the living quarters for adults, the second for children of various ages from toddlers to sixteen-year-olds.

Tightly intertwined with both arms of the cross were the diversified communal services—encompassing everything from daily necessities, libraries, scientific work, individual studies ("for scholarly work and in-depth reading"), lecture rooms, workshops, and leisure quarters. They implicitly catered to needs of both intellectual and manual workers, thus representing a complete cross-section of a classless, but diversely specialized society. The cells for adults were transformable from single to double occupancy.

Unlike Ginzburg's "transitional type," this level of dwelling flexibility was the most the setting could offer. There was no kitchen of any kind beyond an incorporated foldable table as a tea spot—an essential Russian staple. The dining room tables were linearly distributed along both sides of a conveyor, which brought in the meals and took away used dishes. Consonant with the Five-Year-Plan and accelerated industrialization based on the rationalization of production, from Mil'utin's linear city to the Baršč-Vladimirov linear *Dom-Kommuna* and Leonidov's Magnitogorsk, the assembly line was the obvious reference. Not intended for immediate application, this project could be read as a manifesto of the fully socialized *Dom-Kommuna* type.

By the end of 1929, all the "design brigades," the architectural societies, and the economic and social institutions were compelled to adopt a position regarding such a societal model. While projects were numerous, realizations were understandably much fewer. Yet this was still a time when arguments were tested and the discourse developed. The numerous projects included G. M. Dankman's student hostel;[65] the "Phalanstery High-rise" by Pokcičevskij;[66] and the very original tripartite *Dom-Kommuna* with services at the juncture of the three arms by students K. Ivanov, F. Terecki, and P. Smolin[67]—a type Le Corbusier would later adopt for his never built "Patte-de-Poule" high-rise designed in 1935 as a model housing project for the Paris International Exposition of 1937.

Noteworthy among the built work similar to the Narkomfin was the 1930 collective house by Solomon Lisagor, 1900–1937)[68] and E. Popov in Saratov, and a number of pilot projects by Ginzburg to be discussed later. What was exceptional here was not only the multitude of proposals, but also the variety of typological solutions presenting a promising open field of non-dogmatic projects, still open to debate and testing.

They called for standardization in diversity. Beyond the projects themselves, debates among professionals on the merits of collective life flourished.

Even lesser known figures such as S. Motoljanskij looked at historical precedents in search for the utopian roots of the current movement. The latter celebrated nineteenth century collectivist ideals, but, paradoxically, treated Howard as "the illuminated theoretician of capitalism" while branding William Morris as a "petit-bourgeois socialist." Morris was compared to Ohitovič, the ideologue of the "disurbanization." To counter Morris and Howard, Motoljanskij invoked Edward Bellamy's anarcho-socialist novel *Looking Backward.* Relying on an implicit 'license' from an article Pravda published on December 2, 1929, which invited planners and designers to ". . . get inspired by the great utopian socialists in their search for city building models . . . ," Motoljanskij emulated Charles Fourier's projections.[69]

The models of "utopian socialism," and in particular Fourier's *Phalanstère*, frequently figured in the discussions about the socialist future of the Soviet society—a rather puzzling affinity, given that the so-called "father of scientific socialism," Karl Marx, branded these authors as "utopian."[70] The very low level of Marxist critical thought in the Soviet Union, or perhaps a repressed awareness that the Bolshevik revolution itself was highly utopian, might perhaps explain this oddity.[71] On the other hand, the repudiation of NEP's crass commercial materialism, which invigorated the economy but dashed away the revolutionary dreams, may have reawakened by contrast a taste for farfetched ideals.

In a form of "*fuite en avant*" (forward retreat), Markovnikov, one of the architects most involved since 1918 in the search for the definition of a housing model, concluded in January 1930 (the year of the Central Committee's repudiation of all form of new byt experimentation), that

Socialism is not anymore the ideal of a faraway future, but rather a practical problem. . . . A settlement of a new type from which new forms of community life will spring through the development of economic areas capable of responding to the needs of the population, [while] undermining the foundations of an idealistic, petit-bourgeois life, represents in itself a step towards the realization of socialism.[72]

Possibly anticipating an imminent Central Committee backlash against the new *byt* movement, a well-connected Markovnikov published an attack against all previous projects, including his own residential Garden City model. While still reaffirming the central role that collective housing should play in the Five-Year Plan, he condemned extant experiments by claiming that

The types of dwellings we have seen around thus far, either in the bourgeois countries or in our own, all represent without exception individual lodging types, with smaller or greater isolation. . . . All the villas, from multistoried communal-lodgings to workers' "cottages" or other dwellings, are all based on a bourgeois capitalist model. In this era of building[73] *socialism to which we are all contributing, these kind of forms require a radical revision.*[74]

The Sibylline ambiguities of these utterances seem to indicate a hope that his criticism could fit any imminent Central Committee disavowal without losing face.

It is one of the paradoxes of this historic moment, at the juncture between 1929 and 1930, that a decade of investigation now reaching its apogee should fall prey to blanket rejection by the Central Committee. This was the time when the just-completed Narkomfin was becoming an obliged point of reference, and the volume of publications about the *Dom-Kommuny* (already inscribed in the policies of the Five-Year- Plan) had reached its highest level in both operative and theoretical terms. One utopia (the collectivist project) was about to be replaced by another (accelerated industrialization) whose forced implementation would result in tragedy.

The Strojkom and Ginzburg's Search for New Typologies

The manifestation and formation of an authentically modern workers' way of life, which thus far has changed little and which we can envisage only to a certain extent, will determine the remaining unknowns as well; only as a result of this process will it be possible to define this still vague ideal.
M. Ginzburg, *Style and Epoch*, 1924

Moving to the forefront as the basic task confronting modernity is the development of solutions for all the architectural organisms associated with the concept of labor—workers housing and

houses of labor—*and all the innumerable problems they generate.*
M. Ginzburg, *Style and Epoch*, 1924

In 1928, the STROJKOM invited Ginzburg and the "Rationalist" ASNOVA to perform a vast study for the standardization of new *byt* lifestyles. The laboratory work of the OSA, away from the more theoretically oriented ASNOVA founded three years earlier, reflected Ginzburg's inclination for a "logical and rational art, simple and sober, a vocational one, rather than inspired by enthusiasm."[75] The "scientific investigation of domestic life" and of its most economical solutions was undertaken for the first time at an official, governmental level. The primary goal was to improve the quality of workers' dwellings on a mass scale. Exposure to light and fresh air at a time of endemic tuberculosis was paramount. The form and proportions of the dwelling spaces were carefully studied. They were derived from patterns of movement and the rational distribution of furniture and house amenities. Given the economic realities of the time, where several families shared a single apartment (one family per room), efforts were made to find affordable ways of achieving the goal of one family per apartment. Transferring part of the traditional functions of an apartment into common living spaces was a way of rationalizing individual space while promoting collectivism.

The professional maturation of this Constructivist endeavor was best expressed in Ginzburg's first Moscow apartment building on Malaja Bronnaja Street in 1927 (Fig. 17). The project was commissioned by the State Insurance Company. Program-wise, it combined traditional apartments of various sizes with collectivized quarters on the fifth, roof top floor: twelve rooms with a large common kitchen, two baths and two separate toilets—a feature he would replicate in the Narkomfin. Stores occupied most of the ground floor.[76] The building was designed and built before the

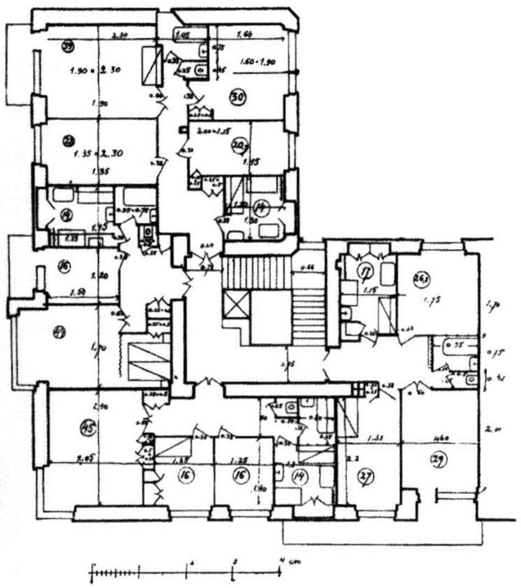

Fig.17 Ginzburg, Apartment building in Malaja Bronnaja street, 1927

termination of the NEP. So the idea that carried the design was primarily an exercise in modernist housing, catering to the so-called Nepmen, the business class that came about with Lenin's reintroduction of a form of market economy. The apartments were lavishly equipped with built-in closets, transformable beds, modern kitchen amenities and a roof garden.The twelve collective rooms on the fifth floor apparently mirrored the nineteenth century Parisian mansards in bourgeois apartment buildings, which housed the service personnel.

This did not mean, however, that Ginzburg was not already reflecting on innovative ways to engage the idea of new housing concepts for the working class. The first issue of the architectural journal *SA* (which he founded with A. Vesnin in 1926) proclaimed the need for contemporary architecture "to crystallize the new socialist way of life." The journal invited other architects to take part in "a comradely competition for [the best] design in workers' housing."[77] A central question was asked: could the quality of socialized housing be raised without reducing quantity? Ginzburg's response was that this would be possible by eliminating superfluous (not inhabited) spaces of traditional dwellings and channeling them into community-used areas. The approach also implied the introduction of modern materials, the rationalization of the building process, and the standardization of dwelling types.[78]

The results of the competition were published in the journal, and in June 1927 the projects were displayed at the First Moscow Exposition of Contemporary Architecture. Ginzburg described his own project as "an experiment in new types of dwelling that favors space combinations of fully individualized lodging spaces with a series of socialized functions (dining room, resting hall, children's day care, nurseries, laundromat and so on)."[79]

The *Dom-Kummuna* itself comprised two parallel housing blocks linked by a perpendicular double-floor bridge on the top floor, projecting the second level of the bridge over the roof of the contiguous building. The two bridge floors accommodated the common dining room, a library with a reading room, a club, and a meeting hall. The daycare facility and nursery were located on the ground floor. Longitudinal hallways, each serving two floors, ran, unlike in the Narkomfin, through the core of the building. The dwelling spaces offered great flexibility, as each volumetric cell could accommodate one single, large four-bedroom apartment of 2.6 meter-ceiling heights for the bedrooms, and one 5.20-meter double- height space with mezzanine for the living room. The volumetric cell could also be divided into two small apartments and a larger one with the same double-height ceiling in the parlor area. Not only could the cells adapt to specific family sizes, but also an independent smaller apartment, or simply a single independent room, could be separated from the whole as the structure of the family changed. The competition entry showed two variants of that cell: one as a large apartment with its interior stairs and the other divided into three smaller dwellings. Evidently, those variations affected the exterior. Depending on the case, one façade could have three rows of longitudinal windows and another façade could have six.

This first project of a *Dom-Kommuna* was included the following year in Ginzburg's research laboratory for the Strojkom. The group garnered architects, engineers, economists, hygienists, and others, all working under Ginzburg's supervision. Looking primarily for affordability, the vast study Ginzburg undertook, following his first *Dom-Kommuna*, went in two directions. One approach consisted of downsizing traditional apartments by reducing as much as possible the surface of ancillary areas such as kitchens, baths, and passageways. These belonged to type A (A-2 and A-3 [Fig. 18], depending on the number of rooms), and type B-2, which also reduced the height (and thus the cost) of ancillary spaces. The reduction was achieved by flip-flopping the orientation of both stacked and contiguous apartments. However, the obvious problem of type B-2 was that such apartments were more difficult to build, and that, between two floors, due to the flip-flopping, a bathroom would inevitably end up over a bedroom, raising technical problems and costs. Ultimately, even with alcove-kitchens and bathrooms without bathtubs, the economists in Ginzburg's team concluded that, given the economic level of the country at the time, such traditional apartments would still be too costly to be occupied by only one family.[80]

The other solution was to reduce the costs by assembling all ancillary facilities into common spaces (either within or outside the apartment block), and reducing the number of circulation hallways, each serving two floors (type F), like in Ginzburg's first *Dom-Kommuna*, or three floors (types E and E-1 [Fig. 19]).[81] Ginzburg concluded that the only way of avoiding the nightmare of shared apartments was to create one-bedroom type F apartments for just one family each.[82] The advantage of the latter over all other types (including derived variants called C and D) was that the common circulation hallway did not reduce the surface of the apartments since the corridor serving two floors had both an apartment above and one under it. In addition, the corridors, which now ran along one façade rather than within the building's core, like in Ginzburg's first *Dom Kommuna*, received a direct exterior light in compliance with required norms for the prevention of tuberculosis, a lesson Le Corbusier did not learn in his Marseille housing block of 1946.

In his report to the Building Committee, in November 1928, Ginzburg emphasized that the F-type cell offered the opportunity to create *Dom-Kommuny* that only partially shared their domestic amenities with their socialized forms.

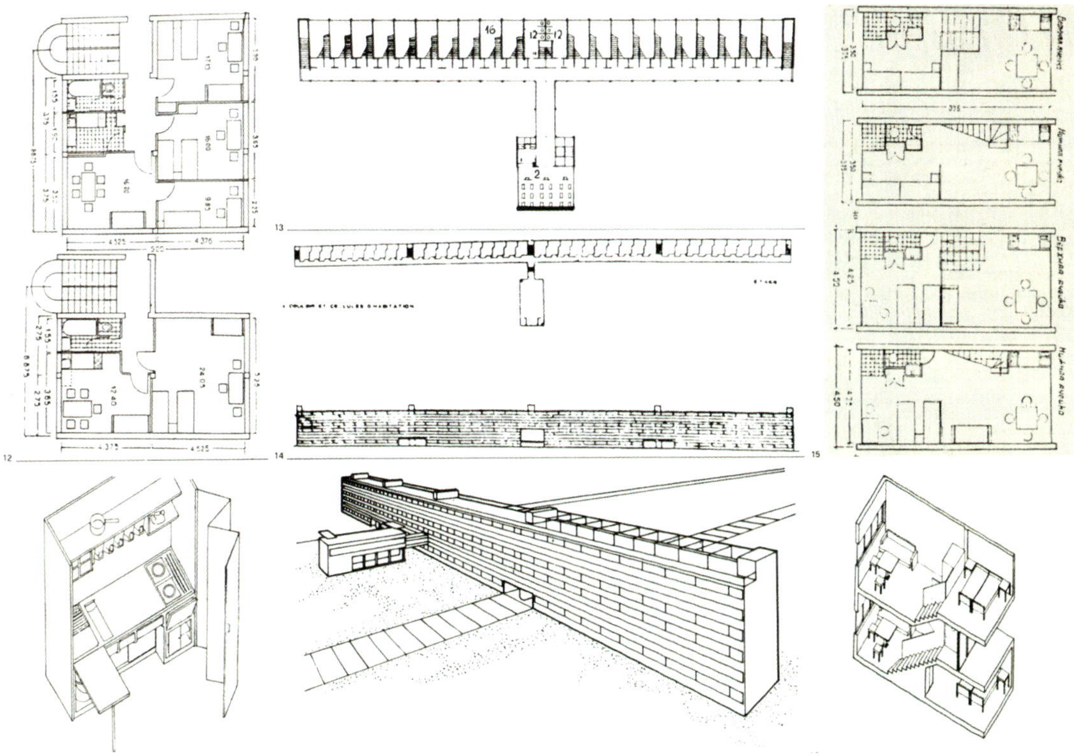

Fig. 18 Type A apartment (A2 and A3) and F-type for the Strojkom.

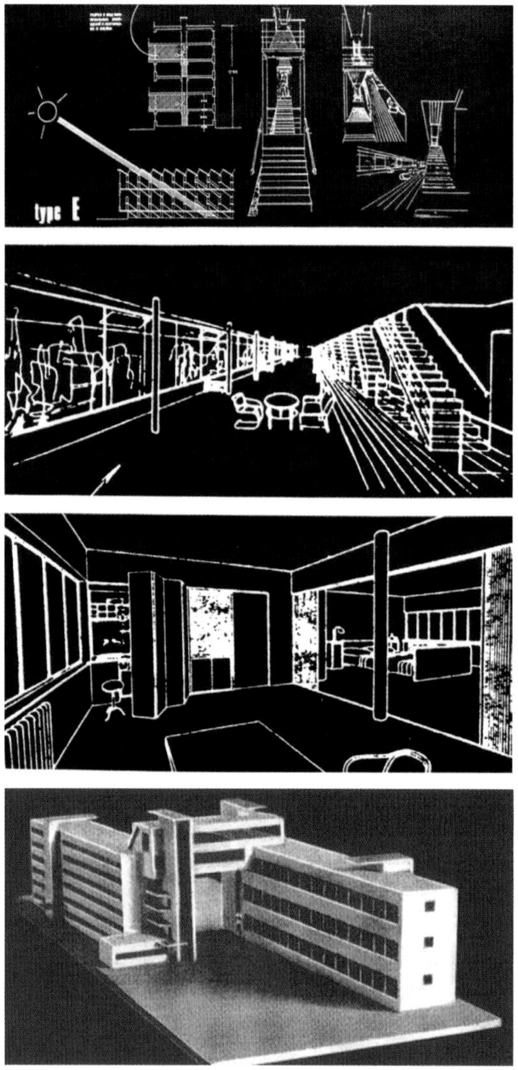

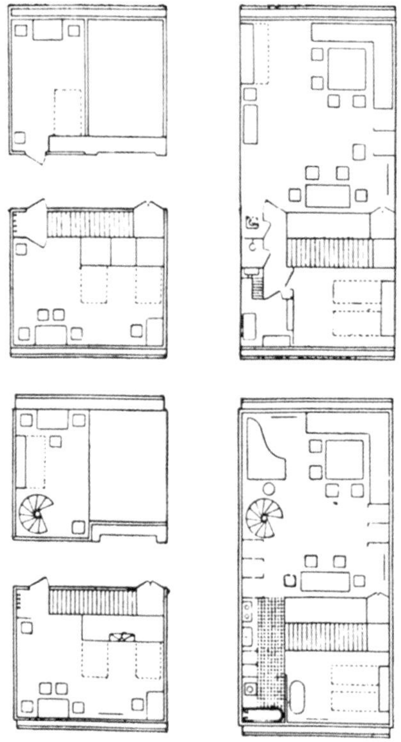

Fig. 19 Ginzburg, "Comradely Competition" Type E entry, First Moscow Exhibition of Contemporary Housing, 1927

They were expected to have a gradual effect on people's habits of thinking and living, from traditional private ("bourgeois") ways of dwelling, to more communitarian lifestyles, while immediately liberating the woman from "domestic slavery." It is in that sense that type F housing facilities were considered as "dwellings of an intermediary type." With non-dogmatic plurality in mind, catering both to social expectations of the moment and to diversity in standardization, Ginzburg envisioned that, beyond the dominant type F dwellings, buildings should also incorporate, among other types, standardized traditional apartments. In other words, to avoid uniformity, he advocated, "standardized elements to be combined in plural ways leading to a significant typological variety."[83] Echoing Constructivist and Russian Formalist principles of reassembling the given into new semantic series (applied most effectively in cinematography),[84] Ginzburg preferred to speak about "montage," rather than "building" of *Dom Kommuny*. Indeed, he experimented with aggregations of standardized living cells into novel dwelling types and buildings, the way cinematic frames, shots, and sequences are montaged into new visual meanings.

Likewise, Ginzburg's concept of housing communities was not limited to the lodging block itself, with its canteens, lounges, collective baths, and the like. He considered the living unit as part of a broader community system of several *Dom-Kommuny* enjoying facilities of a more general urban character such as clubs and sports facilities, daycare facilities and laundry rooms.

The completed work was published in a 1930 almanac *Tipovoj proekty i konstrukcii žiliščno-go stroitel'stva* (Standard Housing Projects and Buildings).[85] Based on this study, several of his *Dom-Kommuny* of a transitional type were "montaged" in Moscow, Sverdlovsk, and Saratov, three of them under Ginzburg's direct responsibility. They were intended, as the Building Committee put it, ". . . to give a home to millions of workers. . . ."[86] The most interesting among them was the apartment block commissioned by the People's Commissar for Finances, Nikolaj Miljutin, for the employees of his ministry, the Narkomfin, or Narodnij Kommissariat Finansov.

The Narkomfin 1928–1932

It must be realized that workers' housing, that is, modern *in its standard mode of formal expression, is a problem whose solution still wholly lies ahead.*
M. Ginzburg, *Style and Epoch*, 1924[87]

Designed by Moisej Ginzburg and Ignatij Milinis, the "montage" of the *Dom Narkomfin* was launched at the start of Stalin's Five-Year-Plan, the year the NEP was replaced by a planned economy, a form of "state capitalism," to use Gramsci's expression.[88] It was set on a prestigious location, parallel to the Novinskij Boulevard (the main inner Moscow circular avenue) (Fig. 20). Raised on a 'forest' of shiny black columns (Fig. 21) at the edge of a wooded hill, it overlooked Moscow to the west. On the eastern side, just across from Chaliapin's nineteenth century townhouse on the Novinskij Bulevar, the Narkomfin faced its communal facilities, dispersed in a picturesque park. The facilities included a club with a canteen/restaurant (Fig. 22), daycare facility (never built), and a central laundry service, set at the edge of the boulevard. A second housing block was planned on an east-west axis along the other edge of the park and connected to the club.

The main north-south axis of the pristine white bar was soon to be known as the "The Steamer" for its hundred-meter-long white ribbon sills

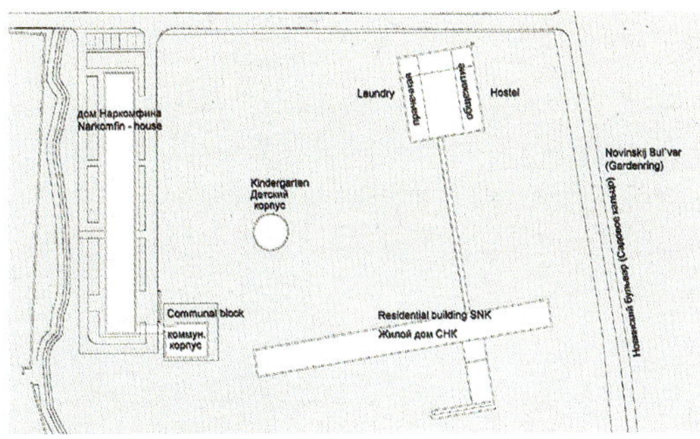

Fig. 20 Site plan of the Narkomfin with two apartment buildings (as planned); the Club annex; Daycare (as planned), and Laundry Pavilion.

Fig. 21 Ground floor with black shining pilotis

Arial view: Park, Chaliapin's house, and, perpendicular to the NKF, the building raised by S. Leontovič in place of the second Communal building. Courtesy of State Museum of Architecture, Moscow.

Fig. 22 The club and restaurant, exterior

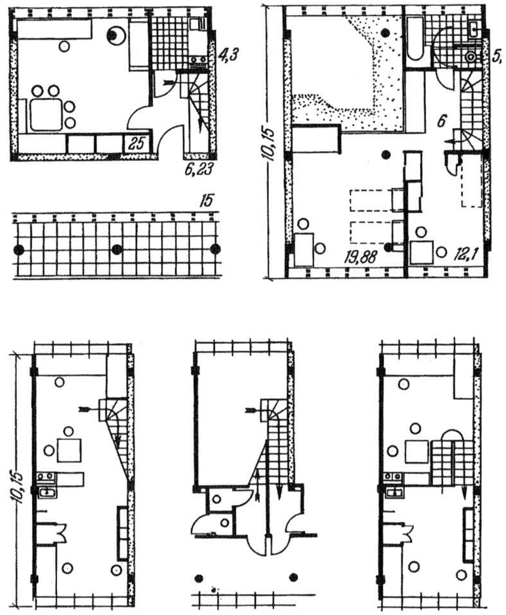

Fig. 23 Floor Plans of K-Type (second and third level) and F-Type apartments (third and fourth level)

stretched from end to end of the building on each of the six floors. The other bar perpendicular to it was never built, victim of the May 1930 Central Committee declaration repudiating experimental *Dom-Kommuny*. The building's design, snapped away from Ginzburg's hands, was commissioned from one Leontovič who built instead a replica of nineteenth century bourgeois rental housing.

The brief transition period between the NEP and the centrally planned economy, when the Narkomfin was built, featured two analogous, if opposing, social formations with similar stylistic predilections: the nouveau riche eclecticism of the Nepmen and the parvenu eclecticism of the rising "nomenklatura."

Much was said about the Narkomfin's alleged "plagiarism" of Le Corbusier's "pilotis" and "fenêtres en longueur." The use of such formal devices, however, followed none of the Swiss architect's dogma. It was actually primarily intended to reflect the specific logic of the building and its site. Situated in the center of a natural park, the building's dark pilotis echoed the trunks of the surrounding trees, while blending into their Arcadian setting. They also facilitated an uninterrupted visual flow from one part of the park into the other. Even the oval, glazed north entrance, which recalled Le Corbusier's entrance to his contemporaneous Villa Savoye, enforced both transparency and visual continuity, while reflecting the shimmering light of the woods. None of this was the case in the villa at Poissy, set on the flat treeless expanse of a meadow, boasting the architect's a priori. The ribbon windows, on the other hand, were used, not because, as Le Corbusier claimed unscientifically, that human vision was horizontal, but because technically such window arrangement provided the best ratio of light to glazed surface. Seeking the absorption of a maximum of light in the most economical way possible was paramount. Yet, the real innovation of the Narkomfin was the introduction of double-height, two-level apartments, fed by a single, heated façade corridor.[89] Four floors were thus fed by two corridors with, on top of it all, a roof garden, which the people's Commissar Miljutin modified during construction by adding a two-floor diminutive villa of his own design. The one corridor, or "street," per two levels allowed Ginzburg to achieve considerable savings, while transforming small, one-bedroom apartments into exciting, dynamic spatial experiences. The double height of the parlor room situated on the west side of the building, with its huge wall-to-wall glazing, invited the entire park and its vistas on Moscow into the apartment's interior space—a veranda in the summer, and a source of maximum light in long Muscovite winters. Depending on the unit, one either descended a full floor into the apartment's living space, with a bedroom niche tucked under the building's access corridor, or climbed a short flight into the parlor, while a second parallel flight led to the bedroom, this time above the corridor. The resulting generous cross-ventilation not only helped cool some hot Moscow summers but also invited air and light. In themselves, these type F units addressed a broad spectrum of social, technical, and architectural issues related to perceived affordable workers' housing. The south and north extremities of the building featured two-level spacious Type K apartments with mezzanines for families with children—eight "transitional" apartments in total. The first two floors above the pilotis featured more two-level Type K apartments as well with different spatial arrangements (Fig. 23). These arrangements of Type K model allowed for a great diversity among them. Twenty years later, Le Corbusier retooled the concept at Marseille, keeping, however, a double-fed corridor within the core of the building.[90]

The building was designed as a commune for fifty families (roughly 200 people), "organically integrated" into the common facilities, as Ginzburg would put it. The facilities, set in a four-floor cubic building, included a club with reading, exercising, and dining rooms—all accommodated over mezzanines and double-height spaces with a huge floor-to-roof glazed wall facing the park (Fig. 24).[91] The club was connected to the living quarters by a heated bridge. Whereas the laundry building (also including a garage and car-repair area for the Commissariat's officials) functioned over several decades, the club was immediately turned into a children's daycare facility to replace the one planned, but never built, in the center of the park.

It stayed this way until the mass evacuation of Moscow in October 1941 and never reopened.[92] In practice, an apartment at one extremity of the housing block was turned into a communal restaurant where most inhabitants came just to pick up their meals, preferring to "eat at home."[93]

It has sometimes been claimed that what defined the "transitional" character of the Narkomfin was the existence of Type K apartments, large three- or even four-bedroom apartments spanning, as mentioned, the second and third floor, and two levels each on the north and south ends of the building. However, like the Type F, they also featured internal stairs to negotiate the double height of the living rooms below the mezzanines, which, according to Ginzburg, sets them apart from traditional abodes (Fig. 25). Both the Type F and Type K maintained some traditional features, the Type F intended for couples without children appearing closer to the fully collectivized type. Each still had a kitchenette and a shower, making them technically into autonomous living units. It is important to note, however, that this reflected an articulated political demand, harking back at least as far as to Kollontaj's ideas, translated into architectural typology. As Ginzburg explained in 1934,

Fig. 24 Western façade showing double height glazed openings of type F and type K apartments

"We were entrusted with the task of studying the social and existential conditions of the transitional period." The entire architectural complex deployed on a horizontal plane was split in two halves: one half (the apartment of a large size—Type K) was intended to fit a family, which had fully kept its old ways of living, while the other half (the dwelling of a smaller size—Type F) was intended to fit a single person or a couple without children. In keeping with this, it was assumed that the "lower" half would transcend more easily the traditional household: therefore the Type K apartments had a small kitchen that would allow one, in case of need, to fix individual meals, but would already be endowed with an auxiliary character.[94]

Yet, the Type K apartments came with various numbers of rooms and arrangements, some more expansive than others, with more spacious mezzanines or, in the case of the south apartments, with large semi-cylindrical balconies asserting individuality. In other words, some Type K apartments were less "transitional" than others. How was this to be explained?

Until the end of the NEP era, Party cadres had salaries, in a Leninist fashion, no bigger than specialized factory floor workers. Best paid were the desperately needed engineers and specialists, predictably of bourgeois extraction. With the gradual abating of the revolutionary fervor of the early years, resentment regarding such disparities grew. The trumped up trial in 1928–29 for alleged production sabotage against a fictional "Industrial Party" (a term possibly borrowed from a Saint-Simonian agenda) involved those well-paid engineers. This could suggest that the trial may have been intended in part to vindicate discontent, while questioning the privileged status of the engineers and other bourgeois professionals. A second step in the reversal of Leninist policies was the revocation of what came to be known pejoratively as "*uravnilovka*"—the early, idealism-based egalitarian system. The Nepmen had shown the way with their market economy, which brought ever-sharper social differentiation. As he revoked the NEP, Stalin put under his control, like everything else, the benefits of such social stratification by introducing a tightly managed meritocratic system. A new privileged class was rising, composed of apparatchiks, meritorious "shock workers," "heroes of socialist work," "people's artists," decorated scientists, and above all, top political leadership—the so-called "professional revolutionaries." The same way the tsars honored their nobility with "dachas" (donations of property), Stalin rewarded his deserving subjects with special apartments, vacations in elite resorts, and a collection of flashy medals.[95]

The Narkomfin, commissioned by the commissariat of finances for its own functionaries, has to be considered in this context. Large Type K apartments, luxurious for their time, surrounded the core of the Type F models, while the People's Commissar Miljutin had his "villa" on the roof garden. The villa was not initially part of Ginzburg's design, indicating clearly how the "meaning" of the building was changing as changes in societal priorities were occurring at this crucial turning point in Soviet history. Moreover, Ginzburg set on the roof twelve individual rooms with common baths and no kitchens, comparable to those he built for the service personnel on Malaja Bronnaja street during the NEP era. The nanny of Miljutin's daughter Katja occupied one of them.[96]

In this sense, the Narkomfin reflected the newly stratified society as much as it did the collectivist, emancipatory ideals. The traditional "bourgeois" building that replaced Ginzburg's never-built second project on the Narkomfin's site confirms the claim. If a transitional building at all, the Narkomfin ended up embodying, ironically, a transition not to the future, but to the past.

Interior of a type K apartment with mezzanine

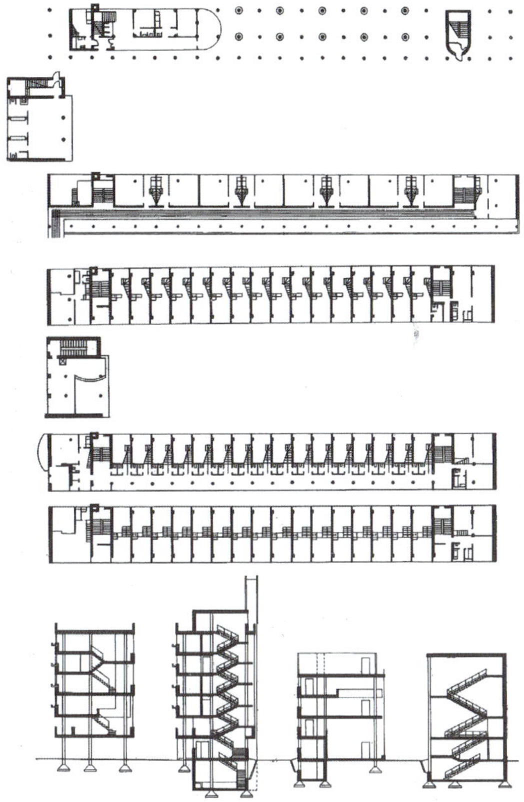

Plans, sections, and elevations of the apartment building and the club

Model showing an upper and a lower type F with section of access hallway situated under and above an apartment

Refurbished type F apartment in Lisagor's Gogolevskij Boulevard. The access hallway can be seen through the open door. Architects Milinis, Vladimitov, Orlovskij, and Pasternak

S.S Suafev, a 1927 cooperative, Moscow

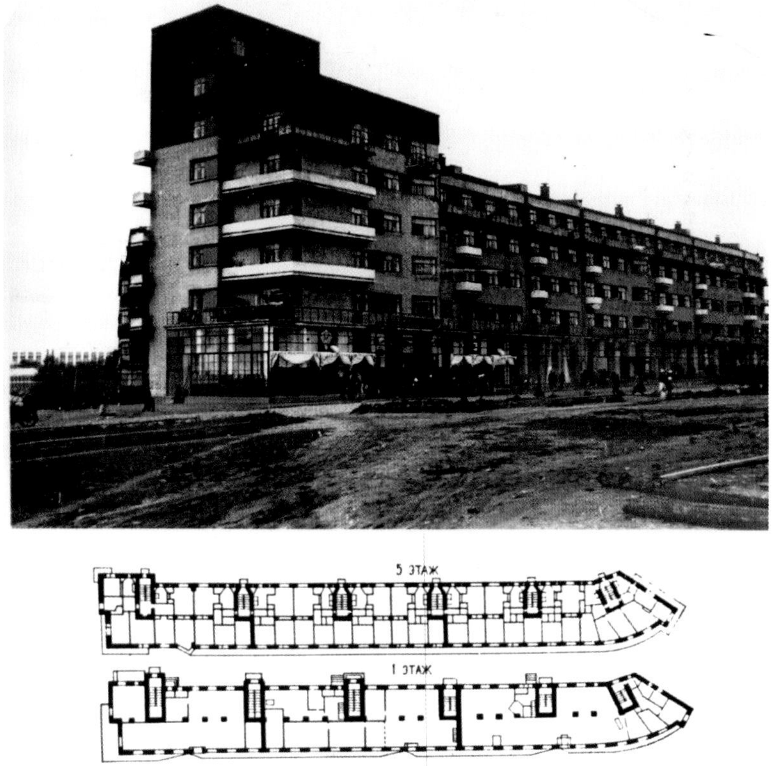

Daniil Fridman, "Dom Korablij" in the city of Ivanovo 1927–1930

1. Aleksandra Mihailovna Kollontaj (1872–1952), was the first woman in modern history to become a State Minister (later also first female ambassador). A Bolshevik feminist, Kollontaj was the most prominent woman in the Soviet administration, best known for founding the *Ženotdel* or "Women's Department" in 1919. Her social ideas influenced the work of Wilhelm Reich, who, like her, advocated the abolition of the family.

2. Like most important women among Marxist revolutionaries, such as Nadežda Krupskaya, Roza Luxemburg, Klara Zetkin, and Angelika Balabanova, Alexandra Kollontaj came from the upper class. The oppression of women from the petite bourgeoisie, the rural and industrial Proletariat, was such that barely any had managed to free herself from the coercions of inherited worldviews. Like these women, Kollontaj spoke for them, as she had in her earliest youth, according to her autobiography, the opportunity to become fully conscious of the suffering of millions of women who were not yet able to speak in their own name.

As a government minister and later a diplomat, she played important political roles, albeit devoid of the sense Trotsky (Trockij) or Lenin had to accede to power and maintain it. Kollontaj is credited for the signing of the armistice and peace between Finland and the young Soviet Republic. She is also credited with advising Lenin and convincing him of the necessity of granting independence to Finland. See Irving Fetscher, afterword, in Aleksandra Kollontaj, *Autobiographie einer sexuelle emanzipierten Kommunistin* (first published in Munich, 1926). In English The Autobiography of a Sexually Emancipated Communist Woman, New York, 1971, p.201.

3. The Narkomfin, also referred to as the "NKF," stood for Narodnij Kommissariat Financov (People's Commissariat for Finances), a government ministry.

4. The concept of kibbutz has analogous roots.

5. Klara Zetkin, a German member of the Executive Committee of the Third International, focused her activity in particular on women's emancipation in the Soviet Union.

6. Kollontaj was also a close friend of the American Louise Bryant, a dedicated feminist and partner of the American journalist and revolutionary John Reed, who described his involvement in the Bolshevik Revolution in a famous diary, *Ten Days That Shook the World*. Reed died in Moscow from typhoid in 1921 and is buried in the Kremlin walls.

7. See Elizabeth A . Wood, *The Baba and the Comrade: Gender and Politics in Revolutionary Russia*, Bloomington and Indianapolis, Indiana University Press, 1997

8. *Pravda*, No. 2, January 4,1918; *Izvestija*, No. 2,1918.

9. See Friedrich Engels, "The Housing Question," first published as a pamphlet in 1872 for the Co-operative Publishing Society of Foreign Workers. It was transcribed by *Zodiac* in June 1995. See also Karl Marx, "The Nationalization of the Land," in The International Herald No. 11, June 15, 1872,.and Friedrich Engels, *The Origin of the Family, Private Property and the State*, London, 2010 (first published 1884).

10. His discourse included calls for women governance, cultural development and opposition to "patriarchalism," and other topics involving the issue of women's emancipation.

11. The Worker's Opposition, a faction within the Bolshevik Party, was critical of the bureaucratization of the Party and its severance from the actual working class base. Kollontaj wrote, among others, "The freedom of criticism and freedom of thought . . . at times assumes farcical features with us. What self-initiative has ever existed without the freedom of opinion and thought? . . . We fear the self-initiative of the masses, we fear any and all criticism, we have ceased to trust the masses—this is the source of our entire bureaucratism." Quoted in Iring Fetscher, afterword in *Kollontaj, Autobiographie*, op. cit. p. 126.

On the Worker's Opposition see further M. Zorkij, *Rabočaja Oppozicija: Materialy i Dokumenty*, 1920-1926, Moscow, 1926.

12. Pasini, Ernesto, *La "casa-comune" e il Narkomfin di Ginzburg* (Rom: Officina Edizioni), 1980, "Preface." Text initially published in *Pravda*, 6 November 1919.

13. Kollontaj, *Autobiographie*, op. cit. p. 128.

14. See Zetkin's *Lenin on the Woman Question*, New York, 1934.

15. The editor of *Pravda*, the main Communist daily, Nikolaj Buharin (also a member of the Politburo until expulsion in November 1929), wrote lucidly, free of utopian voluntarism regarding the new socialist dwelling, as early as 1919: "It is difficult to say at this moment what kind of lodging will be the most appropriate. Will these be vast houses with all the comfort of modern amenities and gardens, community restaurants and so on, or would these be small, well situated homes. . . . But one thing is certain: Whatever the housing program, these will not prevent the integration of agriculture and industry. They will have to help the distribution of the population throughout the periphery of the city. This will prevent the overcrowding of millions of people in the city centers lacking air, severed from nature, and condemned to early death." Nikolaj Buharin and S. Preobraženskij, *The ABC of Communism*, London, 1969 (first published 1919). Leon Trotsky published his own articles about the reform of everyday life in the 1923 *Pravda*. See, among others, Leon Trotskij (Trotsky), "The Struggle for a New Way of Life," *Pravda*, 17 May 1923. A large part of Trotsky's writings on the topic are collected in *Problemy Byta* in Lev Trotsky, *Sočinenija* Vol. 1921, Moscow, 1927, pp. 22–6, pp. 39–43.

Regarding the sources of the collectivist ideology see also Anatole Kopp, *Changer la vie, changer la ville: de la vie nouvelle aux problèmes urbains, URSS 1917–1932*, Paris, Collection "10/18," 1975.

16. Cf. A. Kollontaj, "Novaja Moral' i Rabočij Klass" in *VCIK*, 1918 (The New Morality and the Working Class), and, "Semja i Kommunističeskoe Gosudarstvo" (The Family and the Communist State), in *Kommunist*, Moscow/Petrograd, 1918.

17. Pasini, op. cit. p. 10.

18. Quoted in Iring Fetscher afterword to Kollontaj's *Autobiographie* by Kollontaj, p. 110.

19. Krupskaja resisted collectivization, calling on Lenin's claim that it was an absurdity to create huge cooperatives before the country would have at least 100,000 tractors. See RGASPI Lazar Kaganovič archives, quoted in Kaganovič 1930 papers, Moscow, RGASPI. Stalinism's final victory over all other options in the Central Committee was reached in 1934, at the 17th Party Congress, "The Congress of the Victors."

20. The measures Stalin and his acolyte in the Politburo, Lazar Kaganovič, were to articulate amounted, as Buharin warned the Central Committee, to "the creation of a police state."

21. In 1935 it was even scheduled for demolition. See Yuri Volchok's essay in this monograph.

22. Leonid Sabsovič was an economist and collaborator of Ginzburg's in *Sovremenaja Arhitektura*. In 1929 he sparked a debate about the future of Soviet cities he published in *Planovoe Hozjastvo* (Planned Economy). He adopted a middle-of-the-road position in the debate between "urbanists" and "disurbanists" arguing against decentralized linear cities.

23. *Pravda*, 29 May 1930. No. 145. For a discussion of the "urbanist" vs. "disurbanist" debate, see Yuri Volchok's essay in this manuscript.

24. *Pravda*, 29 May 1930, No.146. Ginzburg reproduced this article in SA's double issue 1–2, 1930.

25. Something similar occurred in agriculture, where a massive famine was provoked in 1931 by the confiscation of the entire production of wheat to be exchanged in the West for machines.

26. On the dwellers' persecutions see Vladimir Paperny's chapter in this monograph.

27. It is entirely possible that this "exile" saved her from Stalin's retribution and purges; her two male former companions perished in the Gulag.

28. Ginzburg's keynote address at the first OSA conference in 1928.

29. See in particular his reasoning on color, argued by Alla Vronskaya in this collection of essays.

30. Moisej Ginzburg, Style and Epoch, Cambridge, MA, 1982, p. 80. First published in the Soviet Union in 1924.

31. Ibid., p. 8–9.

32. See V. E Hazanova, the collection of documents she published in 1970 *Iz Istorii Sovetskoj Arhitekturi*, 1926–1932: *Dokumenty i Materialy* (Moscow: Akademija Nauk SSSR), 1970; M. Astanaeva, in *Arhitektura SSSR*, 1970; M. Tafuri in *Archithèse*, No. 7, 1973; *Rassegna Sovietica*, No. 1, 1974; and *Lotus* No. 8, 1974, p . 77ff.

33. It is worth noting, nevertheless, that while Ebenezer Howard was immediately embraced by the Revolution—feeding into the rising disurbanist movement—by 1924 his theories were declared a bourgeois invention. The still evolving concept of the Dom-Kommuna balanced hesitantly between the two.

34. As they attempted to interpret Friedrich Engels's theories on the elimination of differences between town and countryside, urban and peasant living conditions, with the aim of establishing a theory of socialist urban development, the avant-garde split around 1929 in bitter disputes between advocates of limited development of cities and the proponents of "disurbanization" in the form of linear cities. Sabsovič and the brothers Vesnin supported the former thesis, while Ohitovič and Ginzburg adhered to disurbanism.

35. In Russia, the building was soon nicknamed the "Parohod," or the "Steamer."

36. The Strojkom was a government Building Committee supervising innovative design ventures.

37. See, for example, the 1918 city decoration for the celebration of the first anniversary of the October Revolution designed by the brothers Vesnin or Il'ja Golosov's 1919 Crematorium, which evoked the work of Claude Nicolas Ledoux, or Ginzburg's 1921 competition entry for the Palace of Labor.

38. The "Rationalists" in Russia, unlike their namesakes in Central and Western Europe, adhered to a Gestalt psychology to explain the role of architectural space and form in revolutionizing the mentality of its users.

39. I owe Alla Vronskaya the insight regarding Ladovskij's debt to German Expressionism.

40. The Formalists, principally Šklovskij, uninterested in the philosophical or sociological content of an artwork, be it literature, art, architecture or film, claimed that a *new form* was the true content of art. In that sense, art played a subversive role against the banality of everyday life. Echoing this position, Ladovskij himself favored the effect of form in architecture, rather than any specific functional solution for his Dom-Kommuna.

41. Incidentally, this discrepancy may give us a clue regarding the credits of each of the three Vesnin brothers in their later collective works. The *Leningradskaja Pravda*, for example, was clearly derived from Aleksandr Vesnin's revolutionary stage designs produced at the time with Ljubov Popova in Mejerhold's theater; it had little to do with the concepts of the other two brothers, Viktor and Leonid.

42. See Hazanova, *Iz Istorii*, op. cit. , p. 46.

43. The MAO, in existence before the Revolution, was reinstated in 1923.

44. Ginzburg, Op. cit. p. 80

45. Manfredo Tafuri, "Verso la Città Socialista: Ricerche e realizzazioni nel'Unione Sovietica fra la NEP e il Primo Piano Quinquenale." *Lotus* No. 8, 1974. p. 74.

46. Without elaborating, Manfredo Tafuri has compared this board to a Kandinsky painting. Cf. Tafuri op. cit. p. 85.

47. The members included the group of architects from the Lef, Aleksandr Vesnin, M. Baršč, A. Burov, I. Sobolev, N. Krasil'nikov, and others; and of Ginzburg's followers, students at the VHUTEMAS. In 1926 the group started publishing the architectural journal *Sovremenaja Arhitektura* (SA), edited by Vesnin and Ginzburg, and designed by one of the founders of Constructivism, Aleksej Gan. The latter was arrested in the mid-1930s and never returned.

48. *Stroitel'stvo Moskvy*, No 12, December 1929. The entire issue is devoted to the Dom-Kommuny with articles by David Arkin, V. Lavrov, S. Ajzikovič, and Daniil Fridman. See in particular the article by modernist Daniil Fridman, who had won the same year the first prize for the Lenin Library in Moscow (later retracted probably under pressure by Lazar Kaganovič) "Dom-Kommuny ili kvartal" (House-Communes or Commune-settlements) in *Stroitel'stvo Moskvy*, No. 12, December 1929, p. 15.

49. For Nikolaev's project see Editorial "Za socialističeskij princip planirovki Žil'ja" (For a Socialist Principle of Housing Planning). *Stroitel'stvo Moskvy*, No. 12, December 1930, p. 11., p. 1.

50. Stalin's re-foundation of the Soviet Union along totalitarian rules was also known as "Perestroika" (Reconstruction) or "Cultural Revolution." Less euphemistically, the totalitarian system Stalin introduced was referred to as "revolution from above."

51. Ohitovič, a sociologist and collaborator of *SA*, was arrested in 1934 as a "Trotskyite adventurer" and shot soon after.

52. The students not only had the choice between several avant-garde schools and traditional Beaux-Arts teaching, but also discussed the work of their professors, whom they had the power to dismiss.

53. About the destiny of the city in later years under Stalin, see Stephen Kotkin, *Magnetic Mountain: Stalinism as a Civilization*, Berkeley, 1995.

54. See S. O. Khan-Magomedov, Ivan Leonidov, Moscow, 1971.

55. See S. Ajzicovič, "Dom Kommuny v Moskovskoj kooperacii in *Stroitel'stvo Moskvy*, No. 12, pp. 6–10.

56. For comparison, Ginzburg's Dom-Kommuna was designed for 200 inhabitants.

57. For Nikolajev's project see in particular Nikolaev, "Studentčeskij Dom-Kommuna v Moskvy," 12 December 1930, p. 11. Also Nikolajev, "Opytnaja postrojka studentčeskogo doma kommuny" in *Stroitel'stvo Moskvy*, July 1930, pp. 30–33.

58. Op. cit p. 7. In a detailed description of the daily activities, which sound like a day for military cadets, Nikolaev says: "The ring of a bell wakes up everybody and the student in pajamas goes down to the gym or up to the flat roof for open air to exercises, depending on the season. At that point, the sleeping booth is subjected to vigorous ventilation that lasts all day. Access to the sleeping booth is forbidden until bedtime. After having exercised the student goes to the locker-room to pick up his clothes. Next to it the student has access to the showers. After having readied himself, he goes to the canteen where he consumes his breakfast. From there he is allowed to use his time at will: he can go to classes or go study in the common study room, or else, if he is preparing his exams he can use his own study booth. After lunch make-up classes are offered to students who fell behind in their studies or their social work. The student is free to use his evening time at will. The day ends at a ring announcing the collective strolling. When back from walk the student goes to his wardrobe and takes his pajama to his sleeping booth. The booth is ventilated through the night by central air conditioning. During that time an ozone maker is activated without excluding the possibility of adding something more to promote sleep."

59. See *SA*, No. 3, March 1930, p. 7.

60. Even so, the 2x2-m cubicles were intended for two students.

61. Toward the end of his life Baršč received a commendation for his entry to the Paris George Pompidou Center international competition.

62. Founded as VHUTEMAS in 1919. He graduated in 1926.

63. See M. Baršč and V. Vladimirov, "Dom-Kommuny," *SA*, No. 4 April 1929, p. 122. See also K. N. Afanasaev and V. E. Hazanova, *Iz Istorii Sovetskoj Arhitektury*, op. cit. pp. 126–127.

64. It was supposed to accommodate 1000 adults and some 680 children, of which 360 were preschoolers and 320 were children between ages 8 and 16.

65. G. M. Dankman, "Obščežitie Studentov Kommunističevskogo Universiteta Nac. Menšistv Zapada." (Student Hostel of the Communist University for the Western Minorities) in *Stroitel'stvo Moskvy*, No. 6 (June 1929), p. 9.

66. S. N. Pokcičevskij, "Dom-Kommuna, Mnogoetažnij Falanster," op. cit.

67. K. Ivanov, F. Tereckij, and P. Smolin, "Proekt Kommunal'nogo Doma," *SA*, January 1929, pp. 31–32.

68. In 1937, Solomon Lisagor, who worked with Ginzburg, like Ohitovič, was arrested during the "Great Terror," never to return. We lack information, unfortunately, on the impact that tragically losing two close collaborators in a three-year span had on Ginzburg.

69. Motoljanskij "Problemy gradostroitel'stva v socialnyh utopiah" in *Revolucija i kul'tura* No. 4, 130, quoted by Pasini. Also reproduced in "I problemi dell'urbanistica nelle utopie sociali," *Rassegna Sovietica* no. 4, 1975, pp. 67–72. Such interest for the "utopians" resurfaced in the Soviet Union in the 1960s.

70. As opposed to the work of the "utopian socialists," Marx considered his own work to be "scientific" because he grounded it on the historical and economic analysis of capitalism, without developing any specific vision of future socialist, that is, communist societies.

71. In 1917, Antonio Gramsci wrote: "The Bolshevik Revolution . . . is a revolution against Karl Marx's *Capital*. In Russia, Marx's *Capital* was more the book of the bourgeoisie than of the proletariat." Milan edition of *Avanti!*, 24 December 1917. Gramsci later declared to Lenin that his revolution was not Marxist, and that the best he could hope for in Russia was the emergence of "state capitalism" under the control of a workers' government to avoid the cruelty of the first accumulation of capital in the Western countries. It is possible that the introduction of the NEP was in part Lenin's response to Gramsci's remarks.

72. Nikolaj Markovnikov, "Dom-Kommuny v prošlom, nastojaščem i buduščem" (The House-Communes, in the Past, Present and Future) in *Stroitel'naja Promyšlenost* N.1, January 1930, p. 1.

Most of his extensive writings, throughout the1920s, were published in this journal. Markovnikov was a member of Ladovsky's ASNOVA—a leading avant-garde society—and more tamely, the vice-president of the prerevolutionary MAO (Society of Moscow Architects), reinstated in 1923 with architects who were already professionally established in the Russian Empire.

73. Little-veiled allusion to Ginzburg's investigations and of other architects' experiments in and around the Strojkom.

74. Ibid., *Stroitel'naja Promyšlenost* N.1, January 1930, p. 2.

75. Selim Omarovič Khan-Magomedov, *M. Ja. Ginzburg*, Moscow: Gosizdat, 1972.

76. With the abolition of the NEP and the introduction of Five-Year-Plan distribution monopolies, the very concept of street stores disappeared.

77. *SA*, 1926, No 3.

78. *SA*, 1926, No 5–6.

79. *SA*, 1926, No 4–5.

80. In practice, however, even those F-types ended up occupied by two families, creating far worse living conditions than sharing a traditional apartment. According to statistics of the country's Planning Committee, the country could afford to offer one family per two- or three-bedroom apartments only to 40% of the population. The remaining 60% had to share apartments at the rate of one family per room. See Khan-Magomedov, Ginzburg, op cit., p. 120.

81. Type E-1 was a variant that replaced the corridor by the repetition of staircases that individualized the access, leading alternatively to either the apartments or the common spaces such as dining rooms and collective lounges, as two flights of stairs served three floors simultaneously.

82. In reality, for decades to come, that is, until Nikita Khrushchev (Hruščëv) developed in the 1960s a program of inexpensive mass construction of housing blocks, derided as "Hruščëvki," even the F-types in many cases were occupied by more than one family or by extended families.

83. Quoted by Khan-Magomedov, Ginzburg, op. cit. p.127.

84. See the method the filmmaker Dziga Vertov used in his newsreels, or more specifically his 1929 Constructivist film *Man with a Movie Camera*.

85. Ginzburg reproduced his typological studies in a 1934 book *Žilišče* (Housing)—this time, however, not as a manual for action but as a reflection on an aborted dream.

86. Han-Magomedov, *Moisej Ginzburg*, Milano: Franco Augeli 1975, p.120.

87. Ginzburg, op cit p. 79.

88. Stalin's idea of a "planned economy" aimed at "building socialism in a single country" was antithetic to Marx's political economy.

89. Since Le Corbusier replicated this more rudimentary system of hallways in his Marseille Unité d'Habitation, one could wonder if he had seen at all the more sophisticated plans of the Narkomfin on his 1928 visit to Moscow.

90. Anyone who had the opportunity to experience both buildings and their apartments could appreciate the vastly more elegant, relaxing, and unrestrained sense the F-types offer in comparison to the small units at Marseille.

91. Part of the glazing surface in the lower part of the building has been blocked by a wall defacing the proportions and diminishing the salutary light on the ground floor.

92. See Katja Miljutina Rappaport, ''Moja Žizn' v Narkomfine'' ("My Life at the NKF"), a manuscript published in Moscow in 2013 by the daughter of Nikolaj Miljutin. Interview May 2012. This contradicts Buchli's claim that this facility was never used as intended. After the war the connecting bridge became a dormitory for single people.

93. May 2012 interview with Katja Miljutina-Rappaport. One common joke was that, if invited for a meal, the guests would invariably enjoy at the host's apartment the same meal they would have at home.

94. Moisej Ginzburg, *Žilišče* Op. Cit., p. 82.

95. Dachas (common root with "donations") were land and country houses presented to deserving aristocrats.

96. May 2012 interview with Katja Miljutina-Rappaport..

Residential area "Krasnij kamen" in Nižnij Tagil. Team of architects under Ginzburg's supervision, 1935.

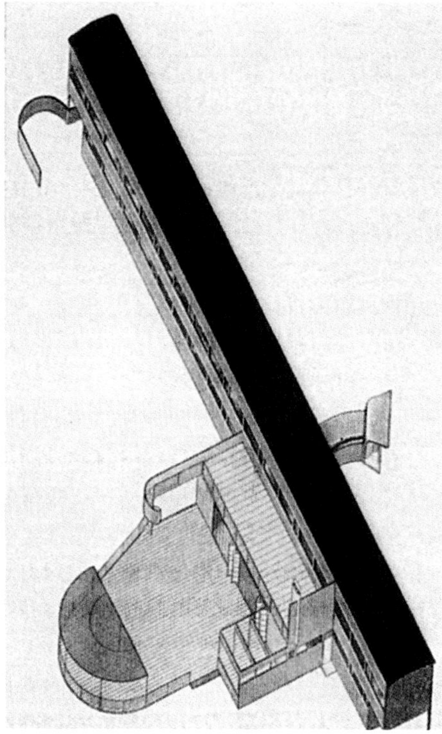

Dom-Kommuna, 1929.

Moisej Ginzburg and Soviet Residential Architecture

Dmitry Khmelnitsky

At first sight, it might seem that architect Moisej Ginzburg had a completely satisfactory career as an architect. From the very beginning of the 1930s, he stood right at the top of the Soviet architectural hierarchy. He was a professor at institutes of higher education, one of the founders and heads of the largest and most influential artistic society, the Association of Modern Architects (OSA), the author of several books on theory, and the creator of numerous outstanding designs, including one of the best-known pieces of Soviet architecture, the Narkomfin building in Moscow. At a time when physical survival was an achievement in itself, he was neither arrested nor sent into exile. He did not fall victim to a savage campaign of criticism. He died in 1946, at a young age (53), but of natural causes and as an Academician of Architecture.

However, one only has to put Ginzburg's projects into chronological order and look at them closely to realize that the success of his career as a Soviet architect concealed what was actually a tragic failure in his creative output. The 1920s were his heyday. This was a period when he produced books and designs, and realized buildings, all of which were world-class. The very end of the 1920s and the beginning of the 1930s saw him creating designs that were strange, removed from any kind of reality, and yet they went down in textbooks and in the history of architecture.

After 1932 a rapid degradation took place, and his creative output suffered a catastrophic failure. Designs he signed continued to appear, but architect Moisej Ginzburg—the Ginzburg who had existed in the 1920s—no longer was. In this respect, however, Ginzburg was no exception. His uniqueness, beyond his outstanding talent, lies in the fact that he was one of the few architects who tried, even if only for a short time, to withstand state policy in the field of architecture.

These attempts were doomed to failure from the outset, but the designs that emerged during this process constitute one of the most striking and heroic episodes in the history of Soviet architecture. It is this resistance offered to state housing policy during the second half of the 1920s that, in this author's opinion, one finds reflected in the concept and floor plan for the Narkomfin building on Novinskij bul'var. And it is this resistance that will be examined in the present article.

For all Moisej Ginzburg's fame, his life has been studied very little. Only one monograph on this subject exists—*M.J. Ginzburg* by Selim Han-Magomedov, published in Moscow in 1972. In spite of the great significance of the material it contains, this monograph cannot be regarded as either exhaustive or sufficient to form an adequate impression of Ginzburg's work during the period of Soviet architectural history with which he is associated.

Very little is known about where Moisej Ginzburg worked and in what capacity, what lay behind the turnarounds in his life, how he got along with his colleagues and state organizations, and how his career developed. Many important facts relating to his life can only be guessed at. Equally unstudied is the short life of the OSA, the organization that Ginzburg founded with the Vesnin brothers. The facts relating to both the founding and liquidation of the *Sovremennaja Arhitektura* journal are likewise obscure.

From the information given in Han-Magomedov's 1972 monograph, one may conclude that there are very few known works by Ginzburg and still fewer realized designs. Only nine of his designs for buildings were actually built or partly built (including a pre-Revolutionary mansion in Evpatoria and the Crimea Pavilion at the 1923

Moscow agricultural exhibition). Of these, five are from the end of the 1920s. With the exception of the Government House in Alma-Ata, all the other buildings from the 1920s are residential buildings.[1] There can be no doubt that residential architecture was Ginzburg's primary focus. In fact, the whole of Europe at this time was preoccupied with the problem of mass housing and urban planning, especially with housing for the working class.

To judge by *Sovremennaja Arhitektura* (*SA*), the journal Ginzburg edited from 1926-1930, his views (and those of his colleagues at the OSA) were no different from those of his CIAM colleagues (one of whom, his collaborator Nikolaj Kolli, was also a CIAM member). It seemed that the only way to solve the housing problem was to develop industrial types of minimal, low-cost housing in the form of individual apartments. *SA* is full of buildings by Le Corbusier, Geritt Rietveld, Frank Lloyd Wright, Walter Gropius, and other Western architects.

However, the possibilities that existed in the West for tackling the housing problem were absent in the USSR because of its political system. The small amount of comfortable housing built in the 1920s was usually intended for civil servants or military personnel.

The Soviet government never, even during the relatively prosperous period of the New Economic Policy, set itself the objective of fundamentally improving the housing situation in Soviet towns and cities. No serious work was ever done to establish programs of mass construction of workers' housing. What was usually built under the name of "workers' settlements" in the 1920s were residential complexes for Soviet civil servants, military personnel, or members of the secret services.

The official sanitary standard in Soviet towns and cities was approximately 8 m^2 of so-called living space (i.e., space in the apartment's main rooms, excluding the kitchen, toilet, bathroom, and other ancillary spaces) per person. The average per capita norm in the mid- and late 1920s fluctuated between 5.6 and 5.9 m^2. The average amount of living space available to workers was much lower, as little as 4–4.6 m^2 per person.[2]

Even during the NEP, plans for residential construction did not promise any solution to the housing problem in the foreseeable future. However, when the industrialization program was adopted in 1927 and especially after realization of this program began in 1928–1929, the situation deteriorated rapidly. Private business, private trade, and independent crafts were eliminated, with the result that construction of housing by private persons or cooperatives practically ceased. Formally, the housing cooperatives continued to exist, but in effect, they became state organizations engaged in construction of departmental housing.

One of the causes of the disastrous situation with housing was the sharp influx of people from the country into cities that were being modernized. The First Five-Year Plan called for millions of peasants to be forcibly moved to towns and to workers' settlements attached to new industrial enterprises. The principal program of the First Five-Year Plan, adopted in 1928, called for the urban population to increase by 2.5 to 3 million people. According to the official results for the First Five-Year Plan, the urban population in fact increased by 13.9 million, while 27 million m^2 of housing (probably an exaggerated figure) were built, i.e., approximately 2 m^2 per new urban resident.

In order to solve the housing problem, new, mass-produced, and inexpensive types of housing urgently needed to be developed. The funding allocated to housing by the first moderate five-year plan was based on a slight decrease in the amount of square meters allocated to each resident and a dramatic reduction of 33% to 50% in the average construction cost of a square meter of residential space.[3] In effect, this meant the introduction of abrupt social differentiation in types of housing.

In 1928–1929, as industrialization and collectivization were getting under way, a new mandatory slogan was devised: "communalization of living." The slogan implied that there was no longer such a thing as a single-family apartment. The country's entire urban population was to be housed in hostels (commune houses), without private kitchens and with no opportunity for inhabitants to lead a family life or bring up children. The official ideology propagated the idea of commune houses and communalization of living, justifying this with the need to liberate women from the stresses of family life and involve them in cultural life and production.[4]

In reality, however, the policy had two hidden motives:

1. The state's readiness to finance mass housing only in the form of primitive common barracks without proper facilities—and even then in insufficient quantities.

2. The desire to make maximum use of the labor of women and youths (even in heavy industry and in dangerous industrial processes).[5]

For the small part of the population in a privileged position, the authorities continued to build apartment blocks with full or partial facilities, but in secret. Mass housing—built to house more than 90% of the population—took the form of wooden communal barracks of various types, without running water or sewerage ("standard houses," to use the terminology of the time), and earth huts. This kind of housing was considered to be temporary given that it did not meet the sanitary standards, but no plans to replace it with anything more permanent existed until the middle of the 1950s. Workers housed in such barracks were allocated 3.5 m^2 of living space each, at best. At the beginning of the 1930s the average per capita allocation of living space in Soviet cities fell to 3–3.5 m^2 (and in certain exceptional cases even to 1.7 m^2) per person.[6]

It was this desperate situation that Ginzburg, together with a group of his pupils and colleagues, tried to change by 1926.

Almost all Ginzburg's important designs and buildings date from the relatively prosperous years of the NEP, a period also known for its artistic freedom (up to the early 1930s). All his residential buildings were "departmental," which is to say that they were built for Soviet civil servants of various ranks. However, the objectives that he set himself were focused on large-scale housing.

The Gosstrah [State Insurance] building on Malaja Bronnaja street in Moscow is considered to be the first residential construction project realized in Soviet times. This was a five-storey house, elegant and very well thought out, with two four-room apartments. The top floor was a twelve-room communal apartment with a shared kitchen, two bathrooms, and two toilets. It is likely that the latter apartment was intended for lower-ranking employees without families, while higher-ranking employees were allocated separate apartments.[7]

In January 1929 Moisej Ginzburg was appointed head of the Standardization Department of the Construction Committee at the Economic Conference of the Russian Soviet Federative Socialist Republic (EKOSO RSFSR; the conference had been set up at the beginning of 1928).[8] As Mihail Baršč remembers, it was Ginzburg himself who came up with the idea for the latter department:

With his characteristic talent for organizing a team and for directing its work towards the given objective, Ginzburg was able to convince Vel'man, chairman of the Construction Committee of the Russian Soviet Federative Socialist Republic, to set up a special group at the committee to develop new types of housing. This team comprised M.J. Ginzburg, A.L. Pasternak, G.R. Sum-Šhik, G.A. Zundblat, V. Vladimirov, and me.[9]

The objectives of the department headed by Ginzburg included "standardization issues; development of structures and standards; experimental construction; training and re-training of technical personnel."[10]

The Construction Committee was dissolved in March 1930, but Ginzburg's team continued its work under the aegis of the department of social housing at Gosplan RSFSR and then in the Baškiria department [State Institute for Urban Planning].

In his book *Žilišče* (Dwelling), which came out in 1934, Ginzburg described the activities carried out by the standardization department as follows:

The main objective confronting us involved developing types of housing which would allow us to minimize capital expenditure on construction, taking into account the need to provide millions of workers with a civilized habitation.[11]

Clearly, Ginzburg and his team were in reality not at all concerned by dreams of new forms of living or the ennobling influence of collective housing—dreams that were then being intensively promoted in the Soviet press. On the contrary, their objective was to design low-cost, extremely compressed, individual residential units, in order to allow for one apartment per family, instead of the prevalent apartment sharing, a room per family. The forced replacement of the kitchen with a kitchen niche in some of the projects was also dictated only by the need to save money, not by official ideology.

On the one hand, the emphasis on making housing less expensive could be seen as conformity to Party directives. On the other hand, no amount of cunning in designing layouts could make the non-communal apartment (i.e., apartment for individuals or individual families) sufficiently cheap to be included in the proposals for the First Five-Year Plan as housing to be built on a mass scale.

In 1929 the Construction Committee [Strojkom] at EKOSO RSFSR published a collection of essays entitled *Tipovje proekty i konstrukcii žiliščnogo stroitel'stva* (Standardized designs and buildings in residential construction) in which it presented the results of the work carried out by Ginzburg's group. In addition to the various designs for low-cost wooden apartment buildings and residential units, the book also included a design by M. Baršč and V. Vladimirov for a communal house with fully collectivized living. There can be no doubt that this wonderful design for a residential complex was created under Ginzburg's influence. However, we may suppose that it is the absence of non-communal housing that compelled Ginzburg to renounce authorship of the project and any personal involvement in the design.

The Green City project of 1930 included, among various types of low-rise light housing, a design that closely resembled in its construction and shape the barracks of that time, a "temporary hostel for people without children." But even this included one- or two-person units with washbasins; a sun-lit corridor linked to the units with a bedroom mezzanine above it.

Several extravagant designs for communal hostels/barracks were published in Ginzburg's *Žilišče.* One of these was a 38.5 m by 8.45 m building with a single central entrance and four staircases that opened into a corridor-like public space serving as both a vestibule and communal dining room. The ends of the building contained toilets and washrooms. The ground floor had six rooms of 15–17 m^2 (evidently, each intended for two persons);[12] the second has another 16 rooms, with four on each staircase. This structure had no corridor on the second floor. The building was intended for 44 persons.

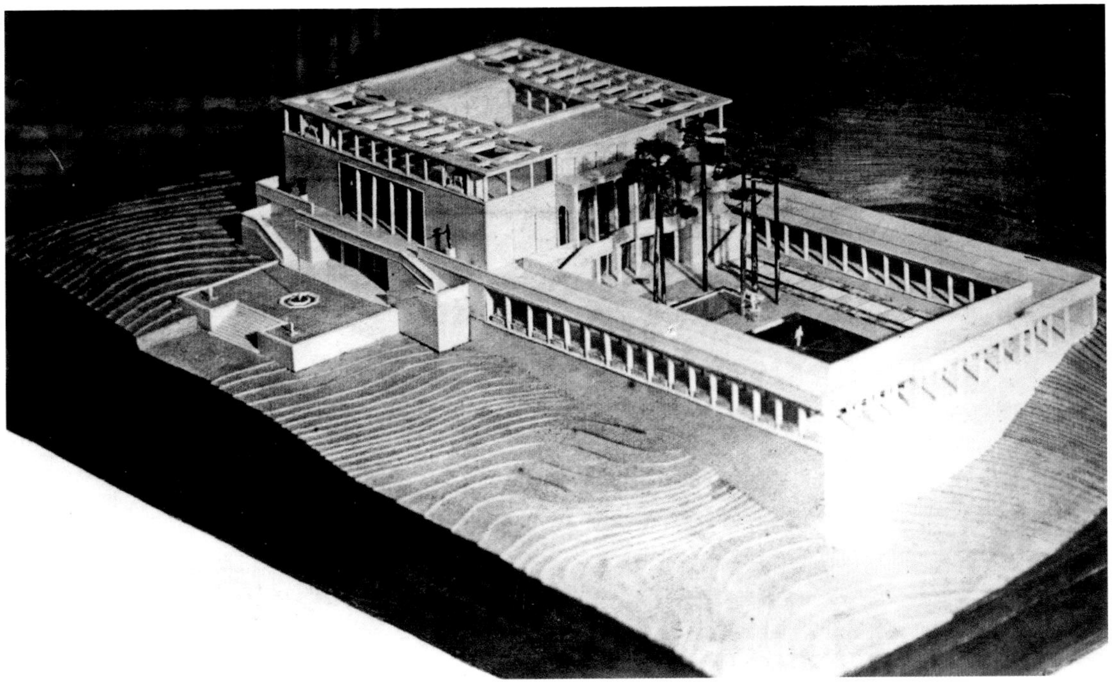

"Dača" for the People's Commissar at the Kislovodsk Sanatorium, Model, 1935–38.

It is interesting to compare the latter design with "normal" building designs of the time. For instance, *Sbornije derevjannije doma (konstrukcii)* [Prefabricated wooden houses (structures)], a book published in 1931, gives a design for a wooden plywood barracks building for 50 persons. The dimensions of a one-story building were 33 m by 5.9 m, 150 m^2 of living space, and a footprint of 199 m^2, which means that the building was intended to provide 3 m^2 of sleeping space per person. The barracks had a central communal dining room and drying rooms (approximately 40 m^2 for 50 persons), but there was no running water or sewerage. Barracks for 100, 200, or more persons were designed following the same principles. A two-story brick hostel (dimensions: 34.8 m by 13.45 m) published in the same collection had 36 rooms of 16 m^2, two staircases, and toilets and bathrooms on both floors at the ends of a corridor running right along the length of the building. This design was for more privileged inhabitants.

Both of the aforementioned designs may be considered examples of the most common types of mass housing then in existence. Comparison of these designs with the work done by Ginzburg and his team shows us the extent to which Ginzburg's activity as an architect went against the reality of that time.

Ginzburg's activities for organizations at the Council of People's Commissars of the Russian Soviet Federative Socialist Republic (RSFSR) are insufficiently studied. We may suppose that Ginzburg's initial patron and supporter was Nikolaj Miljutin while still the People's Commissar for Finance until 1929.

In 1928 Miljutin commissioned Ginzburg's best-known work, the Narkomfin building on Novinskij bul'var in Moscow. This is probably also the best-studied residential building in the Soviet Union. It consists of spatial units designed by Ginzburg's team at Strojkom's Department of Standardization. In July 1929 Miljutin ceased to be the RSFSR People's Finance Commissar and was appointed to the less important position of Chairman of the Minor Council of People's Commissars of the RSFSR.[13] He headed (evidently at his own initiative) a short-lived campaign to design "socialist towns" consisting of well-equipped residential complexes with fully communalized living. Involving almost all the leading architects in the USSR, this campaign and the related theoretical issues came to be known as the "debate about socialist settlements."

By the autumn of 1929 Miljutin had begun working on his well-known book *Socgorod*. It promoted residential complexes of the aforementioned kind (including ones designed by Miljutin himself) and modern architecture as the means by which these complexes could be created. *Socgorod* was published in the second half of 1930 and was then quickly forgotten in the USSR. Miljutin's idea was that his book would serve as something like a code of building regulations and standards for the entire Soviet Union. Yet the designs for mass housing that Miljutin adduced, along with the financial evaluation of these designs, made a poor fit with the Politburo's orientation on minimizing construction costs for housing by rejecting the installation of even minimal conveniences.

Indeed, in the spring of 1930 the Central Committee of the Communist Party issued a resolution "on work to be done regarding reconstruction of people's way of living" (published in *Pravda* on May 16, 1930, and reprinted in Ginzburg's *Sovremennaja Arhitektura*).[14] The point of the resolution was to make clear that there was, and would be, no money to spend on housing construction and communal services; resources were needed for industrialization.

The resolution made no mention whatsoever about what workers' housing should be like, merely indicating that workers' settlements should have "laundry facilities, bath-houses, child-care facilities, factory kitchens, canteens etc." In reality, this meant there would be neither apartments nor more or less civilized hostels—only the simplest barracks. Public services were to be nothing more than bathhouses and canteens, given that the barracks provided no opportunity to wash oneself or one's clothes or to cook food.

The resolution specifically blamed two people: Sabsovič and, "to an extent," Larin.

The original draft of the resolution prepared by the Organizational Bureau of the Communist Party Central Committee had named Miljutin as primarily responsible,[15] but a patron in the Central Committee shielded him by having his name deleted. Equally, at about this time, the governmental committee for designing Socgorods [Socialist Cities][16] was terminated, and Miljutin himself lost his ability to influence what was happening in architecture.

One may suppose that the activities of Ginzburg's team working for the Government of the RSFSR

Residential building on the Malaja Bronnaja, Ginzburg, 1926–1927

largely depended on what happened to Miljutin. In any case, in 1930, after the Central Committee passed its resolution, Miljutin was demoted to the position of editor of the journal *Sovetskaja Arhitektura* (with the rank of Deputy People's Commissar for Education), and Ginzburg's team was transferred to Giprogor [State Institute for Urban Planning], where for some time, until Stalin's reform of architecture in 1932, it continued to work on utopian projects for mass housing.

Sanatorium "Gronye Veršnij" (Mountain heights) in Kislovodsk (with N. Poljudov), 1945

The work Ginzburg and his team did on low-rise types of mass-built non-communal housing had no practical results; nevertheless, Ginzburg managed to build a number of departmental residential buildings before 1930, including the Narkomfin building.

On the site situated alongside Novinskij bul'var the original intention was to erect two residential buildings, a kindergarten, and a building housing a laundry and hostel. Due to unknown circumstances, only one house and the laundry building (but not the hostel) were actually built. The Narkomfin house was strictly a gallery house raised on pilotis. Its 45 apartments belong to two types of residential units (types K and F, to use the classification invented by Ginzburg), but having a very large number of layout variations.[17]

It is quite clear that Ginzburg and Miljutin exploited the situation in order to test in practice how many different types of residential units they could create. It is likewise clear that their main objective was to work with space. Because they used different levels and ceiling heights, even the smallest units in the house seem extremely expressive. At the same time, one gets the impression that the Narkomfin was entirely devoid of links of any kind (either social or professional) with extant Soviet reality.

Regrettably, it is not known how the apartments in the Narkomfin were allocated or the allowance of living space per person. Nevertheless, it is clear that the building's layout was shockingly inconvenient for its time. To have a two-room apartment consisting of through (i.e., not separate) rooms and a total floor area of 42 m^2 was absurd. For a single four-person family (following the standard allowance of space for privileged members of the society), the apartment would have been inconvenient. And to put two less privileged families in such a space would have been impossible. For Ginzburg it was a matter of principle to exclude communal apartments from consideration, and this was something with which Miljutin initially agreed (although in *Socgorod*, published just before construction of the Narkomfin was completed, he declared the exact opposite).[18]

The lack of a kitchen in the type F units was evidently a concession to Miljutin, who had been preaching communalization of living arrangements since 1929, but this was a requirement that could not, and did not in all other instances, apply to housing for the top and middle-ranking *Nomenklatura*.

The second half of the 1920s and beginning of the 1930s saw the construction of closed departmental housing estates equipped with their own services. These projects followed a clear departmental hierarchy: large apartments, medium-sized and small ones, communal apartments, hostels, and so on. As a rule, the houses consisted of ordinary multi-apartment sections with two or three apartments on each staircase landing.

Ginzburg's Narkomfin stood out markedly, not only from the social conditions of that time, but also from the already existing Soviet architectural tradition of designing housing for the mid-ranking *Nomenklatura*. Central to the latter tradition was the use of more or less standardized multi-apartment sections in which the number and sizes of the apartments and rooms were the only variables.

Ginzburg deliberately departed from the idea of a sectional structure as well as from the practice of having apartments with an unvarying ceiling height. His residential units were on the one hand intended for repeat use, but on the other were extraordinarily variable and permitted the most unexpected play with the structure of the house, evident in the Narkomfin building.

No doubt the Narkomfin echoed and contributed to the architectural discourse in Europe. The first issue of *Sovremennaja Arhitektura* in 1928 contained an article on the Weissenhof Estate exhibition. The article was not signed, which probably means that its author was Ginzburg. The essay was illustrated with drawings and photographs of Le Corbusier and Jeanneret's two-apartment house contained an exposition of Le Corbusier's five points.[19]

There is no reason to doubt that Ginzburg designed the Narkomfin building in part under the influence of Le Corbusier's architecture; almost all his principles were followed in the Narkomfin building. The structure of the type K unit with its central double-height living room clearly resembles the layout of Le Corbusier's villas, including the house in Stuttgart. But the Weissenhof Estate has no analogue for Ginzburg's F-type unit (with a half-floor shift in the unit's levels). One may, with reasonable confidence, assert that Ginzburg scored a first here, at least when it came to realization.

Jean-Louis Cohen rightly adduces as an analogue of Ginzburg's units the residential units in the hostel for single people that Hans Scharoun designed for the Werkbund exhibition in Breslau in 1929. However, this is probably not a case of borrowing, but of parallel development.[20] Furthermore, the layout of Scharoun's units was slightly different from Ginzburg's: the levels had a half-floor shift, but the staircase flights inside the unit were separate from one another and abutted different walls.

In 1926–1927 the OSA organized a "comradely competition" to design a communal house. The results of this competition were published in the 1927 issues 4 and 5 of *Sovremennaja Arhitektura*. We may suppose that the competition's main initiator was Ginzburg and that he formulated one of the key requirements for the competition: "an inventive approach to and rejection of traditional principles."[21] Most of the competition entries that were published show residential units even closer in terms of internal layout to the units at the Narkomfin building than Ginzburg's own competition entry (see the designs by A. Nikolskij, A. Ol', I. Sobelev, N. Vorotynceva, and R. Poljak). Specifically, the design by A. Ol', which structurally closely anticipates Le Corbusier's Unité d'Habitation in Marseilles, built in 1946–1952. However, it is not known to what extent Ginzburg himself shaped the course of the competition. It is possible that his ideas formed the basis of the designs by the other participants.

In order to evaluate to what extent the Narkomfin house was clashing with contemporary Soviet mores and rules, it makes sense to compare it with other residential buildings for mid- and high-ranking Soviet civil servants of the time.

In 1926 architect Arkadij Langman designed a house for the heads of the OGPU (State Political Administration) in Miljutinskij pereulok in Moscow. This building contains nine spacious apartments that resemble the apartments of pre-Revolutionary times, with bay windows, maid's rooms, and back staircases for servants and deliveries. This project had nothing to do with minimizing floor area or building costs.

In 1931 architects Evgenij Levinson and Igor Fomin designed the Lensovet [Leningrad City Hall] on the embankment of the River Karpovka in Leningrad. This is probably the second best-known and architecturally most interesting Constructivist design of the time (after the Narkomfin building).

The house has apartments of various sizes, ranging from two-room apartments with a living space of 35 m² to six-room apartments with up to 110 m² of living space. There are two very interesting two-story apartments with exits onto the roof terrace; these may be considered analogues of the penthouse that Miljutin designed for himself on the roof of the Narkomfin building if one ignores the fact that Miljutin's apartment was a compact two-room apartment, whereas the Karpovka apartments were very spacious five-room ones with a room/niche for a maid, but without a double-height living room. Incidentally, a maid's room/niche next to the kitchen was provided in all the apartment types in the building.

The two-room apartments in the house on Karpovka were intended to have 35 m² of living space, which meant they had a total floor area of 55–60 m². The six-room apartments had 110 m² of living space and a total floor area of up to 180 m². All the apartments were supposed to have a bathroom, a kitchen equipped with a rubbish chute, and (next to the kitchen) a room of 6.5–7 m² for the maid.[22]

There is another fundamental way in which the Narkomfin building differed from the ordinary apartment buildings of that time. Ministerial residential complexes were usually gated and guarded complexes. This was the case of the Lensovet building on Karpovka. The tall entrance leading through to the courtyard might seem to invite one in, but it was actually blocked by a wrought iron fence with security posts on both sides. The staircases were accessible only from the courtyard.

The initial layout of Narkomfin was completely open—like the composition of the Narkomfin building itself, which was demonstratively open and permeable to the surrounding space. Both the entrance areas by the staircases were designed in such a way as to exclude the possibility of a permanent security post. Ginzburg's building could easily be seen as a part of the Weissenhof Estate, which, by accident, ended up in Moscow.

The employees of the RSFSR People's Commissariat for Finance were probably on a lower tier of the Soviet hierarchy than the top management at Lensovet; nevertheless, it is clear that it was the idealism of the client, Miljutin (who gave Ginzburg the opportunity to realize his ideas to the full), that was instrumental in bringing the Narkomfin building into existence.

A contemporary apartment house project. Illustration taken from N. Miljutin's *Socgorod*, 1930

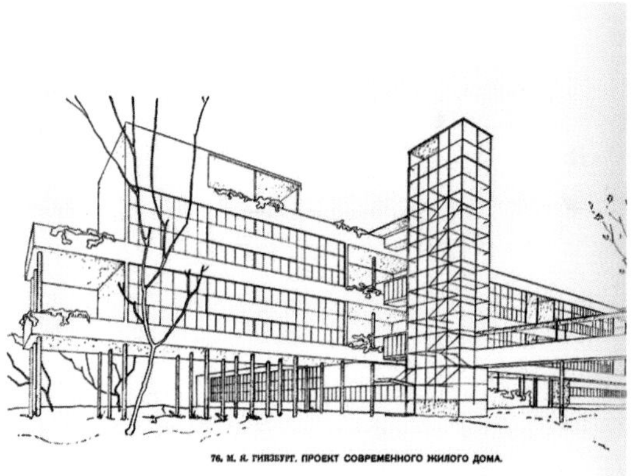

While designing the Narkomfin in 1928–1929, Ginzburg managed to build two other houses with residential units of very interesting design—a hostel for a cotton-wool factory (in collaboration with S. Lisagor and A. Pasternak) and a house for the Sverdlovsk agricultural Sovhoz in the Urals (URALOBLOSOVNARHOZ).

The background of the design of these buildings could have shed much useful light, but unfortunately they are not known. Also, very little is known about the design work on the Narkomfin building itself. The architectural drawings were produced by the *Tech-Beton* Association,[23] and the construction was carried out by *Stroj-Beton*, established in 1929.[24] Ginzburg is mentioned as one of the consultants to *Tech-Beton* in 1925–1935.[25] Neither a design program nor an estimate of construction costs for the building was ever published.

In the chapter "Relative construction costs" in his book *Socgorod*, Miljutin refers to the cost of construction adopted by the Supreme Council for the National Economy as being 20 rubles per cubic meter and to the usual proportion between a building's floor area and volume as being 1:8.[26] One may suppose that the cost of Ginzburg's design did not exceed what was then the average construction cost for housing (160 rubles per m^2).

One bedroom house, exterior view, 1945

For comparison, the cost of one cubic meter of construction of the Lensovet building on the Karpovka in Leningrad was, together with the cost of preparing the plot, 108 rubles (approximately 700–800 rubles per m^2).[27] This was a fairly standard cost for housing for high-ranking Soviet civil servants under Stalin. On page 75 of Socgorod, Miljutin published a perspectival sketch of the second phase of the Narkomfin building (on p. 107 of Ginzburg's *Žilišče*). The perspectival view was captioned "Design for the new block for the second house for the Council of People's Commissars." This project was never built and almost nothing is known about it.

The process of hierarchical differentiation of housing designed in the USSR and the legalization of apartments for the ruling class as the only official form of residential architecture was completed when, on 14 July 1932, *Mosgorispolkom* (the Moscow City Executive Committee) and *Mossovet* (Moscow city hall) passed the resolution "On standardized residential buildings."[28] This resolution cancelled all decisions made previously on this account and stipulated that new housing from that point on should take the form of apartment blocks containing two- to four-room comfortable apartments with large rooms up to 21 m^2 in size, usually with a second (back) staircase with rich and diversely decorated façades. The houses should stand on main streets and serve to embellish them.

The type of house to be built was also specified—with a mandatory full range of communal services (kindergartens, crèches, shops, laundries, storerooms, and the like). The number of floors was to be at least five. The building's architectural design was specified as well; façades were to be unique, each with their own specific decoration. They were to "form and embellish the streets." Another specification was the character of the apartments; they should have comfortable, large rooms; a separate bathroom and toilet; fitted cupboards; standard, specially designed furniture; and high-quality finishes. Furthermore, "all newly erected residential buildings should stand on main streets that are of importance in the context of Moscow."

Taken together, all these stipulations made it clear that the construction of buildings on conspicuous sites in Moscow (and other cities too, since Moscow served as an example to be imitated) were destined to higher officials, i.e., for an extremely small part of the population (2%–3% at most). If these houses were to be inhabited in accordance with the standards that applied to workers at the time, the largest rooms (21 m²) could have accommodated five persons and the smallest (12 m²), three.[29]

The apartment blocks that had been built almost in secret for the leadership now officially represented the whole of Soviet residential architecture, and in the minds of readers of architecture books and journals they took the place of mass housing.

The officially recognized model for architects to imitate was the distinguished tsarist architect Ivan Žoltovskij's house on Mohovaja Street in Moscow (designed in 1932, completed in 1934).[30] This house was a seven-story piece of stage scenery—a multi-columned façade stylized to resemble Palladio's Palazzo del Capitano in Vicenza. The impressive façade concealed apartments that were very large and luxuriously decorated but uninteresting and with primitive layouts (including maids' rooms, of course).[31]

In its 1930 Resolution, the Central Committee expressed alarm in the face of "utopian" and "semi fantastic" experiments that accompanied the work of some architects, recommending to the Government (SNK) to establish in a matter of fifteen days "regulations specifically for the construction of workers' housing (laundry facilities, bath-houses, child-care facilities, factory kitchens, canteens etc.) of its own. . . .[32] Then, from the spring of 1932 forward, Soviet architects were mostly instructed to "revive historical heritage" in their projects, i.e., to stylize buildings to conform to historical styles.[33]

In the first half of the 1930s Soviet architects took part in so-called "creative discussions." These were educational events at which a new professional terminology was developed, and top architects[34] were tested for their loyalty and for their right to continue to be included among

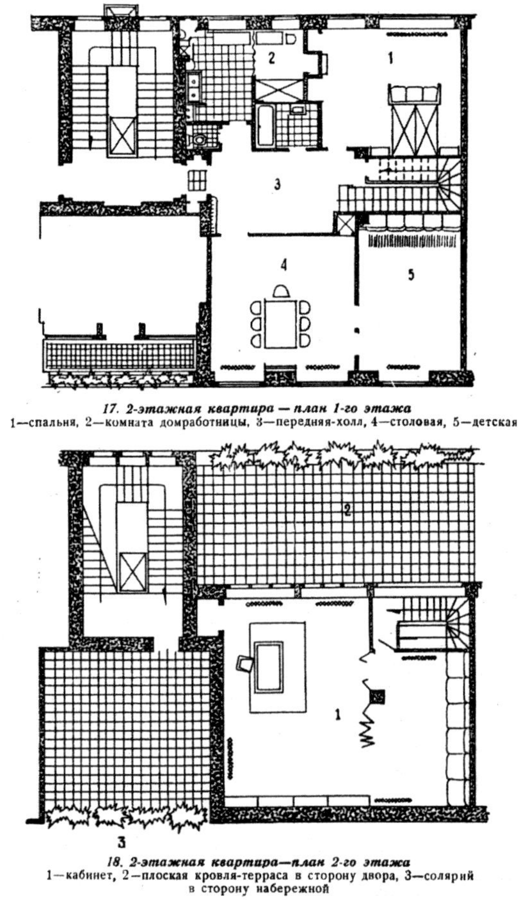

E. Levinson and I. Fomin, apartment house project for the Leningrad City Hall, plan of a two-floor apartment, 1931

those regarded as top architects. During such "creative" discussions held in 1933, Ginzburg offered an opinion for which he was subjected to immediate criticism by the leadership of the Union of Architects: "We must frankly admit that there is today a colossal disproportion between the grand horizons of architectural creativity and the pitiful perplexity in which most architects find themselves."[35]

"Pitiful perplexity" is an unforgivably precise characterization of the state of Ginzburg himself at this time. A year later, during the "creative" discussion held in May 1934, Ginzburg was to say, "Four years ago, we were reproached for being insufficiently socially engaged, but today a building's floor plan is something that cannot be mentioned, just as you would never mention a rope in the house of a hanged man."[36]

The latter words no longer contained any perplexity; they were merely a precise description of the state of affairs. Clients from the ruling class were not interested in buildings' floor plans, so architects too were forbidden to take an interest in it.

Thus the ban on working on floor plans meant the end of architecture as spatial art and its transformation into the art of façade decoration, given that the senior Soviet management, which had by this time taken architecture under its control, was interested only in façades.

After the architecture studios were set up at the Mossovet in 1933, Ginzburg became head of one of them. Gennadij Movčan, an employee at this studio, recalled:

That year, a turn towards Classicism was declared; architecture now had to be enriched. The new architecture was annulled. The changes happened in a painful and difficult manner. I started working at one of the new architecture studios that had been created at the Mossovet [the studio of M.J. Ginzburg]. I can't remember whether anything we created there was actually built. In fact, I think everything we did ended up in the dust bin.[37]

Ginzburg's desperate struggle against the new trend and his attempts to retain at least some of his previous convictions in his designs and statements could—and should!—be the subject of an exciting separate study. In the 1930s Ginzburg and the Vesnin brothers headed the architectural design office of the People's Commissariat for Heavy Industry, mostly building resorts on the Crimean peninsula for the Nomenklatura.

In 1935 Ginzburg designed the "Krasnij Kamen" residential district in Nižnij Tagil, the model for which was published in Han-Magomedov's book. This project was a strange combination of buildings in a distinctly Constructivist architectural style, laid out in a symmetrical, temple-like ensemble of a typically Stalinist character. At the same time, the individual complexes had a geometrical configuration that is uncharacteristic of neoclassical compositions; they consisted of a trapeze, semi-circle, broken circle, hexagon, and so on.

Ginzburg's book *Žilišče Voprosy proektirovanija i stroitel'stva žilyh zdanij* [Issues regarding the design and construction of residential buildings] was published in 1934. The book contains a number of apartment designs prepared by the Third architecture studio at the State Commissariat for Heavy Industry under Ginzburg. He included different options for kitchen layouts (kitchen/dining room, kitchen and separate 4.5 m^2 maid's room, kitchen with a 3.15 m^2 niche for a maid). The design for a "superior type of one-family apartment" was particularly interesting.

The project consisted of a two-storey five-room apartment in a gallery house (with an entrance through a glazed gallery). The lower floor contained a 30 m double-height living room with a polygonal bay window, including a kitchen with

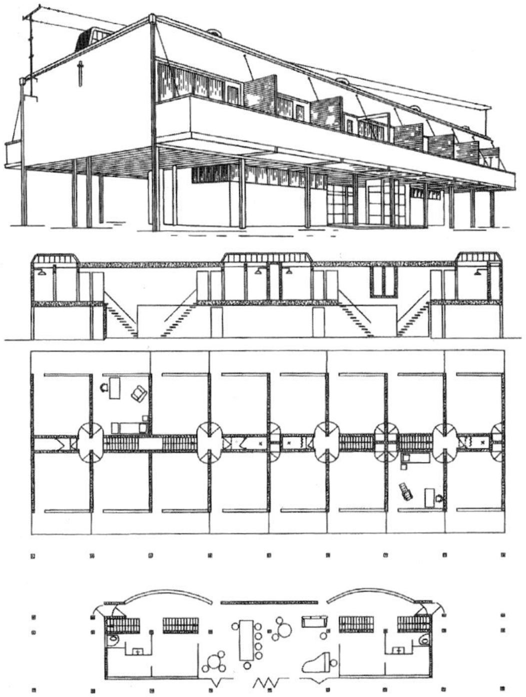

Sixteen-room hostel, 1929

a maid's room (5.8 m^2). The second floor, which was accessed via a semi-spiral staircase, accommodated four bedrooms. At first sight, this appears to be a typical Stalinist apartment, but as a kind of parody of the compact and spatially rich residential units Ginzburg designed at the end of the 1920s. It remains unclear whether such apartments were ever built.

In 1935–1938 a team including Ivan Leonidov and led by Ginzburg built a sanatorium for the People's Commissariat for Heavy Industry in Kislovodsk. The sanatorium was characterized by recidivist traces of Constructivism, visible in the details and in the layouts of the buildings.[38] Famously, the sanatorium included the only realized structure by Ivan Leonidov,[39] an elaborate cascading staircase, which descended through a monumental park.

Ginzburg also designed for the sanatorium a People's Commissar's house, a personal villa for Sergo Ordžonikidze, member of the Politburo, who sponsored the sanatorium project. The villa, however, was never built.[40] The model, first published in 1940,[41] and reproduced by Han-Magomedov,[42] resembled a Roman villa—curiously ill-adapted to the climate of the Caucasus with its atrium courtyard and swimming pool.

Overall, the sanatorium reflected a search for a stylistic niche that would give Ginzburg the opportunity for at least a degree of architectural innovation. Ultimately, the project showed how far behind Ginzburg had left the professional objectives that he had been trying to tackle only a decade earlier.

Several other designs by Ginzburg for residential buildings dating to the late 1930s and the 1940s, a time when he headed a team of architects working on transforming the Crimean coast into a string of vacation resorts. Almost all of these designs were single-family villas. Houses of this kind were designed by many Soviet architects during the war. Usually, they were published in Soviet journals without any indication of the government department that had commissioned them. They were intended for high-ranking civil servants from various departments to which the architects had been attached. Of definite interest was a single-apartment log house/dacha designed and built during the war and published by Han-Magomedov—without indication of the year of construction, client, location, or the source of his information about it. This two-story house
was slightly reminiscent of houses by Frank Lloyd Wright, with simple and elegant floor plans, surrounded by beautifully constructed terraces and balcony. This was, arguably, the only known building by Ginzburg from the 1930s and 1940s in which he did not have to violate his principles.

It is interesting to compare this dacha by Ginzburg with the log villas/dachas that Ivan Žoltovskij designed for the settlement of Krjukovo near Moscow for unknown Soviet dignitaries. Žoltovskij's buildings were not only larger, but also far more monumental than Ginzburg's dacha. And their layouts were much more crude.

Before the war, the paths of Ginzburg and Miljutin crossed one more time. Miljutin, who had been fired from all the positions he had held and escaped arrest by miracle, entered Moscow Architecture Institute in 1935, graduating from it as an extramural student in 1940. His diploma project, supervised by Moisej Ginzburg, was a "Building containing art studios for the construction of the Palace of Soviets" and was designed in the same palace eclectic style against which Miljutin and Ginzburg had fought so hard ten years earlier. It was only in the mid-1950s, after Khrushchev had carried out a sweeping reform of architecture, that mass construction of housing in the literal meaning of that term—i.e., the construction of well-designed apartments for non-privileged parts of the population—recommenced in the USSR. Standardized large-panel houses were now supposed to replace the Stalinist barracks and earth houses.

Khrushchev found himself having to start almost from scratch. According to a secret report "On the condition of urban housing stock in 1940–1952" that was drawn up in August 1953 for L. Kaganovič, in 1940 Soviet cities had had a total of 167.2 million m^2 of housing, almost the same as in 1926, when the corresponding figure had been 162 million.[43] The new housing built during the first pre-war five-year plans had entirely evaporated. It is likely that, even taking into account the barracks buildings, the new construction scarcely made up for natural loss among residential structures. In 1952, according to the above report, the country's housing stock was 221.9 million m^2.

According to official statistics, in 1952 the total urban population in the USSR was 76.8 million. In 1927 it had been 25.8 million.[44] Thus over a period of 25 years the total urban population had increased by 51 million, whereas the total floor area available had risen by a mere 59 million m^2. So the average allocation of living space had fallen over this period from 5.5 to 2.8 m^2 per person.

According to *Narodnoe hozjajstvo SSSR* [The national economy of the USSR], the reference book S.N. Prokopovič compiled and published in 1952 in New York, the situation was not so gloomy: in 1949 there were 4.2 m^2 of dwelling space per urban resident.

Precise and reliable figures with regard to this matter are impossible to establish given the unreliability of Soviet statistics, but one may confidently suppose that the real allocation of housing in the USSR 30–35 years after the start of industrialization did not exceed approximately 3.5–4 m^2 per person.

For all the grand scale of the construction of housing carried out in the years that followed, the Soviet government never managed, before the USSR itself broke up, to attain the sanitary allowance of living space that had been adopted in the 1920s.

Kislovodsk Sanatorium, 1935–38, general view

1. Han-Magomedov, *Ginzburg,* op. cit. Moscow, 2007, pp. 128-130.

2. Han-Magomedov, S.O., Moisej Ginzburg, Moscow: 2007, pp. 128–130.

3. In 1927 *Sovremennaja Arhitektura* published: "Our meager allowance is 8.1 m^2 of living space per person, but this is a remote ideal: in Moscow alone there is a shortage of more than 5 million m^2 of housing, i.e. 1/3 of the city's population [in 1927 the population numbered 2,018,000] has nowhere to live. For industrial centers such as Ivanovo-Voznesensk, Bogorodsk, Nikola-Pavlovsk (Urals) and papermaking factories in Kaluga, the allowance of living space per person varies between 4.5 and 1.5 m^2.

[. . .] In order to maintain the level of 1926, i.e., in order just to keep up with the growth in the size of the population each year and to replace housing stock that is worn out, 2 billion rubles must be spent over the course of five years, but the state spent 145 million rubles from various sources on construction of workers' housing in 1925–1926 (session of the All-Russian Central Executive Committee, 12th convention, comrade Levin) and 162,500,000 rubles in 1926–1927. G. Vegman, "Enlarged housing," in *Sovremennaja Arhitektura*, 1927, no. 1, p. 12.

4. At the end of the 1920s in the USSR the cost of a square meter of an apartment equipped with all utilities fluctuated between 150 and 190 rubles. In 1930 a resolution was passed limiting the average cost of a square meter of living space in the RFSFR to 102.5 rubles. Barracks buildings costing 4–60 rubles per m^2 were built on a mass scale. For instance, the five-year plan for Kazakhstan provided funding for residential construction on the basis of a cost of 60–90 rubles per m^2.

5. "The billions of rubles which we spend on construction of housing and organizing people's living conditions must serve the purpose of instilling a new way of living, i.e. a socialist organization of the cultural and household services provided to the population, which is the condition for liberating women from domestic slavery." Miljutin, *Socgorod*, Op. cit., p. 8.

6. "The adopted five-year plan for the national economy provides for enormous industrial growth based on reconstruction and socialist rationalization, which, in distinction to capitalist rationalization, is not based on exploitation of the workforce, makes it possible to expand, without damage to the functions of motherhood, the use of female labor in production, including in heavy industry. For this purpose the Central Committee considers it necessary that the relevant Soviet and pubic organizations (Gosplan, NKT, VSNH, and the unions) should ensure the realization of the five-year plan's provision for involving female labor in all industrial sectors—by adapting for this purpose plans for training the female workforce and by ensuring continual growth in numbers of women present at all instances involved in producing a qualified workforce (FZU, CIT, evening courses, higher technical institutions of learning)." Central Committee Resolution no. 19 of 15/IV 1929. Cited from Marševa, B., Okuneva, I., "Female labor in conditions of socialist construction" in *Bol'ševik*, Nos. 11–12, 1932, p. 110.

7. The following table shows changes in the average allowance of "living space" (sq. m. per person) in cities in the Urals:

City	**1928**	**1933**	**1937**
Sverdlovsk	5.3	4.2	4.1
Cheljabinsk	4.4	2.2	2.6
Perm	3.9	2.8	4.9
Magnitogorsk	—	1.6	2.6
Berezniki	—	2.5	3.9
Zlatoust	4.6	2.7	2.7
N. Tagil	4.5	3.2	3.7

8. See also the second chapter of this monograph (editor's note).

9. "Strojkom RSFSR was the Construction Committee at EKOSO RSFSR. It was established in 1928, initially as the Construction Committee of Gosplan RSFSR [. . .] In January 1929 Strojkom RSFSR was reorganized, as its six departments were reduced to four. The first of these departments dealt with issues relating to the construction economy, including assessment of efficiency of construction, financing, labor, materials, transport, and target figures used in planning. The second was the Standardization Department, headed by Moisej Ginzburg. . . . The materials published in the album/collection *Tipovye proekty i konstrukcii žilščnogo stroitel'stva, rekomenduemje na 1930 g.* [Standard designs and structures for housing, recommended for 1930] were prepared by the following employees of Strojkom RSFSR and 'authors' engaged from outside: M.O. Baršč, V.I. Vel'man. I.I. Berezubov, V.N. Vladimirov, M.J. Ginzburg, I.S. Gurevič, N.A. Krasilnikov, L.M. Lissitzky, S.V. Orlovskij, and A.L. Pasternak. The committee was disbanded on March 10th, 1930 and its functions were transferred to the Construction Sector at Gosplan RSFSR [. . .] in particular, the work of the Standardization Department had its continuation in the activities of the Department of Socialist Housing at the Construction Department of Gosplan RSFSR." Kazus' I.A., *Sovetskaja arhitektura 1920-h godov: organizacija proektirovanija* [Soviet architecture of the 1920s: how the design process was organized], Moscow, pp. 292–293.

10. MARHI XX Vek (*20th century*), Moscow, vol. 1, p. 105.

11. Kazus', I.A., *Sovetskaja arhitektura 1920-x godov: organizacija proektirovanija*, Moscow: p. 293.

12. And further:
"The work began with an analysis of the range of types of housing in the pre-Revolutionary, so-called 'commercial' apartment building. This analysis showed that, for all its cultural hideousness, this type of housing met to a certain extent the interests of the middle and petty bourgeoisie and was economically more efficient than, for instance, the mass housing built in Moscow in the first years following the Revolution. In order to attain economic balance at the very least, it was necessary to reduce and compact the ancillary spaces. We had to drop the second [back] staircase and the maid's room; but this in itself was insufficient. We had to reduce to an absolute minimum all passages and corridors which serve merely as links. It proved necessary to look in detail at the hall, bathroom, and kitchen.

"The analysis of the latter rooms showed that when their positions, and in particular their fittings, are rationalized, their dimensions may be reduced without any painful consequences. Experiments undertaken by progressive architects in the West confirmed the results of our theoretical analysis. Continuing this rationalizing work, we came to the conclusion that by reducing the dimensions of the ancillary spaces we could increase the economic efficiency 'expressed in cubic volume' by 10%–12% compared with existing buildings (for instance, those built by the Mossovet).

"Analysing further the subsidiary space in the ordinary apartment, we became convinced of the possibility of reducing its volume still further by reducing the height of the ancillary rooms (bathroom, toilet, entrance hall).

"By placing alternately the living rooms in one half of the building and the ancillary rooms in the other, we were able to adjust the height of both types of room at our own discretion. By reducing the height of the ancillary rooms we increased the height of the living rooms (type C). Even taking into account a number of factors that raise the cost (an additional downpipe and additional horizontal pipes), we still managed to obtain noticeable reduction in costs. But in apartments with a small floor area even these measures were insufficient. We had to replace the separate kitchen with a kitchen niche which, while taking up minimal space (1.4 sq. m.), allows housework to be done with sufficient convenience." Ginzburg, M., *Žilišče*, Moscow, 1934, p. 66.

13. Kazus', I.A., *Sovetskaja arhitektura 1920-h godov: organizacija proektirovanija*, Moscow, p. 293.

"The following employees of Strojkom RSFSR and guest 'authors' took part in the development of the graphic and textual materials published in *Tipovye Proekty i Konstrukcii Žiliščnogo Stroitelstva, Rekomenduemje na 1930* [Standard designs and structures for residential construction, recommended for 1930] (Moscow: Gos. tekh. izd-vo, 1929): M.O. Baršč, V. Vel'man, I.I. Verezubov, V.N. Vladmirov, M.J. Ginzburg, A.L. Pasternak." Kazus', I.A., *Sovetskaja Arhitektura 1920-h Godov: Organizacija Proektirovanija*, Moscow: 2009, pp. 292–293. The minimal dimensions per person may be reduced to 10–12 m^2." Ginzburg, M, *Žilišče*, Moscow: 1934, p. 88.

14. "The Minor Sovnarkom was a permanent committee at the Council of People's Commissars (SNK)—the government—in the period 1918-1930. It was set up in November 1917 for the purpose of preliminary consideration of issues in the competence of the SNK and to resolve minor financial and economic questions. The committee comprised 3–4 people's commissars or their deputies, as well as a secretary. The committee had no permanent members. It met when needed. It was finally disbanded in 1931." 'Naselenie SSSR' at http://ru.wikipedia.org/wiki.

15. The type K unit is the largest and the most traditional in terms of layout. This is a three-room, two-level apartment. The first level has a kitchen and double-height living room situated at the entrance from the building's public corridor. The second level, reached by a single-flight staircase, has a bathroom and two bedrooms. The regular type K can reach 145 m² (as in the case of the two largest apartments in the house). For the most part, the type K units have entrances from the corridor on the second floor of the building and occupy the second and third floors; at the two extremes of the building, however, they are found on other floors as well.

The type K unit is similar to the penthouse apartment, which Miljutin built for himself on the seventh and eighth floors of the house. The F-type units are on the fourth and fifth floors and are accessed from the gallery on the fourth floor. There are two kinds of type F: a lower and an upper. The upper type F unit is on two levels. A small entrance hall with a toilet opens onto a staircase. The first flight of the staircase leads to the double hight living room and the second leads higher, to the bedroom. The type F units have a floor area of 41–42 m². Several apartments in the building are double type F units. The house also contains a number of apartments that do not belong to any particular type, but have different levels with a great variety of ceiling heights. Editor's note: On this subject see also second chapter.

16. Me'erovič, M.G,"Discussion about Social Housing and New Materials', http://archi.ru/agency/news_current.html?nid=45601

17. Socialist Cities.

18. A detailed analysis of all types of apartment in this house has been carried out by Johannes Cramer. See: Johannes Cramer/Anke Zalivako, *Das Narkomfin-Kommunenhaus in Moskau 1928–2012*, Petersberg, 2013, p. 39f. See also the second chapter of the monograph.

19. "By creating public dining rooms, crèches, kindergartens, boarding schools, laundries, and repair workshops, we shall truly and fundamentally break away from existing property relations in the family and thus create economic conditions for liquidating the family as an economic unit. This means that when deciding what to do with residential units in new buildings, we may treat these units as housing for individuals who have been joined together to form a collective in which the family, if it still exists, exists not as an economic unit but as a free association of people linked to one another by personal, kinship, and other such ties. People's intimate relations with one another will be their own business and divorced from property relations of any kind." Miljutin, N., *Socgorod*, Moscow: 1930, p. 8.

20. The same issue of *Sovremennaja Arhitektura* contained an article by I. Gurevič entitled 'Contemporary housing', in which Gurevič wrote: "for the most part, the layouts used at Weissenhof can in no way serve as prototypes for layout designs for workers' houses in the USSR" (*Sovremennaja Arhitektura*, 1928, No. 1, p. 36). This is an indication of the circumstances in which Ginzburg and his colleagues worked.

21. Jean-Louis Cohen, "Einordnung in einen europäischen Kontext" in Johannes Cramer/Anke Zalivako, *Das Narkomfin-Kommunenhaus in Moskau 1928–2012*, Petersberg: 2013, pp. 150–151.

22. Ibid. pp 150–151.

23. Levinson, E., Fomin, I.I., *Arhitektura i Stroitel'stvo Žilogo Doma Leningradskogo Soveta*, Moscow: 1940, p. 3.

24. "Tehbeton was a regional industrial cooperative construction association. It was established in 1925 under the name 'Tehnik-betonščik' [. . .] Projects designed by the association before 1930 included: Uralmaš [. . .], seven diesel pumping stations for the Baku to Batumi oil pipeline, a cinematic film factory in Šostka, a plywood factory in Kukmor, a fabric factory in Vjazniki, the tool block of Stalingrad Tractor Factory, the Palace of Culture at the Stalingrad Regional Professional Council, three chemicals factories for Centrohimtrest, refrigerators for Sojuzriby in Kiev, Nižnij Novgorod, and Voronež, the buildings of the executive committee, professional council, pedagogical college, and day-care facility in Elista, the Narkomfin building on Novinskij bul'var in Moscow, the Uraloblsovnarhoz building in Sverdlovsk, a workers' club in Kolomna, the steam-power station of Centrobumtrest in Okulovka, and a tanning factory in Sarapul. . . . In 1935 the association became the state group Mospromproekt." Kazus', I.A., *Sovetskaja arhitektura 1920-h godov: organizacija proektirovanija*, Moscow, 2009, pp. 298–299.

25. "Strojbeton was a regional industrial and cooperative construction association. It was set up in 1929 and was part of Moskoopstrojsojuz. It carried out work 'involving construction of all types of buildings—including factories, housing, retail buildings, and clubs—from hollow-core cinder blocks." In 1929 Strojbeton built the experimental Narkomfin building on Novinskij bul'var in Moscow to a design by Tehbeton." Kazus', I.A., *Sovetskaja arhitektura 1920-h godov: organizacija proektirovanija*, Moscow, 2009, p. 292.

26. Kazus', I.A., *Sovetskaja arhitektura 1920-h godov: organizacija proektirovanija*, Moscow, 2009, pp. 101.

27. Miljutin, N.A., *Problema stroitel'stva socialističeskih gorodov. Osnovnye voprosy planirovki i stroitel'stva naselennyh mest* [The problem of construction of socialist towns and cities. Principal issues relating to planning and construction of settlements], state publishing house, Moscow-Leningrad, 1930, p. 74.

28. Levinson, E.A., Fomin, I.I., *Arhitektura i stroitel'stvo žilogo doma Leningradskogo soveta* [Architecture and construction of the house of Leningrad Council], Moscow, 1940, bldg. 6.

29. "The resolution of the Presidium of the Moscow City Executive Committee and the Moscow Council of Workers' and Peasants' Delegates of July 14th,1932." *Stroitel'stvo Moskvy*, 1932, Nos. 8–9, inner front cover page.

30. "Joint Decree of the Prezidium of the Moscow City Executive Committee and of the Moscow Soviet (Council)" R.k. and k.D. 14 July 1932 r. *Stroitel'stvo Moskvy* (1932), No 8–9.

31. Editor's note: This trend encountered some resistance as criticism of the "Renaissance revival," and Palladian "plagiarism" appeared in professional and satirical journals, at least until 1937. Stalin favored a different trend altogether, that is, American corporate architecture. The term "principled eclecticism," as a correct approach, as opposed to the unprincipled one, further murkied the water. Cf. Danilo Udovički-Selb, "Between Modernism and Socialist Realism: Soviet Architectural Culture under Stalin's Revolution from Above: 1928–1938" in *Journal of Architectural Historians* 68:4 December 2009.

32. Both the client who commissioned this building and its cost are unknown. There is reason to suppose that it was designed for the top management of the NKVD, but soon after completion was handed over for use as the US Embassy.

33. See Directive of the Central Committee of the Communist Party (Bolshevik) "On the work regarding the reconstruction of the *byt*," 16 May 1930. Published by *Pravda* on May 29, 1930. Ginzburg published it verbatim in his journal *SA* 1–2 1930.

34. This is what German architect Rudolf Wolters said, who worked in Novosibirsk in 1932: "For all architectural details the supreme authorities in Moscow prescribed the 'classical style' as the only style possible: star-shaped floor plans and Greek facades!" Rudolf Wolters, *Spezialist in Sibirien*, Berlin (1933), p. 83.

35. For more detail on the reeducation of Soviet architects at the beginning of the 1930s see: Hmelnitskij, D., *Arhitektura Stalina*, Moscow, 2007, pp. 129–209.

36. Arhitektura SSSR, No. 4, 1933, p. 12.

37. "Lessons to be learnt from the architecture exhibition in May," *Arhitektura SSSR*, 1934, No. 6, p. 12.

38. Editor's note: Ginzburg actually reinterpreted the Milanese Noveceuto style on the main façade. Only an ingenuitive visitor, however, could discover that the side and back façade are frankly modernist. Ginzburg quotes Gropius, Le Corbusier, Mies van Der Rohe, and his own Narkomfin building.

39. MARHI, vol. 1, p. 148.

40. Editor's note: Ordžonikidze, a jovial and good spirited "enfant terrible" of the Politburo, apparently refused to accept such privilege. He committed suicide under obscure circumstances in February 1937.

41. Editor's note: See M. Ja. Ginzburg, *Arhitektura Sanatorija: NKTP v Kislovodske*, Moscow: Gosizdat, 1940.

42. Editor's note: The villa was first published in M. Ja Ginzburg Arhitektura Sanatorija: NKTPV Kislovodske, Moscow: Mosobegolit,1939.

43. Report of the Central Statistics Office of the USSR to L.M. Kaganovič on the state of the urban housing stock in 1940–1952, August 18, 1953. *Sbornik dokumentov Sovetskoj žizni 1943–1953. Sostaviteli: B.J. Zubkova, L.P. K Šeleva, G.A. Kuznecova, A.I. Minjuk, L.A. Rogovaja*, Moscow, ROSSPEN, 2003.

44. V.P. Černyšev, *Pjatiletnij plan razvitija narodnogo hozjajistva SSSR*, Moscow: Gosizdat 1928, pp. 80–83.

Nikojaj Miljutin's penthouse, watercolor by Ellena Ovsianikova

Condition in 2008.

Invisible Colors: The Narkomfin House-Painting Experiment

Alla G. Vronskaya

Designed and built during the First Five-Year Plan (1928–1932), at the moment of a pivotal turn from a relatively liberal New Economic Policy toward the creation of a centralized industrial economy, Moisej Ginzburg's Narkomfin House by no means remained ideologically neutral. But how can one capture its ideology without reverting to the clichés of a comeback of social utopianism and the emergence of Stalinian totalitarianism, which—impregnated with a negative ethical appraisal and a prediction of an inevitable collapse—still serve as the analytical models for the discussions of Soviet architecture of the period? One possible approach to analyzing ideology was offered by architectural historian Michael Hays, who introduced the notion of "posthumanism" to characterize a perceptual shift within modernist architecture, a shift that marked the emergence of a fragmented, depersonalized subjectivity that was a result of industrial capitalism.[1] Similar to Hays, in this essay, I will turn to a study of subjectivity; however, I will explore the internal dynamics of the new subject, analyzing it as from the point of view of the user of a building, a user constituted by the very architecture that he or she inhabits. Interpreted as an instrument of the production of subjectivity, the Narkomfin will reveal not a political stance vis-à-vis the regime, but architecture's self-assigned social mission. Moreover, as a part of the European modernist tradition, Ginzburg's ideology needs to be dissociated from its Soviet political context. In order to do so, I suggest focusing on a particular part of the Narkomfin project—the collaborative work of Ginzburg and leading Bauhaus pedagogue Hinnerk Scheper on the design of wall-painting schemes.

The head of the Bauhaus House-Painting Workshop between 1925 and 1933 (except for his stay in Moscow in 1929–1930), Scheper was invited to the USSR as the foremost specialist in this newly emerging architectural discipline, which he reoriented from its initial subjectivism toward a strictly scientific foundation.[2] He believed that contemporary scientific psychology was the way to overcome the bourgeois individualism of a genius-artist and to create a new subjectivity that fused individual differences with the collective, understood as a biological species. Accordingly, architecture was to become a system of physiological stimuli, which were to trigger identical reflexes and lead to the same psychological responses in all perceiving subjects.

In Germany, this approach led to the emergence of signage systems, architectural prompts that facilitated the orientation of people within a building. Operating on an instinctive, physiological level, these systems most often relied on painting walls into contrasting colors in order to make them immediately distinguishable. Heinrich Koch, for example, employed it in Oskar Schlemmer's house in Dessau, where the doors of adjacent rooms were painted in different bright colors, while Scheper reverted to it in the Bauhaus building in Dessau (both built in 1925–1926).

Ginzburg, who had seen both buildings during his visit to Germany in 1927, admitted the influence of the Bauhaus precedent on his interest in house-painting and on the color schemes applied in the Narkomfin house in particular.[3] Indeed, in the Narkomfin corridors and stairwells color also allowed a quick understanding of the organization of space and an easy orientation among otherwise identical objects. As in Dessau, doors were painted either black or white to prevent residents from confusing their apartments with those of their neighbors; the black and white color applied to steps (black on the horizontal and white on the vertical planes) helped the users of the building not to stumble.[4] Moreover, just as it was in the Bauhaus building in Dessau, each level of the building received a distinctive color: here orange, light blue, green, cobalt, vermillion (red), and Veronese green (emerald). The bright colors, however, were predominantly applied on the ceilings, whereas the rest of the surfaces were painted in light grey.[5] Moreover, Ginzburg radicalized the Bauhaus agenda not only by adapting the results of psycho-physiological investigations to architecture, but also by furthering these investigations themselves. In particular, he was interested in the impact of color upon the energy and working capacity of a person, continuing the experiments started by such physiologists as Charles Féré, who explored the influence of color upon working energy and the strength of muscles.[6]

As Anson Rabinbach has demonstrated, by the 1840s, following the developments in the theory of electromagnetism, the concept of energy (*Kraft*) appeared in German philosophical discourse as one of its foundational notions. Energy was interpreted as the source of all mechanical, and thus human, work. In the 1860s, however, the discovery of the second law of thermodynamics added a pessimistic note to this idea. The law postulated an inevitable loss of energy during the process of its conversion and the ensuing entropy. Energy was now understood as a scarce and ever-diminishing resource that had to be economized.[7] As the decrease of energy was associated with the feeling of fatigue, the concepts of energy and fatigue became the tropes of nineteenth-century psychology and physiology, subsequently leading to a host of various psychological and sociological disciplines and practical methods of organizing industrial work—including Féré's research.

Aspiring to turn architecture into a tool of economizing and restoring the energy of the dweller,[8] Ginzburg suggested treating the surfaces of the Narkomfin interior walls as color screens of psychological laboratories: "From the color discs of Féré [we have to move to] color screens (large surfaces of color) and from color screens—to their spatial combinations, enclosing [*zamikajuščie*] the perceiving subject."[9] As Ginzburg established earlier that bright colors exercised a tiring effect upon an inhabitant of an architectural space, the palette applied in the Narkomfin was pale in comparison to the one used at the Bauhaus.[10] In the Narkomfin, Ginzburg and Scheper tested two (opposite) ranges, the warm and the cold.[11] An axonometric drawing of an apartment of type K (a larger apartment for families with children), demonstrated bright blue color on the ceilings, whereas the rest of the surfaces were painted in much calmer hues: light grey for the kitchen, almost white for the living room, and a warmer, pinkish tone for the bedroom on the upper level of the apartment.[12] A more traditional central perspective drawing illustrated the warm palette that was applied to a small, studio-like F unit (an apartment for single persons and childless couples).[13] The ceiling was painted a dark yellow; the external wall was given a pale lemon-yellow color above the window and a white color below.

Floor Plan Detail

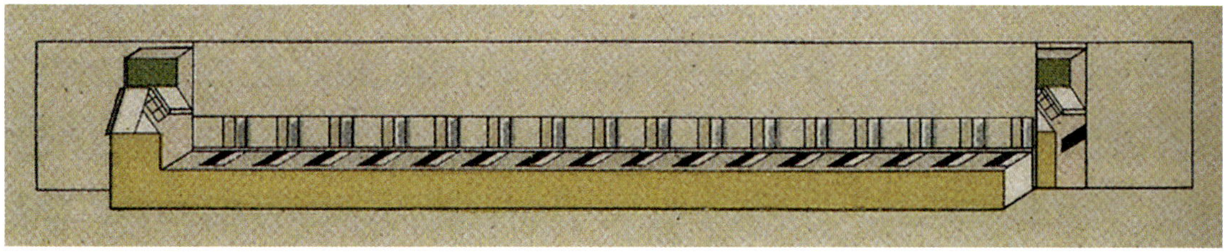

The other walls were painted into subtle warm hues. In contrast, the screens enclosing the staircases leading up and down were given various shades of grey to accentuate the properties of the architectural space—its size and the relationships between architectural volumes.

As in the circulation areas, bright colors, generally avoided in the interiors, could nevertheless be

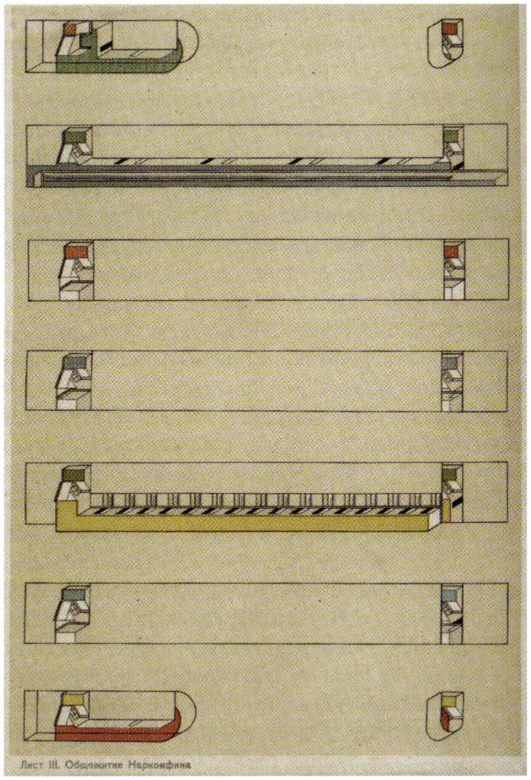

Circulation Analysis

found on the ceilings. According to Ginzburg, the surface of ceilings "penetrated into the consciousness only in individual, separated [*otdel'nije, prepyvistje*] visual images."[14] The glances that one threw on a ceiling, in other words, were too brief for the color to enter the cognitive sphere and thus would exhaust the individual. The walls, on the contrary, were given an "invisible coloration" [*nevidimaja rascvetka*], which was nevertheless perceived by the subject without consciously registering it:

this was achieved by means of "extremely little-noticeable spatial-color shades of the same, almost monochrome range."[15] *In an example suggested by Ginzburg—and indeed followed in the Narkomfin house—a room with a light-blue ceiling could have walls of cold-white, pale-gray, or pale-yellow colors, whereas a greenish ceiling could have white walls with just a slight shade of green. If the colored surface of such a room were observed for a short period of time, Ginzburg continued, the color of the walls remained practically unnoticed and the room seemed white. However, after the person had been subjected to the coloration for a longer period of time, it began "to exercise an effect—a deep and half-conscious one, which did not produce any noticeable visual irritation—on the subject's perception [*oščušče-nie*], becoming not so much as a factor of color per se, as a purely spatial sensation."*[16]

The word "half-consciously" [polusoznatel'no], explained by Ginzburg as "a non-visible . . . yet perceptible" [*nevidimaja, no oščuščemaja*] coloration that entered the mind of the subject unregistered by consciousness betrayed Ginzburg's interest in the tradition of studying the basic, precognitive strata of mind and an attempt to communicate with this strata directly. According to this tradition, which formed a part of the discourse of economizing energy, a waste of mental and physical force accompanied thinking, whereas the precognitive, conversely, allowed energy to be preserved. In Russia, the productive power of the unconscious became an object of interest of literary scholars, such as Dmitrij Ovsianiko-Kulikovskij, who in the 1910s argued that the vast majority of cognitive acts took place in the unconscious as an automatic activity, which the consciousness noticed only in its latest stages. In this ability of the unconscious to tacitly perform a cognitive work, Ovsianiko-Kulikovskiu saw in this ability of the unconscious to tacitly perform a cognitive work a great potential for the rationalization of thinking. "This means," argued the scholar, "that the whole work is gratuitous for us, and that we must notice a great economizing of intellectual energy."[17] These theories were well known to Constructivist architects via Viktor Šklovskij and other literary Formalists. By unnoticeably affecting the dwellers of the Narkomfin through the psychological stimuli of colors, Ginzburg and Scheper could hope to help them overcome a possible discomfort and save the energy that would be otherwise wasted in the process of analyzing architectural form.

It was this economizing of productive energy—rather than an aesthetic appreciation of architectural form or even a functional convenience—that comprised the ultimate goal of the architects. Indeed, their house-painting schemes had nothing to do with the habitual way of exploring color by modernist painters (including the color theory courses at both the Bauhaus and VHUTEMAS), such as studying color harmonies and the relationship of colors to each other. The architects lost the status of creative geniuses—instead, they turned into scientists who, working collaboratively (the personal contributions of Ginzburg and Scheper within the project are indeed almost impossible to distinguish), relied on scientific experiments rather than personal tastes. Scheper and Ginzburg strove to make their house-painting schemes unseen and unappreciated by the viewer, whose only response to them was a physiological feeling of refreshment and relaxation, and provided a concrete architectural solution for achieving this goal. The subject, not the building, was the real object of their architectural work. The architects redefined their creative subjectivity as radically disjointed from that of the user, who was reduced to an element of the psycho-physiological mechanism; as a result, they assumed the claims of power, which they idealized as a scientific machine of effectiveness.

Warm Scheme (above), Cold Scheme (right)

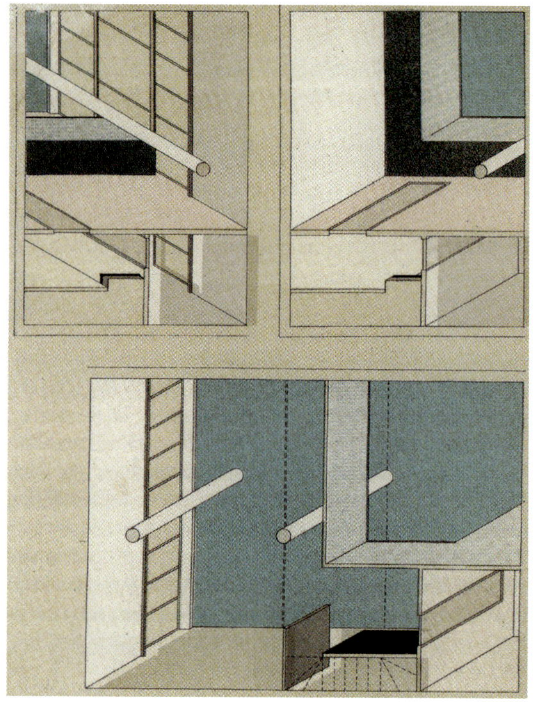

I thank the Getty Research Institute for generous support of this research.

1. K. Michael Hays, *Modernism and the Posthumanist Subject. The Architecture of Hannes Meyer and Ludwig Hilberseimer*, Cambridge, MA: MIT Press, 1992. Emerged as a response of architects to the fragmentation of the individual during the era of industrial capitalism, in particular, in Weimar Germany. Post-humanism, according to Hays, eradicated from architecture a holistic, authorial, and centralized humanist subjectivity.

2. Scheper arrived in Moscow in March 1929, invited by the Supreme Soviet of the People's Economy to become a consultant in a state trust "Maliarstrojproekt" (an agglutination referring to "the design of house-painting in buildings") under the umbrella of the People's Commissariat of Infrastructure. He returned to Germany in September 1931.

3. The date of Ginzburg's visit is given in Renate Scheper, *Vom Bauhaus gepägt: Hinnerk Scheper: Farbgestalter, Photograph, Denkmalpfleger.* Bramsche: Rasch, 2007, 58. For Ginzburg's account of the Bauhaus visit, see Moisej Ginzburg, "Cvet v arhitekture," in *Sovremennaja Arhitektura*, (1929), No. 2, 75–76.

4. Similarly, a staircase in the Bauhaus building was painted black on the horizontal and white on the vertical planes.

5. Ginzburg, "Cvet v arhitekture," 75. Scheper's axonometric view of the Narkomfin house circulation areas was published in the Maljarstroj journal *Maljarnoe Delo* [House-painting] ("Color supplement" in #1–2 list III) A similar approach was applied by Scheper at the Bauhaus building in Dessau, where the color was concentrated on the ceilings and architectural details.

6. See Mihail Baršč, "Vlijanie zritel'nyh vpečatlenij na trudovje processy," *Sovremennaja Arhitektura*, 1928, #2, 72; Mihail Baršč, Cvet i ego rabota," *Sovremennaja Arhitektura*, 1929, #2, 77.

7. Anson Rabinbach, Berkeley and Los Angeles, CA: University of California Press, 1990, 45–51, 61–64.

8. In doing so, it responded to a program, which had been developed by modernist architects at the time, of productively utilizing the time spent outside of the work place, and can be thus compared to such programs as "the park of culture and leisure" (developed in 1928) and, in particular, to Konstantin Mel'nikov's Green City (1930), a vacation town near Moscow, which he interpreted as a "sleeping sonata," a factory of physical and mental transformation of people through sleep. "Such a thing as an absolute rest does not exist," explained Constructivist architect Kuz'min in 1930 on the pages of the Ginzburg-edited *Sovremennaja Arhitektura*. "A person is constantly working (even when he is asleep)." Arhitektor Kuz'min, "Problema naučnoj organizacii byta," *Sovremennaja Arhitektura* (1930) No. 3, p. 14.

9. Ginzburg, "Cvet v arhitekture," 74.

10. Ginzburg's work at the Narkomfin house was a continuation of an experiment that he conducted at MVTU (*Moskovskoe Vysšee Tehničeskoe Učilišče*, Moscow Higher Technical College) several years earlier. The purpose of the MVTU experiment was to define the rules of using color for articulating architectural space and of psychologically compensating for its functional imperfections. The problems to correct in the given situation of MVTU were the darkness of the room, which faced north and overlooked a tiny courtyard, and its visual segregation into small elements by several small vaults on the ceiling. To enhance the luminosity of the light coming from the windows through a stark contrast, Ginzburg painted the external wall black; the same color as the ceiling, aimed to eliminate the perceived partitioning of the room. The wall opposite the windows, on the contrary, received a bright lemon-yellow coloration, which, according to Ginzburg, due to its light absorbing character, endowed even a diffused ray of light with a sunny saturation. The two remaining walls Ginzburg painted orange in order to give the cold and dark room more "warmth" and to provide a contrast to both black and yellow and thereby to accentuate the spatial properties of the room. Although the colors did, indeed, correct the light and spatial conditions, it was noticed that their brightness exercised a tiring effect upon a perceiver and destroyed the three-dimensional character of the space. Moisej Ginzburg, *Žilišče: opyt pjatiletnej raboty nad problemoj žilišča*, Moscow: Gosstrojizdat, 1934, 93-94.

11. Both were published in *Maljarnoe Delo* ("Color supplement" in #1–2 list II, and in #3–4 (1930) list XII, while the original drawings are preserved at the Bauhaus-Archiv Berlin (NachlaßScheper).

12. In a manner typical of the Bauhaus House-Painting Workshop representation style, the drawing omits the floor as the least important area of the application of color. For more on the conventions of house-painting axonometry see Erich Borchert, "Metody proektirovanija maljarnyh rabot," *Maljarnoe Delo* (1931) no. 2, 48–51.

13. Ginzburg described the apartments of types F and K within a Strojkom workshop (Stroitel'nyj Komitet) of the RSFSR Sovnarkom (the government of the Russian Soviet Socialist Federative Republic) alongside El Lissitzky, Mihail Baršč, Vladimir Vel'man, I. Verezubov, Vladimir Vladimirov, I. Gurevič, N. Krasil'nikov, S. Orlovskij, and Aleksandr Pasternak. See Stroitel'naja komissija ĖKOSO RSFSR, *Tipove Proekty i Konstrukcii Žilišnogo Stroitel'stva, Rekomenduemye na 1930 g.* Moskva: Gos. Tehničeskoeizd-vo, 1930.

14. Ginzburg, *Žilišče*, 94.

15. Ginzburg, *Žilišče*, 94.

16. Ginzburg, *Žilišče*, 94–95.

17. Dmitrij Ovsianiko-Kulikovskij, Voprosy teoriii psihologii tvorčesvta. Kharkov, 1914; Dmitrij Ovsianiko-Kulikovskij, "Vvedenie v nenapisannuju knigu po psihologii umstvennogo tvorčestva (naučno-filosofskogo I hudožestvennogo)." Published in N. V. Os'makov, *Psihologičeskoe napravlenie v russkom literaturovedenii.* (Moskva: Prosveščenie), 1981, 111.

Moisej Ginzburg in the 1930s

Ginzburg:
Architect, Architectural Theoretician, Methodologist, Experimenter, Design Practice Organizer

Yury Volchok

Pages from His Biography

M. Ja. Ginzburg's upbringing and schooling, which prepared him for eventually becoming an organizer and leader of Constructivism, one of the leading trends in architecture of the avant-garde era, were largely defined by the fact that he graduated from a business school in Minsk, where the fundamental disciplines were mathematics, drafting, and drawing. These were actively supplemented by his home education: he took painting lessons and read books on history and art. His enthusiasm for literature studies was encouraged. He participated in the publication of a handwritten magazine distributed at his school. His father, a practicing Minsk architect and developer, brought him in to work in his studio and, after his son's graduation in 1911, sought an opportunity to send him to study architecture abroad. Moisej began his search for an attractive architectural school in France. Over the course of several months, he attended classes at the École des Beaux-Arts in Paris and then at the École d' Architecture in Toulouse. However, for his formal education he selected the Academia di Belle Arti in Milan. For several years he studied in a group under the well-known architect Professor Gaetano Moretti, where he received thoroughgoing architectural and artistic training, which he combined with mastering the skills of collaborating in a creative collective, following the principle of the medieval professional-guild communes. He gained an additional daily living experience in a historic city. The receipt of his architect's diploma capped off Moisej Ginzburg's multifaceted humanist education.

After returning to Russia in 1914, he enrolled at the Riga Polytechnic Institute, which had been evacuated to Moscow due to the events of World War I. He graduated in 1917 as a civil engineer. In his first independent work, a private home in Evpatoria (in collaboration with N. A. Kopeliovič), Ginzburg gave modernism its due. It should be noted here that, at the time, modernism was not very popular at Milan's Academia. However, the young architect asserted his will in this instance, trusting his own intuition. Years of study had cultivated in him a harmonious, mutually complementary combination of close and in-depth interest in scientific, technical, and methodologically ordered knowledge as well as an understanding of the value of a cultivated artistic intuition. After this, he worked in Crimea for four years, where he was able to exercise all his acquired professional capabilities. He combined his architectural practice with a study of Crimea's vernacular architecture. This research resulted in his first scholarly work, "Tatar Art in Crimea," in addition to designing Crimea's pavilion on the All-Russia Agriculture and Cottage Industry Exhibit of 1923 at Gorky Park in central Moscow, but he also designed the offices for the protection of monuments of architecture and art that he helped organize in Crimea.

The Historical and Cultural Value of the Experimental Apartment House on Novinskij Boulevard in Moscow

In 1921, Ginzburg returned to Moscow for good, fully prepared to participate in professional life and consciously oriented toward shaping the new architecture. During these years, he devoted special attention to his scholarly work and teaching. By 1923, as a professor at VHUTEMAS (Higher Artistic and Technical Studios), he was teaching courses on the history of architecture and the theory of architectural composition. He was simultaneously lecturing and directing design in the architectural schools at MVTU (Moscow Higher Technical Institute) and MIGI (Moscow Institute of Civil Engineering). Ginzburg was confirmed as an acting member of the State Academy of

Artistic Sciences (GAHN), where he gave many scholarly reports, all of them dealing with a common issue: comprehending the content and characteristics of contemporary architecture. These were used as a reference to a Dictionary of Artistic Terms, compiled at the Academy from 1923 to 1929. Unprecedented in this kind of work was that two authors would give their own definition of the concept of "architecture"—A. G. Gabričevskij (classical) and M. Ja. Ginzburg (contemporary)—resulting in two separate articles for the Dictionary.

Under the GAHN program, Ginzburg led a scholarly expedition to Buhara (Uzbekistan), where he made full use of his Crimean experience in surveying two monuments, while organizing a Museum of Historical Heritage and Art. In 1925, he traveled to Turkey for the Academy to study Byzantine and Islamic monuments. In a certain sense, he repeated Le Corbusier's famous journey to the East in 1911. This trip of Ginzburg's was an important stage in eventually forging a professional friendship between the two men that lasted many years. I will cite one example. A letter from Le Corbusier to Ginzburg was published in the third issue of *SA* (*Contemporary Architecture*) for 1928. The topic was of deep concern to both him and his Moscow colleagues: the relationship between city and countryside, the peasant's fate in the new socioeconomic conditions, and architecture's role in shaping modern urbanism.

The letter's author, aware of its official nature, realized full well that he was not writing a private letter, so he chose his words with great care. Moreover, he did not forget to cite Lenin's authority and created—perhaps for the first and last time in his life—what we would now call a perfectly politically correct text.

In his response, Ginzburg joined in with the tone Le Corbusier had set—gratefully, as I understand it. He thanked his Western colleague for citing Lenin and he himself cited Karl Marx. Through their joint efforts, the authors of the correspondence constructed a protective "façade" against any exterior interference, including censorship. This problem was of decisive importance for the era: making sense of the controversy over "urbanism" and "disurbanism." By giving their text an armor as "official façade," they gained sufficient freedom to formulate organizational methods to the internal profession.

Why was it so important for the authors to bring the topic of their correspondence to the journal's readers? They realized that Le Corbusier's opinion would not go unremarked. It is important to note that this correspondence took place in the late 1920s, and not after 1932, a time of radical shift in the "creative trend" in Soviet architecture. The new understanding of the term "architecture" was rapidly taking hold. The Constructivists, who were basically of like mind, reacted very differently to Le Corbusier's urbanist views. In Socgorod (Socialist City), published in 1930, N. A. Miljutin did everything he could to support and share Le Corbusier's interpretation of urbanism. But A. K. Burov, who stopped the same year in Paris on his way to America—mainly to meet with Le Corbusier—noted with unfeigned amazement that, in his opinion, the Master who had devoted himself intensely to urbanism seemed not to understand much about its essence, especially in social terms.

Quite logically, these differences in shared value affected the approach to the issue of housing, especially regarding the content of the experiments to be carried out. In 1922, Ginzburg published *Rhythm in Architecture*, which in the meantime became known all over the world, as did his *Style and Epoch*, published two years later. In *Rhythm in Architecture*, the author's intention was to describe in geometric parameters the artistic-aesthetic understanding of movement in space, thus allowing us to view this book as an introduction to his theory of contemporary architectural shape-formation, analogous to the contemporaneous *Cinematics of Mechanics* by N. I. Mercalov, an introduction to his theory of machines and mechanisms. However, Ginzburg also wrote that machines and engineering equipment could not serve as a methodological equivalent to a theory of architectural invention, that is,"the spatial resolution that constitutes the true mark of architecture." *Rhythm in Architecture* serves as a "plastic hinge," the coefficient of the transition between the two systems (scientific-technical and artistic-aesthetic) for describing spatial movement theoretically.

Style and Epoch is about contemporary architecture, which the author understood in the context of his era as the Formation Principle of the new Great Style. In 1924, when Ginzburg's book was published, Erwin Panofsky wrote his classic work, *IDEA: Toward a History of Concepts in Theories of Art from Antiquity to Classicism.* Surprisingly, these works had much in common. The main "hero" of both works was the concept of "the beautiful," around which the authors built their theoretical concepts and scholarly ideas. For Ginzburg, as well as for Panofsky, the timeframe of the problem under discussion was important, and as later became obvious, this kind of approach was characteristic of his entire scholarly career.

Ginzburg's efforts focused the reader's attention both on the problematic of duration and on the need to stratify the issues historically—hence, *Style and Epoch*. Hence, as well, the epigraph from Heinrich Wölfflin's *The Renaissance and the Baroque*. The epigraph opens with the word "movement." This was important for Ginzburg. And so is it for us. The conceptual Movement (IDEA), conceived in the 1920s, is still valid today.

If Panofsky's book shapes our knowledge of the movement of "the beautiful" in the historical era, then Ginzburg's book projects it into the future. It is very important to view these works in the continuity of their shared architectonic knowledge. In Ginzburg's work, history is not oriented toward the past, as it usually is, but turned around to face the future. Therefore he precedes the book with a double epigraph. One (Wölfflin's), mentioned above, focuses on the fact that "the old is reborn, drawing us along, and the new style becomes fact." The second epigraph is resolved graphically: a photograph of

Caproni's triplane, reminding the reader about the civilizational innovations of his time. In Ginzburg's understanding, the dialog between the demands of artistic culture and the opportunities afforded by civilization were the foundation of Constructivist thinking and activity. Ginzburg the investigator implemented that dialog in full in his scholarly work, having provided a foundation for the shift "from the atavistic concept of 'construction' to the modern concept of 'montage.'" Moreover, it would take decades to graft the new to culture, and only after that would Wölfflin's formula gradually begin to play out: "the new style becomes fact." According to this logic, however, the epoch of a style, the era of its existence in the most diverse interpretations, truly goes beyond any defined chronological framework. Thus, when we speak about "an epoch's style," we are asserting a characterization that individualizes a given era and makes it special, distinguishable from others. When we talk about a "style's epoch," that is, about extension in time, then rationally, unemotionally (Ginzburg spoke about this as he characterized the difference between the Constructivists' own attitudes toward his method and style), we must talk literally about a mathematical concept—"domain of function."

Ginzburg's approach to shaping the foundations of his concept combining the "style and method" in contemporary architecture was methodologically irreproachable. Confirmation of this thesis can be found in the book itself. The last section of Ginzburg's *Style and Epoch* is about "Illustrations: The New Style's Reflection in Works by Contemporary Russian Architects."

In my opinion, this section has a specific significance for understanding the role of the creative individual in shaping *any new style*. Ginzburg opens his survey of his colleagues' works with examples from the practice of I. V. Žoltovskij. Here is how he explains this choice.

In deciding about the material, the author tried to be as objective as possible and to present various groups of architects in whose works a sense of the new form *had a greater or lesser impact and who, consequently, might have some* inherent significance *in the formation of the new style.* (Emphasis added)

In *Style and Epoch*, he cites five of I. V. Žoltovskij's works. It is worth noting that in this section of the book, the Vesnin brothers are also mentioned five times, although only for two works, Aleksandr Vesnin being represented by his extremely popular theatrical work: his set designs for *The Man Who Was Thursday* at the Moscow Chamber Theater. I think that the fequency with which he referred to Aleksandr Vesnin was conceptually important for Ginzburg. It took several years before the classics of Moscow Constructivism appeared: the author's building on Novinskij Boulevard as well as the Vesnins' department store on Krasnaja Presna, the House of Political Prisoners, the Palace of Culture of the Proletarian District, and others. Thus, Žoltovskij's contemporaries, the readers of *Style and Epoch*, were quite conscious that in his early years Žoltovskij presented, if not embodied, the *emergence of the new style*.

Wise Ginzburg called his book *Style and Epoch*, encoding in the meaningful "and" the diversity of relations between style and method. To this day there is, strictly speaking, no unanimous understanding as to what Constructivism is—a style or a method? Only in our time has it become more obvious that this dilemma should be approached differently. When does Constructivism manifest itself as a style and when as a method? Most people do not perceive the emergence of something new as the manifestation of a new style. In his design practice following the newly constructed methodology, Ginzburg preferred working in the author's collective he had created, maximizing the potential of the devices through dialog among co-authors.

Along with his scholarly work and teaching, Ginzburg designed a great deal and entered virtually every major competition, beginning with the 1922 competition for the Palace of Labor in Moscow, and continuing with the Palace of Labor competition in Ekaterinoslavl', in 1926 (with B. Koršunov); the Palace of Labor in Rostov-on-Don, in 1926; the House of Soviets in Mahačkala, in 1926; the University in Minsk, in 1926; the Polytechnic Institute in Ivanovo-Voznesensk, in 1927; the Government House in Alma-Ata, 1927 (with I. Milinis); the Great Synthetic Theater in Sverdlovsk in 1931; the Palace of Soviets in Moscow, in 1932 (with G. Hassenpflug and S. Lisagor); and Narkomtjažprom (People's Commissariat of Heavy Industry) House in the center of Moscow, in 1934 (with S. Lisagor)—i.e., throughout the

Interior views of the club, historic and contemporary

founding and development of Constructivism, a newborn creative method in architecture, one of whose leaders he became, alongside with A. Vesnin. In 1925, Ginzburg organized the Association of Contemporary Architects (OSA), which included the principal participants in the architecture group of INHUK (Institute of Artistic Culture), LEF (Left Front of Art), and also followers of Constructivism's leaders from MVTU and MIGI.

In 1926, OSA began publishing a journal, *Contemporary Architecture* (*SA*), and its senior editors were Ginzburg and Vesnin. Theorizing this trend fell mainly to Ginzburg, who wrote most of the editorials and theoretical articles for *SA*. During this period, his attention was focused on developing a functional method for architecture and making sense of social problems, primarily in connection with residential construction.

In 1926, he published "A New Method of Architectural Thinking" in *SA*. It was here that the architect expounded on the theoretical foundations for a future-oriented professionalism . . . the method of functional creativity—instead of the old fragmentation into separate, independent and, usually, mutually hostile goals—leads to a unified and organic creative process where one goal flows from another with all the logic of natural development. There can be no element, no part of an architect's intent if that intent would be an isolated element. Everything finds explanation and functional justification in its purposefulness. The whole unites everything, balances everything, and creates models of supreme expressiveness, precision, and clarity where nothing can be changed.

This text by Ginzburg in particular allowed the Italian architect and scholar Guido Canella to entitle the introductory essay to the digest he compiled (with Maurizio Meriggi) from issues of *SA* "Moisej Ginzburg and Euroconstructivism." He argued that Muscovite Constructivism laid the foundation for the International style just as much as Le Corbusier's Functionalism did.

In this same year, Ginzburg designed and built with V. N. Vladimirov a five-story apartment house (with a dormitory on the top floor) for employees of Gosstrah (State Insurance Administration) on Malaja Bronnaja Street in Moscow implementing his "new method"; a year later, in 1927, in co-authorship with I. F. Milinis and engineer S. L. Prokhorov, he began work on a design for an experimental apartment house for the employees of the Narkomfin (People's Commissariat of Finance) on Novinskij Boulevard in Moscow that became a programmatic piece of Constructivism and, more broadly, of the architecture of the Moscow avant-garde. In time, it became an epoch-making monument of the historical-cultural heritage. The unique destiny of the building, which remains complicated to this day, was preprogrammed much earlier. The house was not included in the 1935 General Plan (Genplan) strategy for Moscow's reconstruction. By this time, evidently, the experiment linked to its appearance was viewed as moot. According to Genplan's compilers, the "building of the transitional type" had exhausted its purpose and in accordance with the new concept of residential construction had to yield to another type of—block-based—construction. Fortunately, these plans were not implemented and we still have not lost this monument of twentieth-century architecture.

Ginzburg presented a design for a communal building at the first exhibition of contemporary architecture in Moscow (1927). Later, he had the opportunity to carry out experiments in mass residential construction in state institutions. In 1928, a standardization section was organized under Strojkom RSFSR (Construction Committee of the Russian Soviet Federated Socialist Republic), where Ginzburg shaped the concept of the transition from the building-commune to the communal building, in which apartment-based housing was combined with developed public services. In 1929, a socialist settlement section based on the group that came over from Strojkom was created under Gosplan SSSR (State Planning Committee of the USSR). Here, new approaches to designing housing were shaped in conjunction with city planning issues, that is, ideas such as disurbanism and the linear settlement system that were actively developed at the start of the 1930s.

In 1931, Ginzburg's entire experimental design studio moved over to Giprogor (State Institute for Urban Design). The only person not invited was the economist M. Ohitovič, one of the leading co-authors of the disurbanism concept worked out under Ginzburg's direction. The department where the earlier work was started was named the Section for Assembly Construction and Planning. On the one hand, this name emphasized the programmatic continuity between the urban-planning and spatial planning problems; on the other, it was here that the long and thorny path toward mass prefabricated building construction began. By 1928, N. A. Ladovskij headed up ARU (Association of Architect-Urbanists), which had split from ASNOVA (Association of New Architects), and he was the author of the dynamic city scheme as well as prefabricated housing cell-cubicles. Ladovskij echoes Giprogor's plan for the building's "montage" under the direction of Ginzburg.

Let us turn now to the 'conflict' between the concepts of the urbanists and disurbanists. "Traditionally," the stratification of participants in the Association of Contemporary Architects (OSA) into adherents of the system of socialist settlement and the disurbanists has been perceived in terms of mutual opposition. What is more important is to understand the two conceptually different approaches to human settlement as they were formulated in the first stages of OSA. It was the association's leaders, Vesnin and Ginzburg, who agreed to this experiment, taking upon themselves very strictly regulated roles. The former became the leader of the urbanist trend; the latter represented the interests of disurbanism. The Constructivist method came fully into play in their dialog.

Viewed from the present day, however, the concept of the socialist city (*socgorod*) and disurbanism can be properly perceived only if they "trade places." Strictly speaking, Sabsovič's ideas limited the urban development to a small number of inhabitants. In the proposed logic, his ideas implied that this was a matter not so much of cities as of worker settlements (villages) attached to major production.

Disurbanists were closer to the ideas of genuine urbanization. At the same time, though, no confrontation between disurbanists and their opponents can be read in theoretical "terms." If any conflict did arise, then it was only in the discussion of designs and, above all, in their different perception of relevance to the era. The main group of OSA members was concerned with implementing city-formation in the present. The disurbanists were working for the future. This allowed for the necessity of a transitional period before genuinely urbanist ideas would become truly relevant. There was no conflict between urbanists and disurbanists, nor could there have been, since they were working for different times, complementing each other perfectly. Their time frames meshed methodically and easily. It is very important to preserve the succession of precisely this kind of mutually complementary understanding of the relationship between the urbanists and disurbanists in the shaping of a contemporary interpretation of urban culture's diversity, including on the situational level of the experimental apartment house on Novinskij.

Ginzburg played a significant role as well in shaping the concept of the socialist city and the linear city, and he was close friends with one of the leading authors of their development, Miljutin. During the years when the House was being designed and constructed, Miljutin was the country's finance minister, i.e., director of the ministry for whose employees the Dom was being created. A "penthouse" was designed for the minister that fit organically into the Dom's volumetric-spatial structure. Later, after being relieved of his ministerial duties and publishing *Socgorod*, Miljutin graduated from the Architectural Institute (1939). He wrote his thesis under Ginzburg's supervision.

In 2003, Jean-Louis Cohen translated Miljutin's Socgorod into French, and in 2008, D. Khmelnitsky published this work in Berlin in two volumes, in German and Russian. *Socgorod* is one of the few books (if not the only one) published in the 1920s and 1930s that has been published in the twenty-first century in virtual facsimile, preserving the format, design, and typeface. Behind this "gesture," one sees sincere respect and a desire to understand and preserve the creative efforts of the Moscow architectural avant-garde of the 1920s and to present them to the contemporary reader in their original form.

In 1934, Ginzburg published *Žilišče*. In it he generalizes his theoretical and practical experience designing and constructing housing and residential districts. Special attention is paid to buildings of the transitional type and to experiments in mass residential construction.

In 1943–1944, at the USSR Academy of Architecture, Ginzburg revived this work and created a standardization bureau to elaborate principles for postwar mass residential construction.

A significant journey of "inquiry and experiment" characterizes all of Ginzburg's design art. At the same time, new types of buildings for different purposes were the subject of constant scholarly interest. This manifested itself most fully in health spas, beginning with the design for the Institute for Invalids in Moscow (1931). Next was the resort district on the southern shore of Crimea (1932–1937), the Sergej Ordžonikidze Sanatorium in Kislovodsk (1935-1938), and others. Ginzburg treated each of them as a multifunctional site, created as a self-sufficient "city within a city" offering a high level of comfort. He developed, perfected, and deepened his functional design method over the course of many years. In the late 1930s and early 1940s, he returned to this set of issues in several works that remain to this day in manuscript form, based, as before, on the methodological concept of "function"as understood in the early works of Ernst Cassirer (in particular, *Cognition and Reality*, written in 1910 and published in Russian translation in 1912).

Ginzburg's focus on the problems of design methods in architecture, and the methodological maturity of his investigative and inherently systemic approach to "montage," drew Ginzburg's professional thinking and activities together with the "life and fate" of S. M. Eisenstein in cinematography. Their complementary legacies convey in the fullest the sense of contemporaneity in the time allotted them.

Conscious of this, S. O. Han-Magomedov devoted his first article on the masters of the avant-garde's architecture to the legacy of Ginzburg (1962). Ten years later he published a monograph on the master (1972), the first in Han-Magomedov's multi-year effort to publish monographs about the leaders and pioneers of our country's architectural avant-garde.

The Narkomfin's Building Experiment:
A Dialogue Between Culture and Civilization
Yury Volchok

The experimental apartment house on Novinskij Boulevard by Ginzburg and Ignatij Milinis (1899-1974) and engineer Sergej Lvovič Prohorov remains the principal topic of a great many debates and discussions to this day. Moreover, the house's "life and fate," as a rule, are perceived broadly, especially as they relate to the effort to understand the principal concepts of the "new thinking in architecture" (Ginzburg) that arose in the 1920s.

It was at this time in the early 1930s that the terms "experimental" and "montage" first appeared, as Ginzburg replaced the obsolete concept of "construction" with the modern understanding of "montage."

Today it is indeed important to understand exactly what were the dominant humanist notions of the avant-garde. What did Ginzburg mean by the notions "new," "experiment," "montage culture," "function and form," "time-place-space," "radically altered socio-economic conditions," "life-building," and so forth? An understanding of such architectural values is facilitated by the passage of time, which allows us to delve significantly deeper into the genuine values of this architectural legacy and, as a consequence, to advance our own general historical knowledge.[1]

In our day, any discussion about the Narkomfin usually opens with the statement that it is in terrible operational condition. This is true, unfortunately. Then it is usually pointed out that the House contains multi-level apartments that are small in area (cells F1–F5). This, too, is fair. Then it is pointed out that the House does not provide for kitchens and in general was designed for a way of life for "people from the future" that is difficult to understand and far removed from reality. Here, however, I do not think one should rush to conclusions. The Narkomfin [People's Commissariat of Finance] House was contemplated and executed as an experimental building.[2] What were they supposed to build and how, bearing in mind the era's limited means? The authors had to figure out whether a way of life could be organized in such a way as to answer the new social conditions, that is, to balance in a single spatial whole both private and public interests.

Can we today judge the results of this experiment? Only hypothetically, by examining it in the modern context of our urban life in the capital's megalopolis, but not in practice, because the experimental content in search of a contemporary way of life in the Narkomfin Dom has long been lost. Today one can hardly live in that Dom at all. But one can hardly live in any building, let alone in an experimental one, if it has not been properly maintained for nearly eighty years. This public building has not functioned for a long time, and everything that corresponds to the full-fledged quality of life that we have in our apartments (kitchen, bathroom, elevator, heating) is regularly turned off. No one ends up living in the House out of a proud desire to dwell on a daily basis in the aura of its unique architecture; rather, all too often one lives there out of desperation and the inability to change one's "habitat."

The Novinskij Boulevard Dom experiment presupposed a number of fairly obvious (to the professional architect even in those years) assumptions; the authors sought ways to organize the minimum space necessary for daily life. However, the House belonged to the People's Commissariat of Finance, so the authors were focused on the compact family of Commissariat employees. If the family make-up changed, the way of life could be adjusted, and the housing could be replaced. To this day, we have a hard time understanding such an assumption since the housing market is still not fully formed.

How can we penetrate to the essence of the experiment in daily life in the House if the public building, the laundry, and the garden in front are not functioning? We will pass over the garden in silence, although it is worth recalling that as schoolchildren we played soccer there. Several of my classmates lived in this building. They lived in individual apartments, by the way, and they knew what a wood- and coal-fired heating stove was only by having visited those who lived in "communals" (*kommunalki*). During those years, because kitchens were small, the cultured residents of the Dom suffered more than they have in more recent times. The "kitchen mode" that combines the interests of private and public life was quite widespread in our country in the middle of the last century. Today, in our daily life, we are so used to being able to visit a café and spend time in public that the Dom's public building could well get a second wind and help us return even in our day to a full-fledged reading of the 1920s experiment's essence.

Acquisition of full knowledge about the creative intention and urban-planning placement for the housing complex and the House's volumetric, spatial, and constructive resolution is not only a contribution to historical scholarship but also a documented foundation both for shaping the monument as an object of preservation and for creating a well-argued plan for its restoration.

Let us turn to the archival documents: The siting of the House Commune for Employees of the NKF RSFSR and Rosgosstrah on the Tract Allocated for Its Construction at 113–115 Novinskij Boulevard.[3]

A letter to the Minister N. A. Miljutin dated April 2, 1929, stating that, by order of the Deputy Chairman of the Moscow Soviet, the previously approved tract had been put under construction for a House-Commune.

A letter dated May 3 to the Moscow Construction Oversight Administration and signed by Ginzburg, not as [the project's] author but as a member of the RSFSR Construction Commission. The letter contains several of the plan's definitions and descriptions. When first presented, the plan was called "Plan for an experimental communal apartment house based on the research done by the RSFSR Building Commission for residential standardization." The document states further that the Dom consists of separate buildings:

a) The housing proper
b) The communal center (dining room, physical culture room, reading room, and others)
c) The nursery and kindergarten spaces
d) The service building (laundry, drying room, and so on).

Then the author draws the Oversight Administration's attention to those aspects of the project's aspects that favor an economy of means. Ginzburg justifies the House's corridor (gallery) structure by the need to join the residential and public buildings "using horizontal connections." The lower level comprises two-story apartments, "in the lower part of which a hallway has been cut through, while on the upper row"—as the letter says—"there are small room-and-a-half apartments, where one corridor suffices for two stories, which allows for just two stair enclosures per fifty apartments."

Ginzburg goes on to explain the method that became constructivism's classic calling card, whereby the residential building on Novinskij Boulevard was raised 2.5 meters above the ground, "on individual piers," over the tract's unevenness and the variations in elevation. "Usually in such instances," he writes in the letter, "an extensive plinth has to be made. The decision taken is significantly more economical and moreover preserves the park area untouched."[4]

Preserved in the archive are several general plans for the tract that reflect the process of drafting and constructing Narkomfin's apartment house. One of the first is a general plan dated June 1929 for a fragment of the apartment house on the boundaries of the land allotment.

E. G. Nikulina, director of M. V. Posohin Studio No. 20 for Historical-Urban Planning Research of Mosproekt-1, has published research materials from a stage-by-stage reconstruction of the general plan for the tract used for the House's construction. "Set aside for the complex's placement was the territory of two city plots with extensive gardens and a structure in front facing on Novinskij Boulevard," she writes in one of her articles. She goes on: "To some extent, one can say that the new complex was the successor to the Moscow city plot, with its compositionally and functionally intact world, where the garden was an inalienable part of life. The author placed most of the apartment building on the territory of the garden plots."[5] The general plan makes it clear that the laundry (also raised above ground on piers) was located on the structure's building line along Novinskij Boulevard, since this is where the "central entrance" to the territory of the House-Commune is. The diagonal path through the garden led to the public building, but going straight led to the residential building and, continuing, to an observation platform appropriate here due to the significant difference in elevation between the construction site and the ponds nearby, which later became the Metrostroj Stadium. However, by mid-1929, the project's clients and authors were beginning to have trouble finding the property lines on the site and thus getting approval to start the work. As archival documents show, the client took the decision to begin construction without having obtained the necessary approval. There is a letter to the Hamovničeskij Administrative Commission dated August 1, 1929, demanding that engineer Prohorov be fined for going ahead with the construction work "without permission." Later, the superintendent Prohorov was sued on criminal charges several times. However, the client and the author hurried to complete construction as

quickly as possible inside the boundaries of the originally allocated tract, so that by the time the authorization documents were ready, the House-Commune was virtually complete (except for the kindergarten, which, therefore, was never built). Ginzburg tried to preserve the site's original territory, proposed viewing the already erected volumes as the first line of construction and to develop a new volumetric-compositional solution by adding a second residential building, a dormitory, and a garage. This proposal was not approved, and another traditional apartment building was built by a different architect with no connection whatsoever with the Narkomfin's concept.

A Constructive Resolution for the Experimental House-Commune

The structural engineer Prokhorov, a prominent specialist and organizer of building production, took on the construction superintendent duties for erecting the complex on Novinskij Boulevard because this gave him an opportunity to apply the hollow blocks he had invented on an actual building.[6] In essence, the joint work of architect Ginzburg and engineer Prohorov in designing and erecting the House constituted a practical application and interpretation of Ginzburg's postulate: "It is time to replace the atavistic concept of 'construction' with the modern one of 'montage.'"

The stratification of the building production and of the factory processes were ultimately less a matter of technology than a systemic-organizational problem. The structuring of space was a dialog not so much between two technological principles as between cultural patterns and civilizational possibilities as viewed since the mid-1920s. This dialog did not appear explicitly in the constructive process of the Novinskij Boulevard House, but this did not diminish its significance, i.e., the cultivation of functions: the carcass, the concrete column, and the use of the hollow bricks of Prohorov's invention as ducts for the building's mechanicals. The voids of the hollow bricks were quite multifunctional in purpose: first, they served as ducts for air vents; second, it was also proposed that the metal gas pipes be installed in the ducts during the buildings' montage. However, the fire department would not allow that. They feared damage to the metal as well as gas leaks. The possibility was raised of filling the voids between the metal pipes and the opening in the box with slurry. This method was successfully implemented to a certain extent. Some of the voids were filled with solid concrete, which actually dramatically increased the building's bearing capacity and stability. A future restoration plan of the House will have to take this into account.

Heated Street-Galleries in the House on Novinskij Boulevard

Ginzburg defended the corridor-galleries to the oversight organizations mainly on economic grounds. No less relevant for him, however, was the real-life creation of the heated street-galleries, which significantly improved the quality of daily life in the House, especially if one recalls that they were not able to build the kindergarten. In winter, the galleries became heated streets, a preferred place for children to spend time. This is an incidental aspect of the problem, though. No less significant is yet another point that must be dealt with here. In the 1920s and 1930s radiators were not simply heating devices but a sign of the time, a measure of the level of civilization and the quality of urban life in Moscow. In support of this I would cite the work of Ludwig Wittgenstein, founder of modern analytic philosophy.
In our country, the attention paid to his "logical-philosophical treatise" (1914–1916), which set forth the foundations of analytic philosophy, was quite multifaceted.[7] I would like to draw attention to the fact that in 1928, the year work began on

the House project when he was already an authoritative and popular philosopher, he designed and ordered from a factory a corner radiator for his sister's new house. (His initial education was that of an engineer.) One very important detail is that the author of the heating radiator was not satisfied with the quality of the radiator manufactured at the factory in Austria, so he ordered another version of the item from a factory in Germany.

Unfortunately, many of the radiators in the House on Novinskij have been irreparably lost, including those of Miljutin's apartment and Ginzburg's studio and those of the heated street-galleries the topic of a famous Rodčenko photograph. Even those that have been preserved could hardly be used as technological devices in contemporary heating systems. Still, they should be preserved as tokens of their bygone era.

In shaping this outstanding architectural monument as an "object of preservation" and working on the plan for its restoration, one must bear in mind not only the outwardly obvious realities of the House's construction and structure, but also its cultural foundations of the dialog between culture's demands and civilization's possibilities. This dialog was realized in the most multifaceted and capacious way through the edification of the Narkomfin's experimental apartment house on Novinskij Boulevard in Moscow.

Translated from the Russian by Marian Schwartz

Use of "hollow bricks"

1. S. O. Han-Magomedov. "27 prioritetov sovetskogo arhitekturnogo avangarda" [27 priorities of the Soviet architectural avant-garde], in *Russkij avangard 1910–1920-h godov v evropeiskom kontekste,* Moscow: Nauka, 2000, pp. 216–220.

2. V. Sedov, *Dom Narkomfina: essej o značenii odnoi postrojki* [The Narkomfin House: Essay on the significance of one structure] (Moscow, 2008).

3. CANTD (Central'nyj arhiv naučno-tehničeskoj dokumentacii) g. Moskvy [CANTD (Central Archive of Scientific-Technical Documentation) of the City of Moscow], fond 2, op. 1, t. 11, delo 10024.

4. Ibid., delo 10024, list 6.

5. E. G. Nikulina, "Dom Narkomfina na Novinskom (1928 g. Arhitektory M. Ginzburg, I. Milinis). Realizovannoe i nerealizovannoe" [The Narkomfin House on Novinskij (1928. Architects M. Ginzburg and I. Milinis). What was and was not built], in *Gorodskaja tkan': arhitektura i vremja. Stat'i arhitektora Eleny Nikulinoj*, compiled by I. V. Krymova Moscow, 2011, pp. 150–156.

6. Cf. I. A. Kazus', *Sovetskakaja arhitektura 1920-h godov: organizaciia proektirovanija* [Soviet architecture of the 1920s: planning organization] Moscow, 2009, pp. 101–103, 190, 410–417.

7. Iu. P. Volchok, "Perspektivy sohranenija v XXI veke istoriko-kul'turnogo nasledija sovetskogo vremeni" [Prospects for the preservation of the Soviet era's historical-cultural legacy in the twenty-first century], in *Arhitektura izmenijauščeisia Rossii: Sostoianie i perspektivy*, edited by I. A. Bondarenko, Moscow: KomKniga, 2011, pp. 288–322.

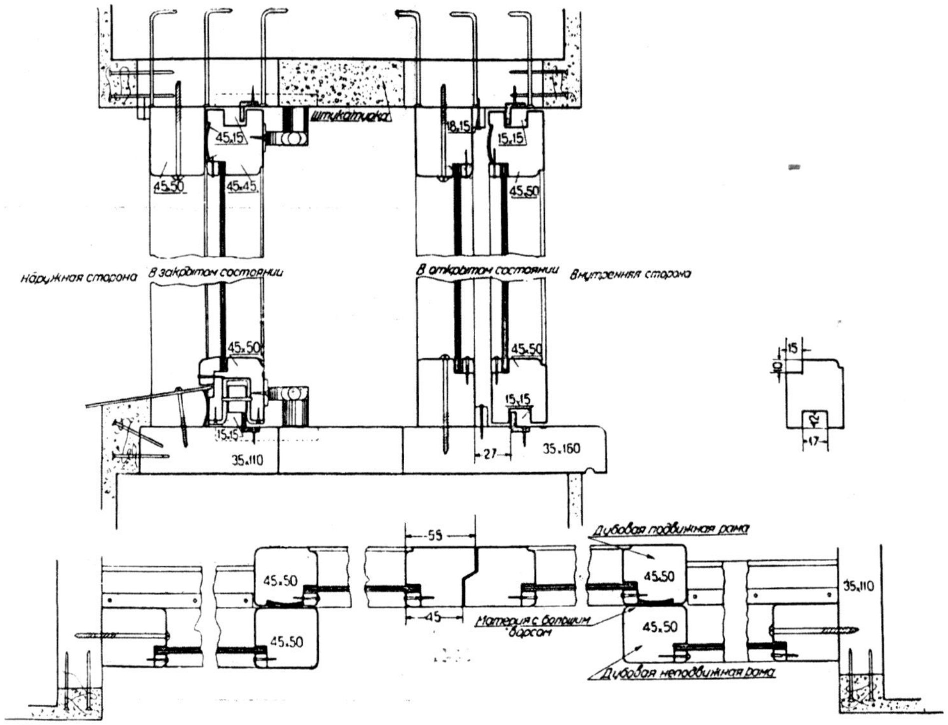

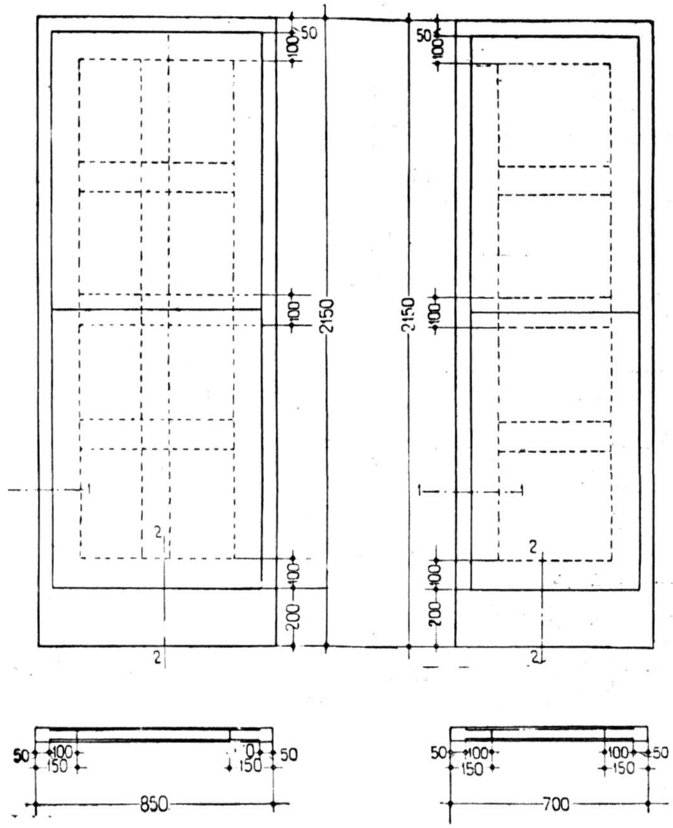

Window detail as published in *Žilišče*

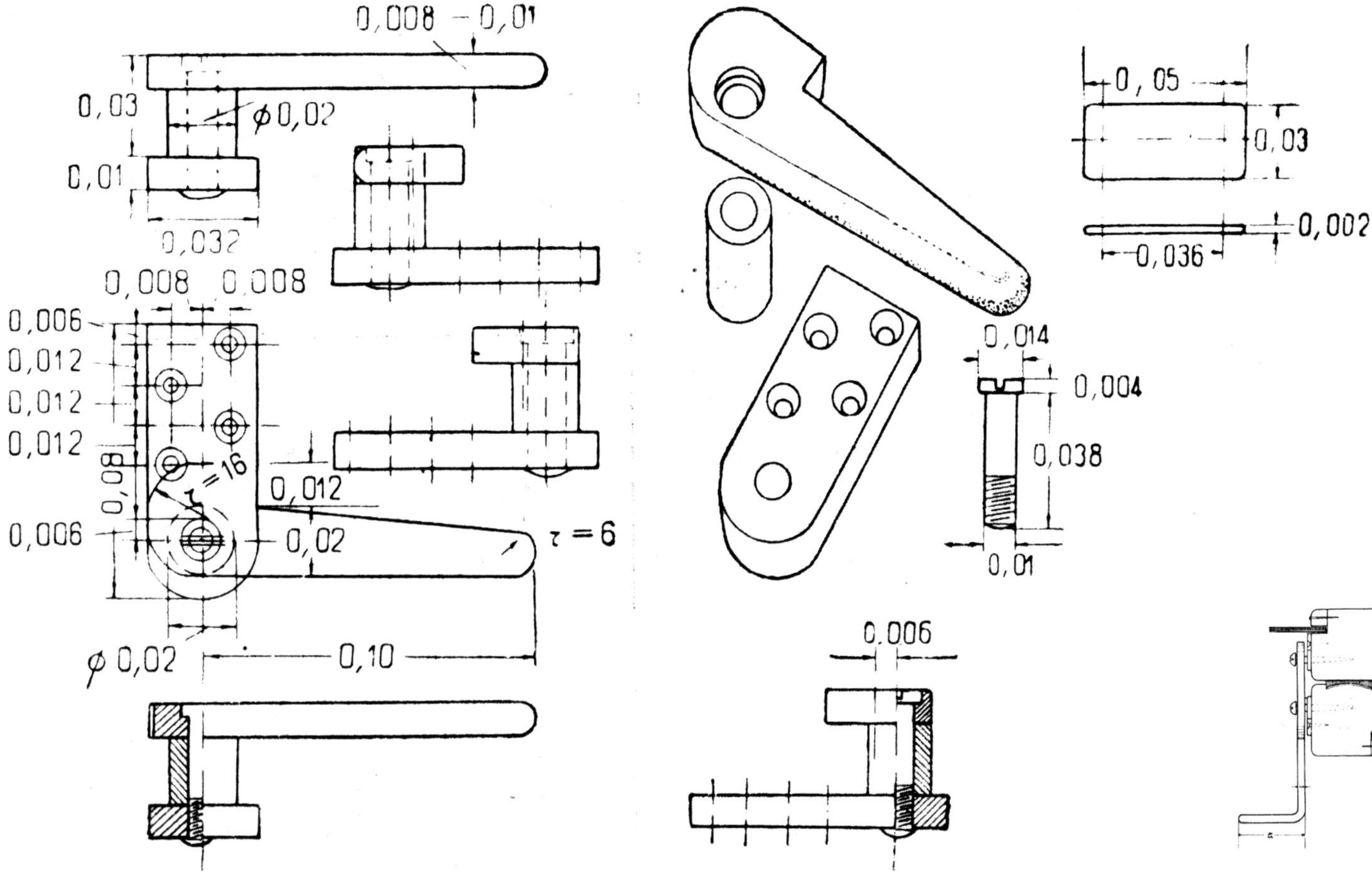

Window detail as published in *Žilišče*

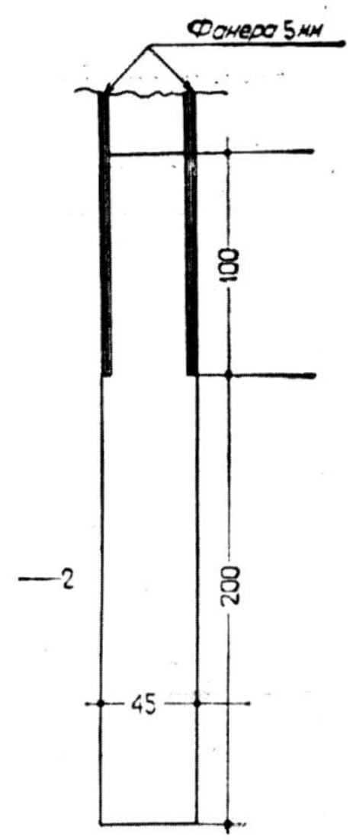

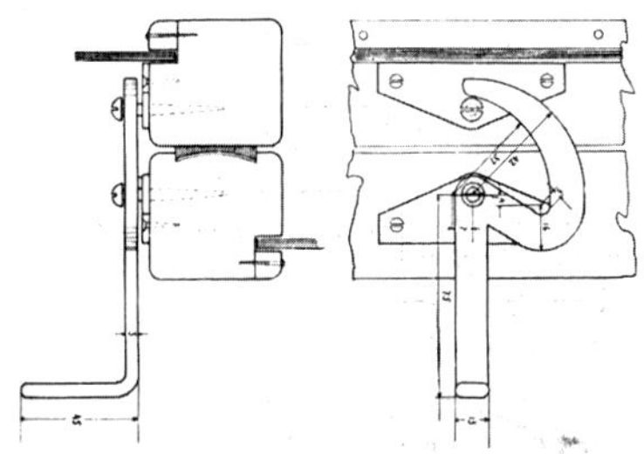

Window detail as published in *Žilišče*

Survey Drawings and Models

Housing of the Narkomfin

Surveyed in 1990 by A. D. Čegodaev and M. Ju. Merkulov

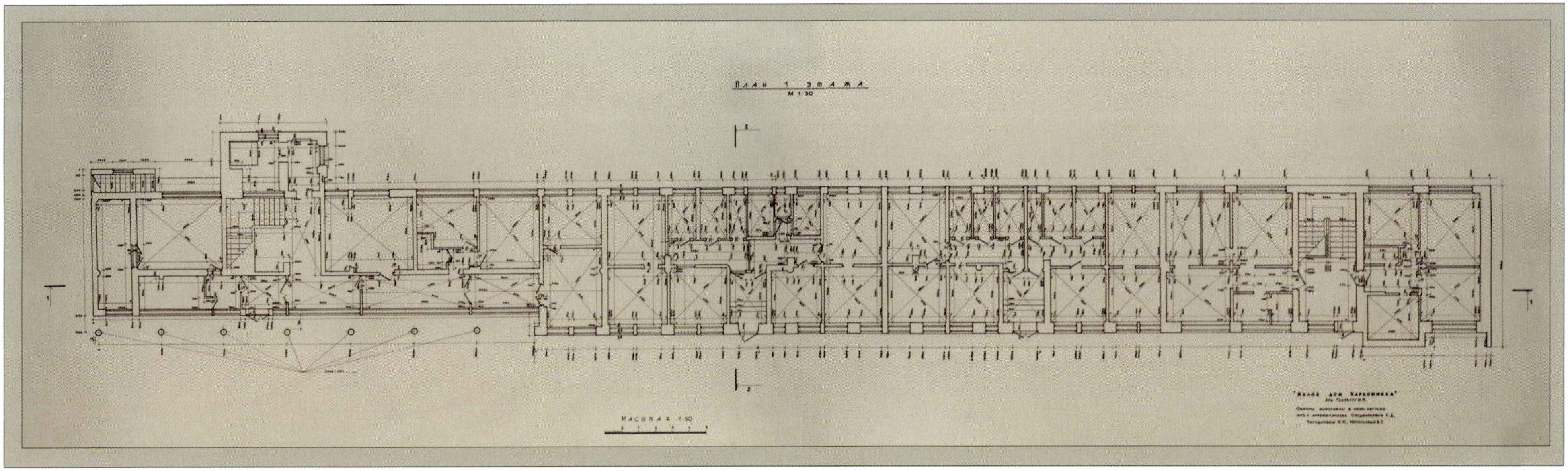

Present condition of the ground level, scale 1:350 by A. Studenikin, M. Čegodaev, A. Merkulov. 1990 (collected by the Ščusev State Museum of Architecture)

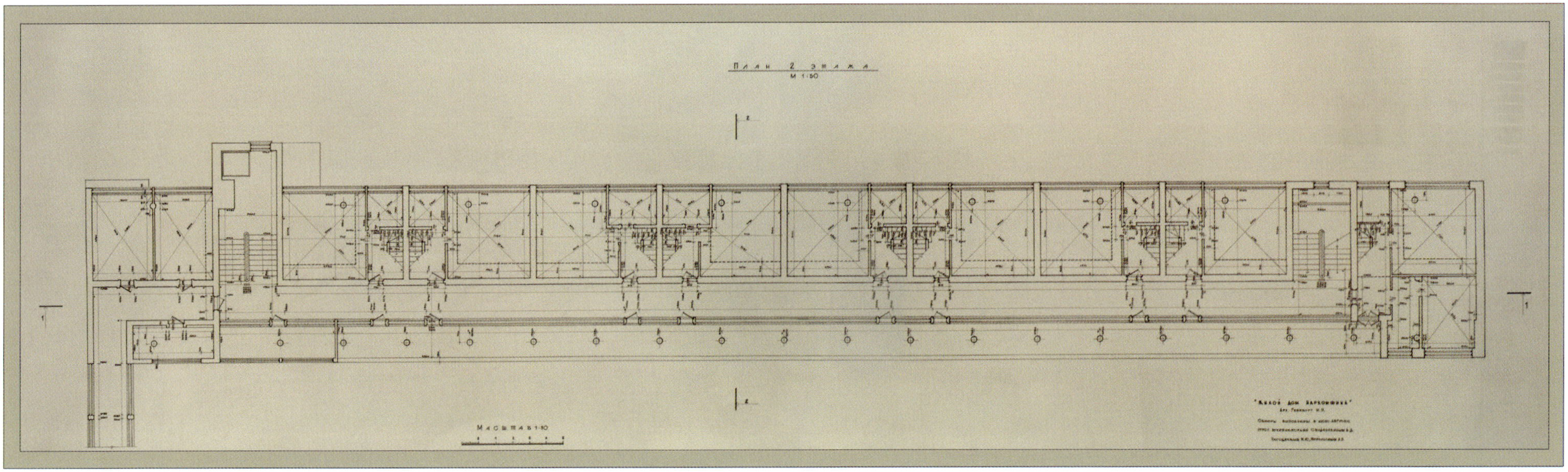

Plan of the second level, scale1:350 by A. Studenikin, M. Čegodaev, A. Merkulov. 1990 (collected by the Ščusev State Museum of Architecture)

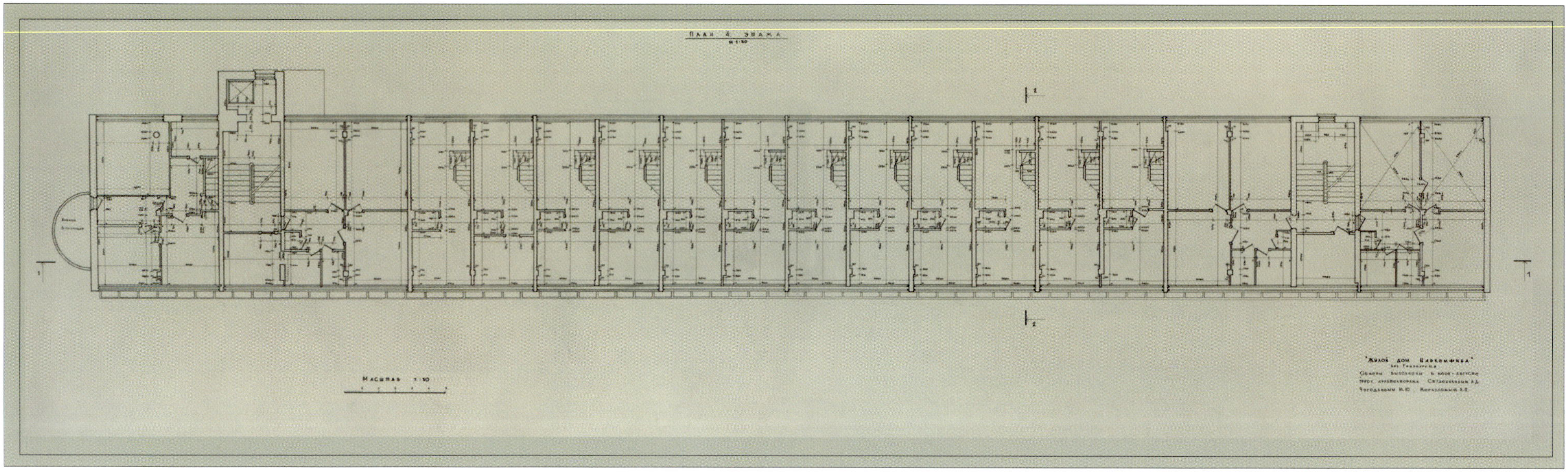

Plan of the third level, scale1:350 by A. Studenikin, M. Čegodaev, A. Merkulov. 1990 (collected by the Ščusev State Museum of Architecture)

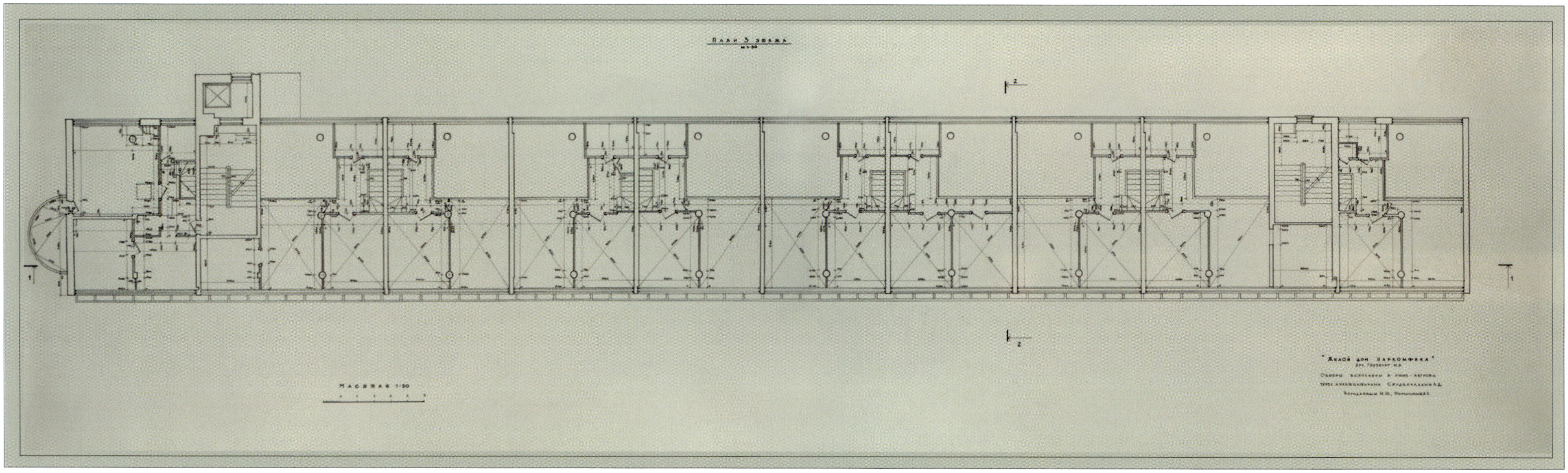

Plan of the fourth level, scale 1:350 by A. Studenikin, M. Čegodaev, A. Merkulov. 1990 (collected by the Ščusev State Museum of Architecture)

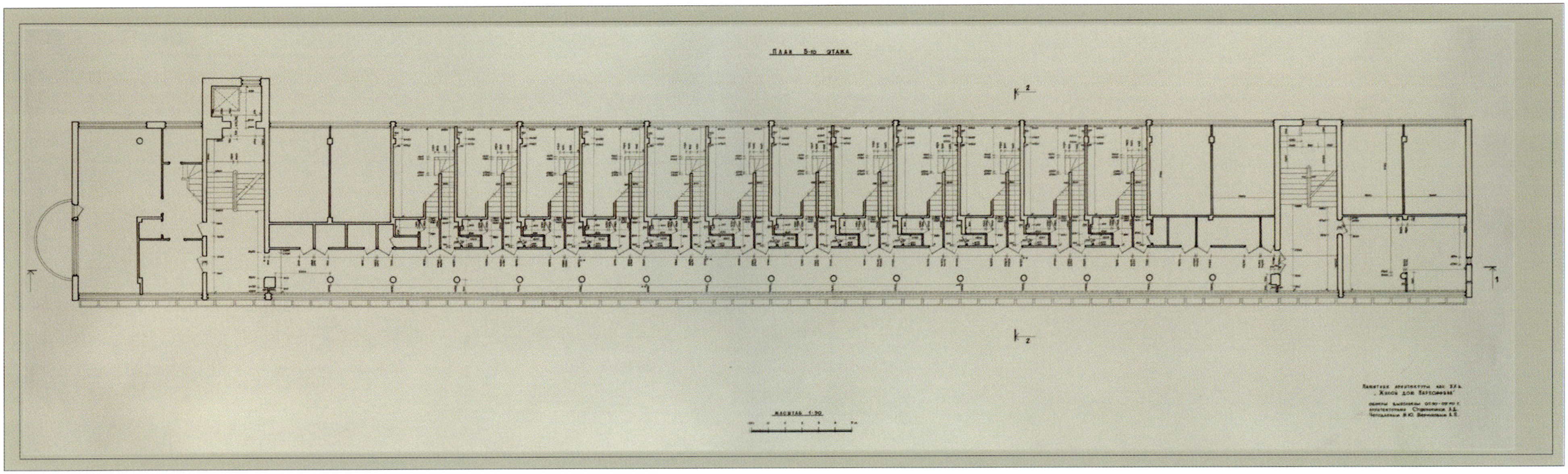

Plan of the fifth level, scale 1:350 by A. Studenikin, M. Čegodaev, A. Merkulov. 1990 (collected by the Ščusev State Museum of Architecture)

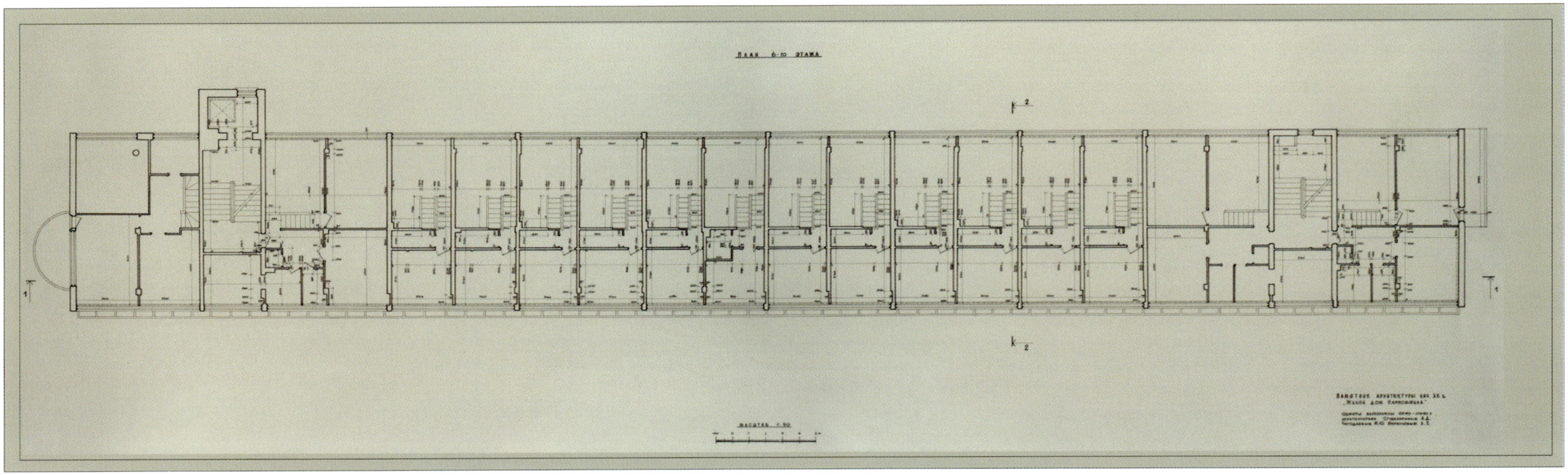

Plan of the sixth level, scale 1:350 by A. Studenikin, M. Čegodaev, A. Merkulov. 1990 (collected by the Ščusev State Museum of Architecture)

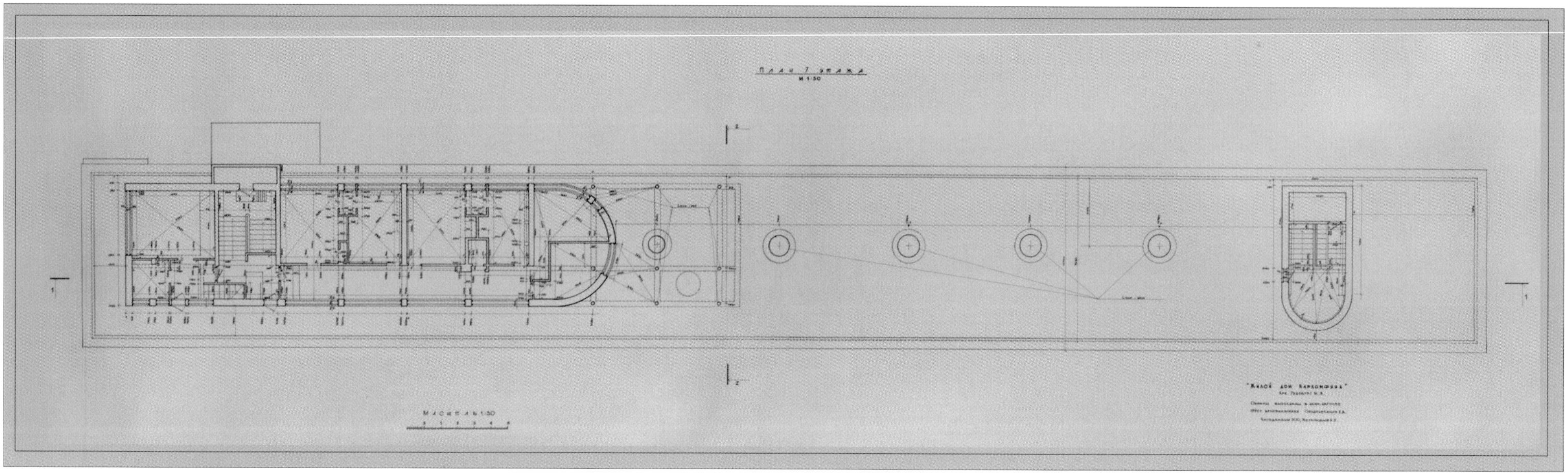

Plan of the seventh floor, scale 1:350 by A. Studenikin, M. Čegodaev, A. Merkulov. 1990 (collected by the Ščusev State Museum of Architecture)

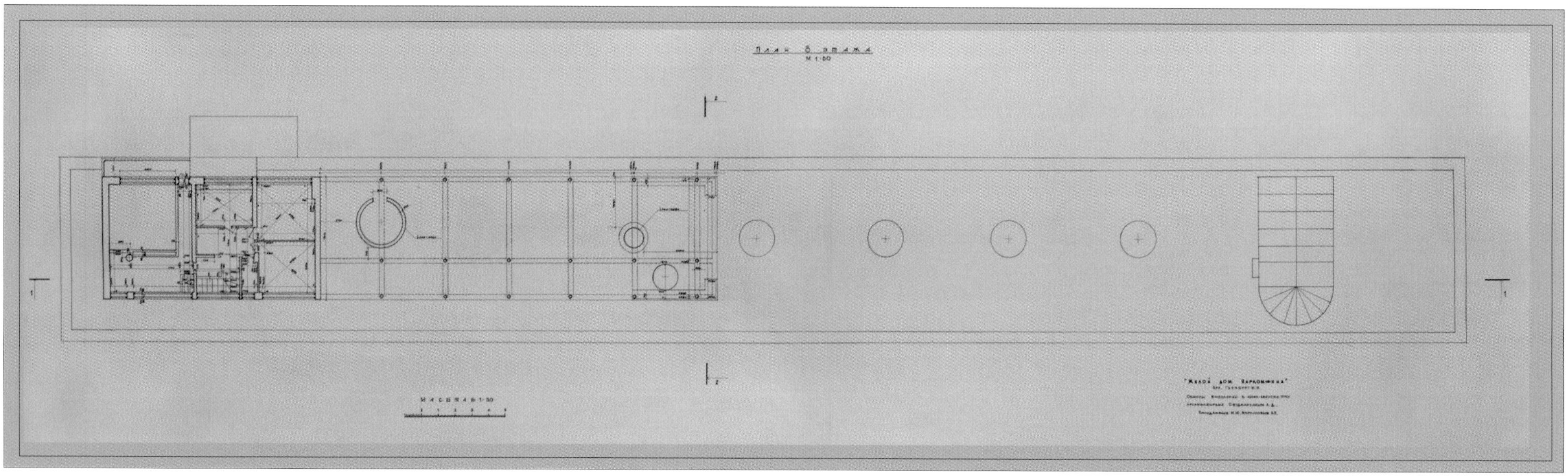

Plan of the eighth floor, scale 1:350 by A. Studenikin, M. Čegodaev, A. Merkulov. 1990 (collected by the Ščusev State Museum of Architecture)

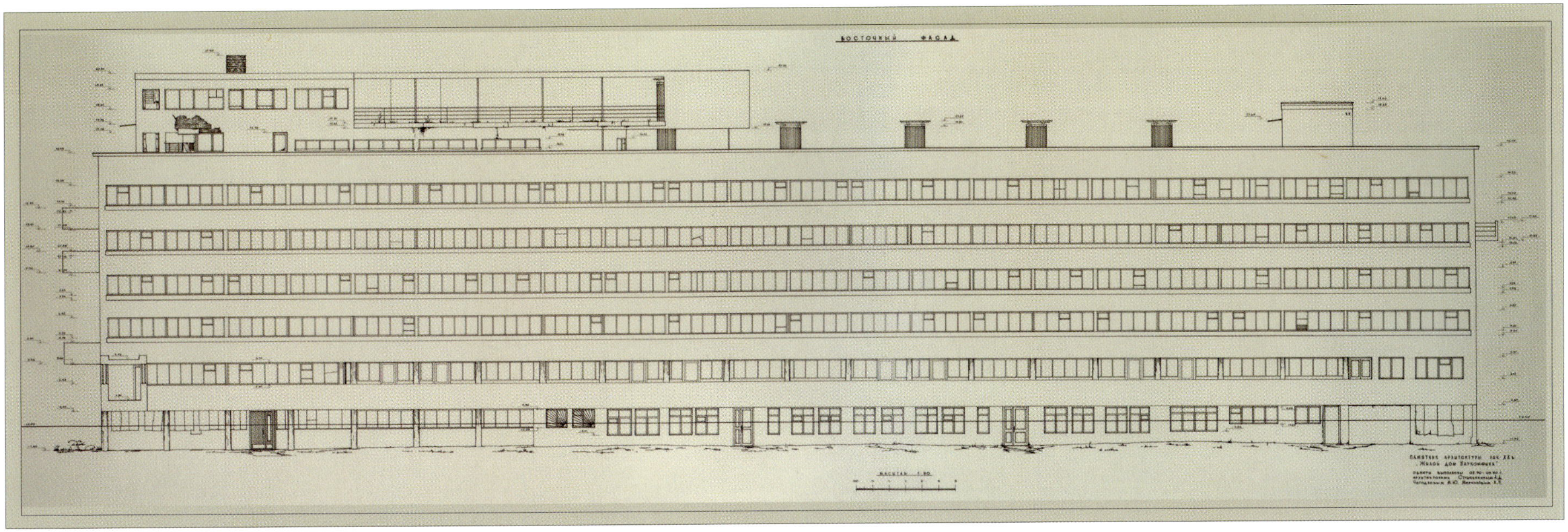

Eastern façade, scale 1:350 by A. Studenikin, M. Čegodaev, A. Merkulov. 1990 (collected by the Ščusev State Museum of Architecture)

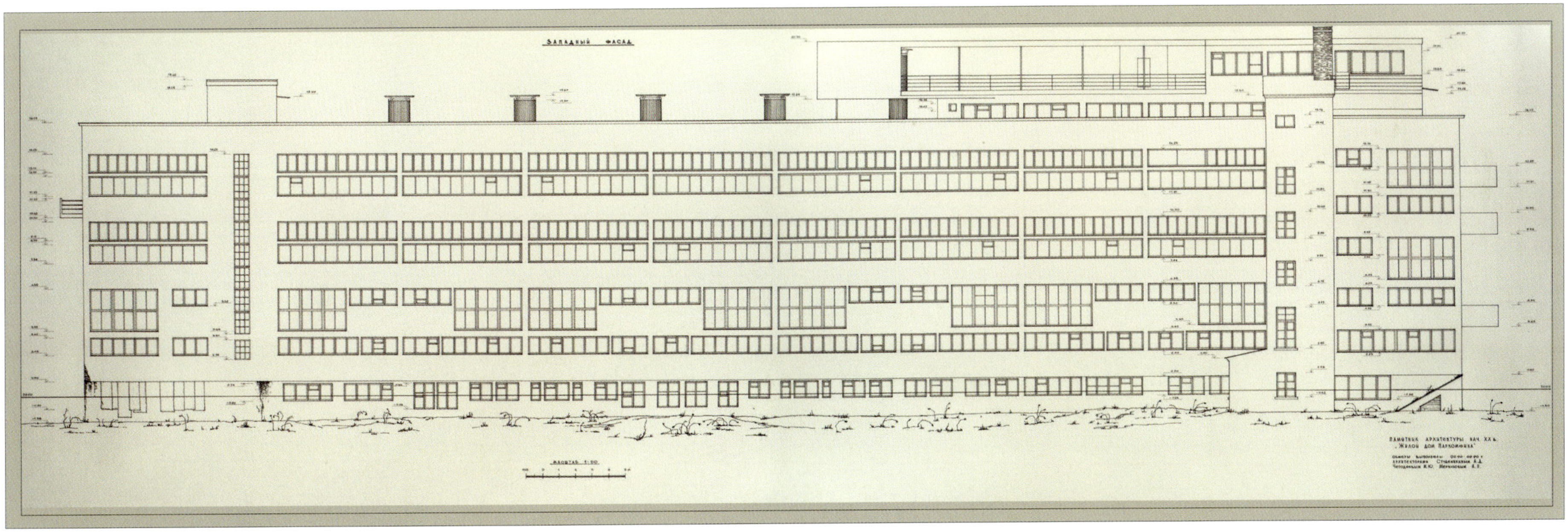

Western façade, scale 1:350 by A. Studenikin, M. Čegodaev, A. Merkulov. 1990 (collected by the Ščusev State Museum of Architecture)

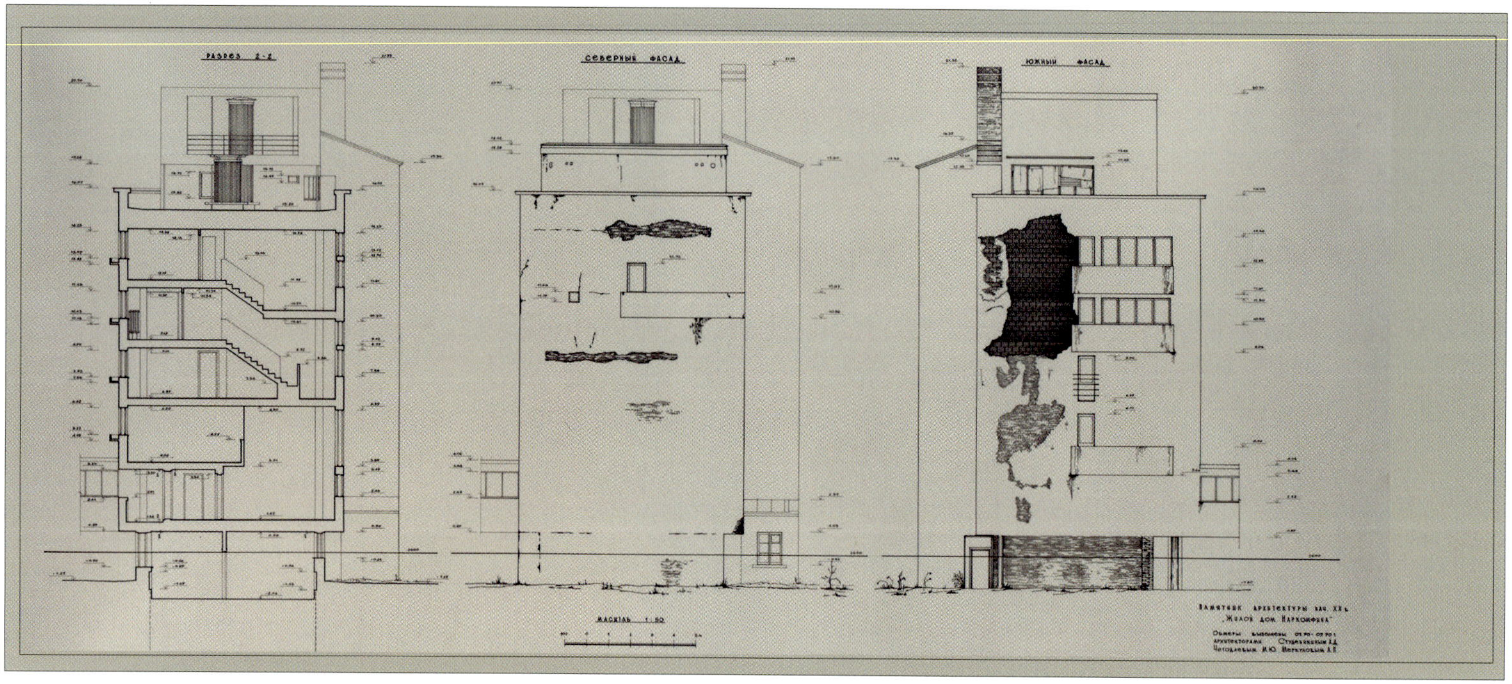

Section 2 - 2; North façade; Southern façade, scale 1:350 by A. Studenikin, M. Čegodaev, A. Merkulov. 1990 (collected by the Ščusev State Museum of Architecture)

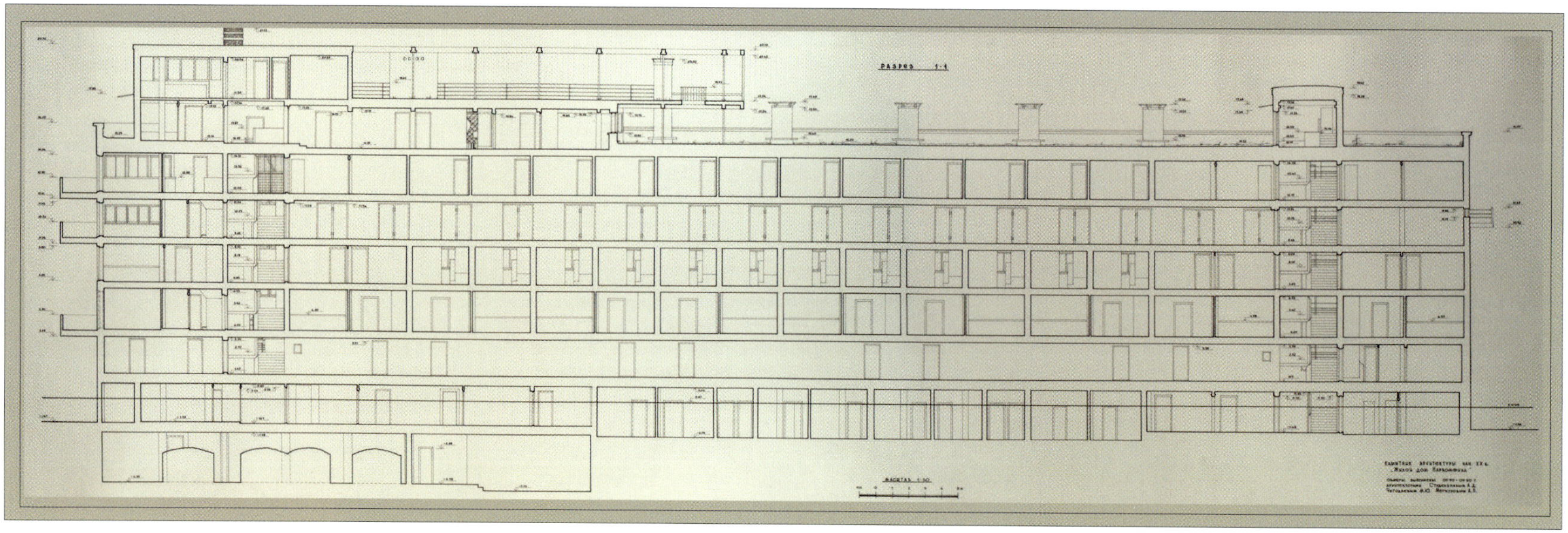

Section 1 - 1, scale 1:350 by A. Studenikin, M. Čegodaev, A. Merkulov. 1990 (collected by the Ščusev State Museum of Architecture)

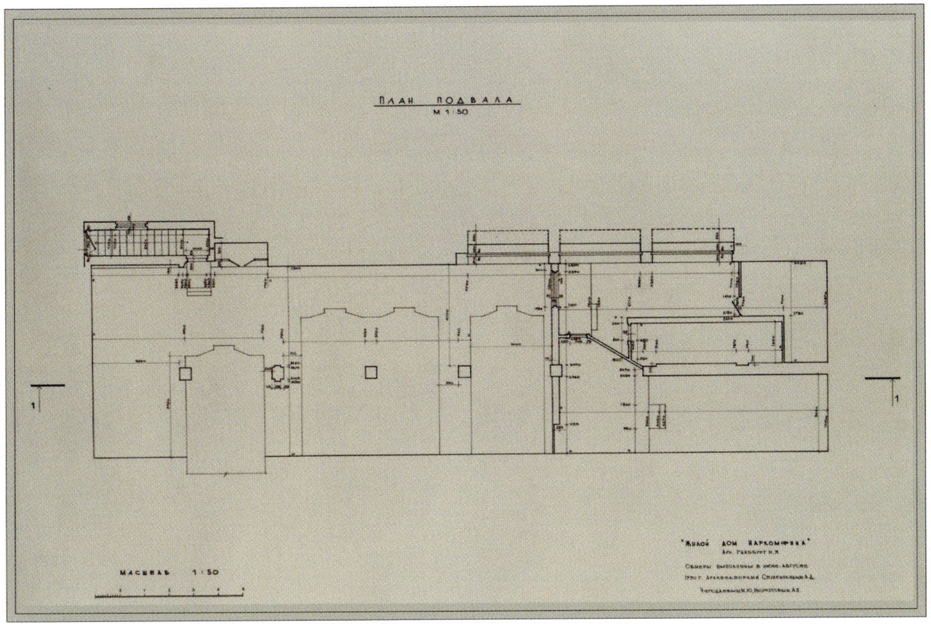

Plan of basement, scale 1:350 by A. Studenikin, M. Čegodaev,
A. Merkulov. 1990 (collected by the Ščusev State Museum of Architecture)

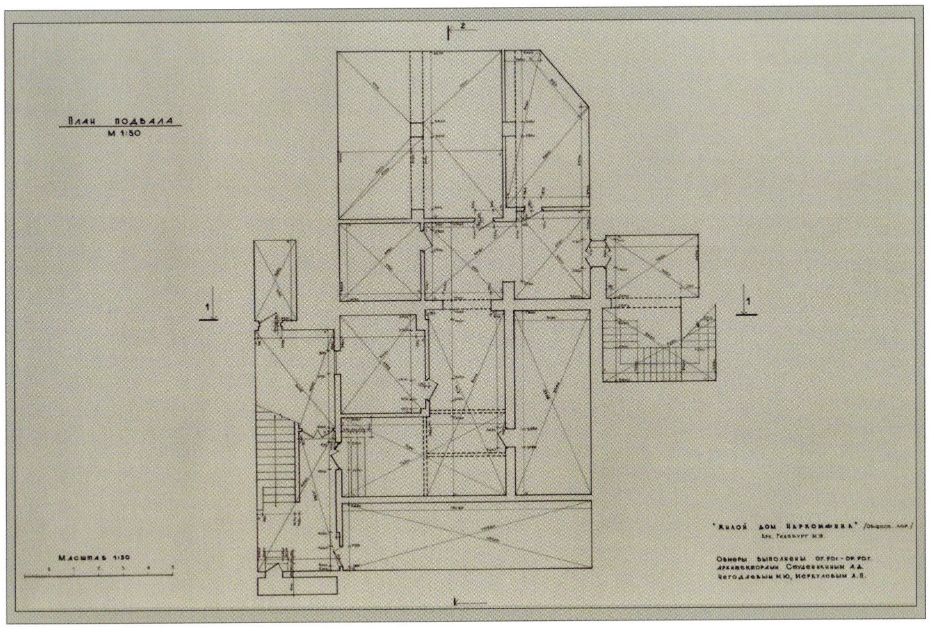

Plan of basement, scale 1:350 by A. Studenikin, M. Čegodaev,
A. Merkulov. 1990 (collected by the Ščusev State Museum of Architecture)

Plan of first floor of club (above ground), scale 1:350 by A. Studenikin, M.Čegodaev, A.Merkulov. 1990 (collected by the Ščusev State Museum of Architecture)

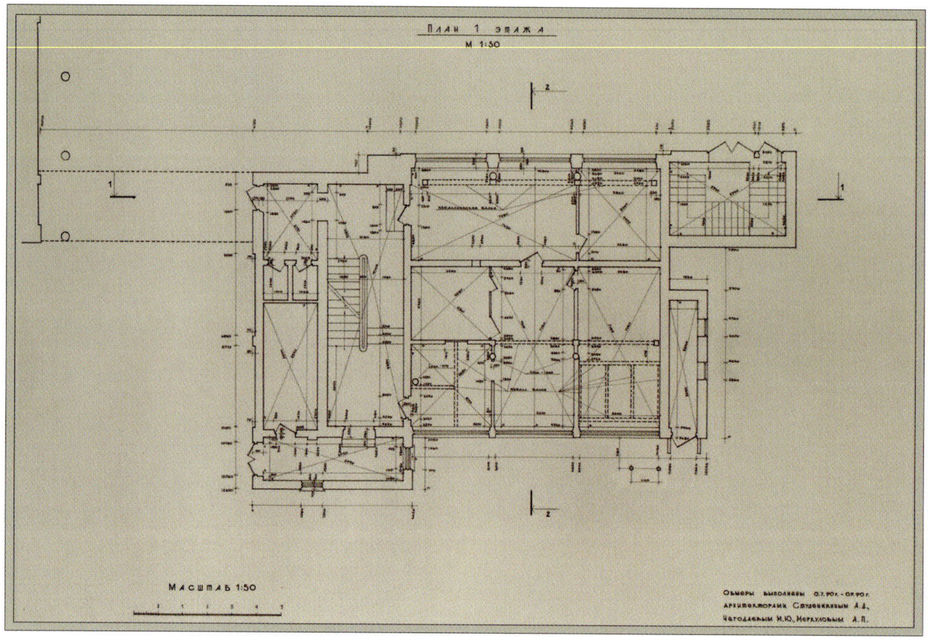

Plan of second and third floor of club, scale 1:350 by A. Studenikin, M. Čegodaev, A. Merkulov. 1990 (collected by the Ščusev State Museum of Architecture)

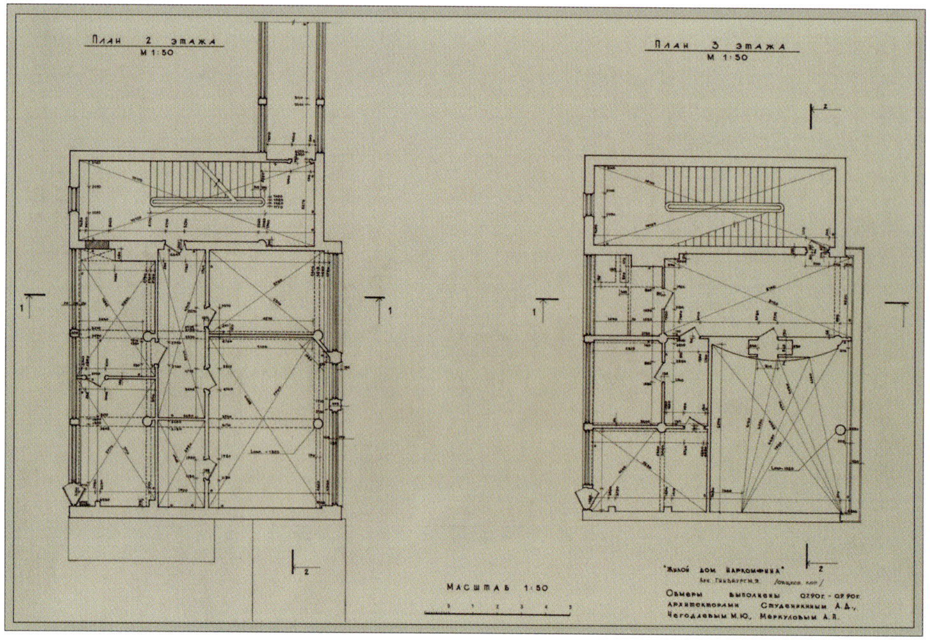

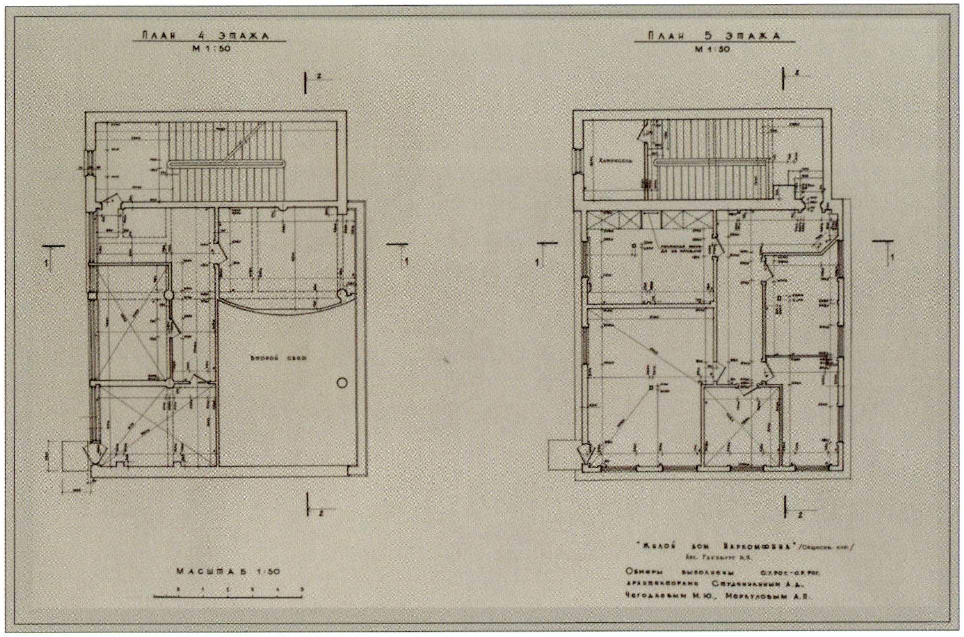

Fourth floor plan (annotation on the plan: "View below on second floor") and fifth floor of club, scale 1:350 by A. Studenikin, M. Čegodaev, A. Merkulov. 1990 (collected by the Ščusev State Museum of Architecture)

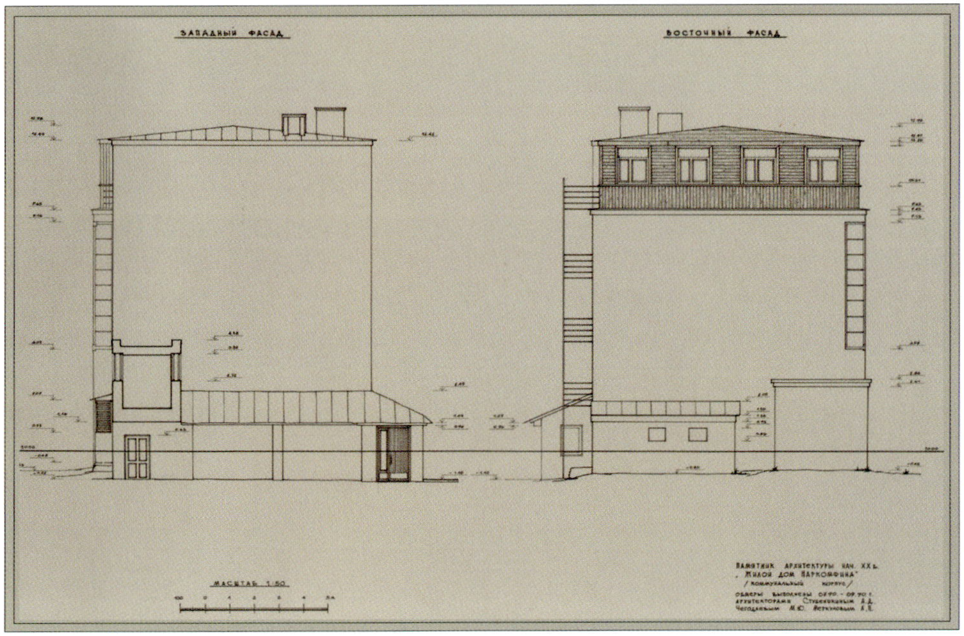

Western and eastern facade of club, scale 1:350 by A. Studenikin, M. Čegodaev, A. Merkulov. 1990 (collected by the Ščusev State Museum of Architecture)

South facade of club with bridge connection
Note: invading structures at ground floor and roof addition, scale 1:350 by A. Studenikin, M. Čegodaev, A. Merkulov. 1990 (collected by the Ščusev State Museum of Architecture)

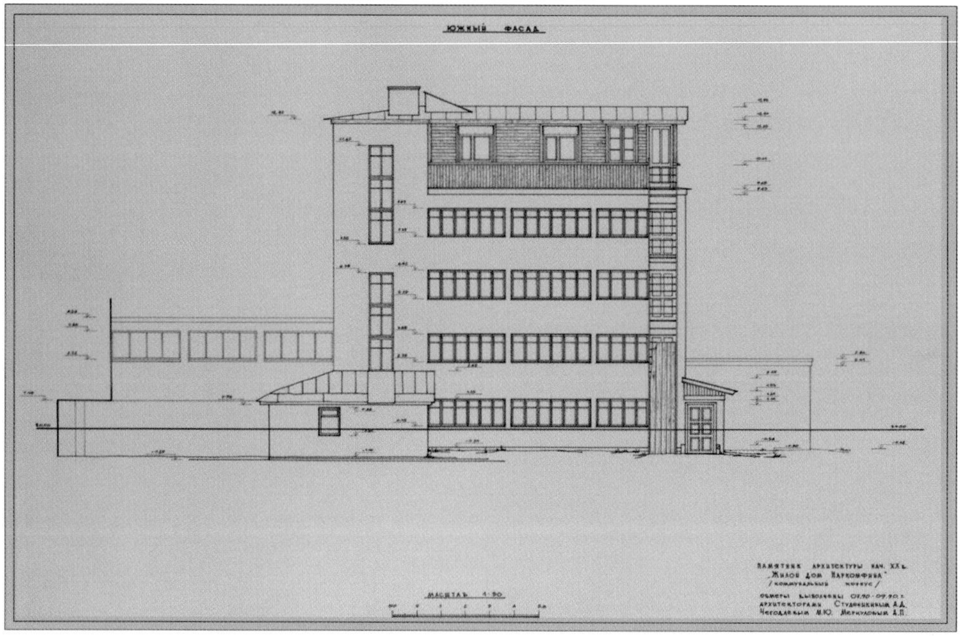

North façade, scale 1:350 by A. Studenikin, M. Čegodaev, A. Merkulov, 1990 (collected by the Ščusev State Museum of Architecture)

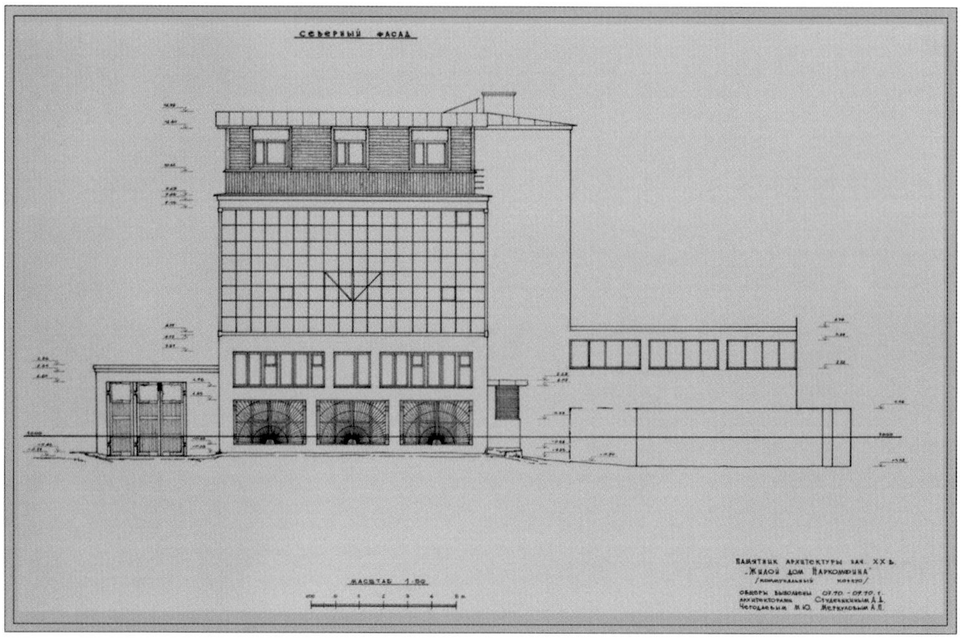

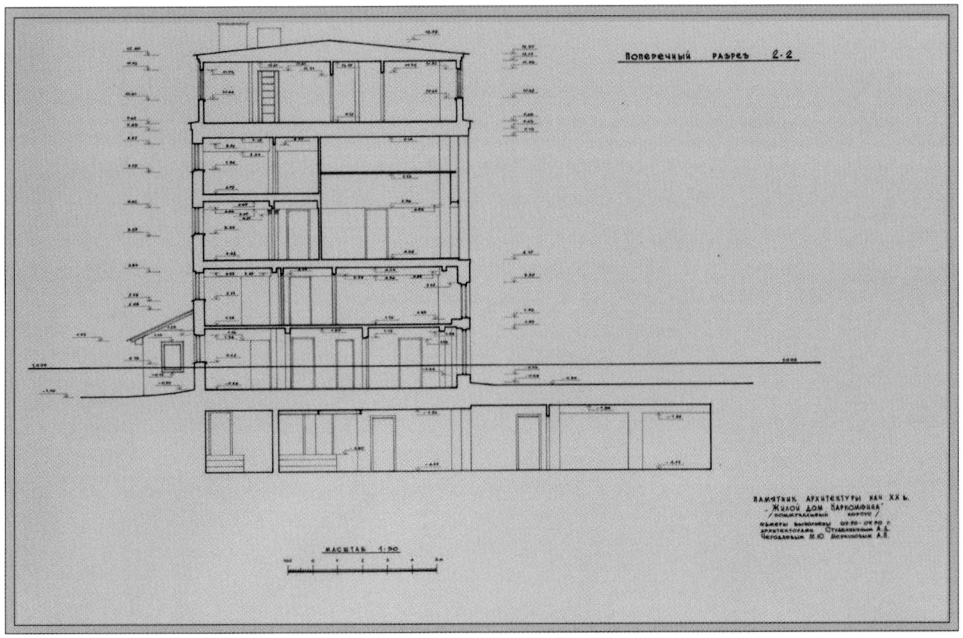

Transversal section 2 - 2, scale 1:350 by A. Studenikin, M. Čegodaev, A. Merkulov. 1990 (collected by the Ščusev State Museum of Architecture)

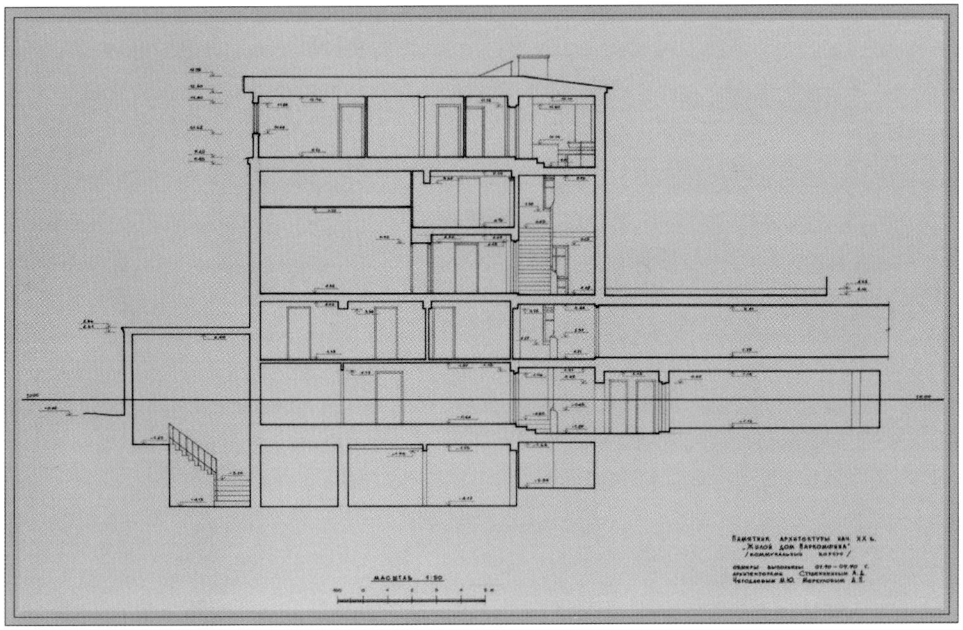

Longitudinal section 1 - 1, scale 1:350 by A. Studenikin, M. Čegodaev, A. Merkulov. 1990 (collected by the Ščusev State Museum of Architecture)

Narkomfin west façade model by Junusov N. A. 1988, Ščusev State Museum of Architecture

Interior of Roof penthouse. Drawing by Nikolaj Miljutin.

Historical Photographs

(collected by the Ščusev State Museum of Architecture)

Post war aerial view of the Narkomfin building and park. Ginzburg's building in first plan; perpendicular to the building by Leontovič instead of the second building Ginzburg had planned

General eastern view through the park. Photo by A. Alexandrov. 1963

South-west view. Top: Nikolaj Miljutin's penthouse. Each apartment opens on both east and west sides of the building for light and cross ventilation.Second and third floors with more spacious K type apartments.

North-east view with added balcony on North facade. Photo taken immediately after completion with trees Ginzburg insisted on preserving. Top south end, Miljutin's penthouse

Detail of east façade with Miljutin's penthouse on top

Center of building seen from the east. Ground floor, entrance to south stair. Photo taken immediately after completion with trees Ginzburg insisted on preserving

East façade seen from the roof garden of the club. Photo taken immediately after completion

View of typical corridor photographed by Aleksandr Rodčenko, 1930.

2011 condition

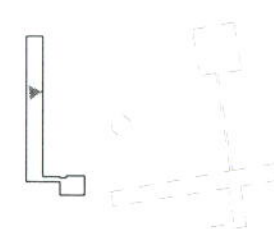

Roof garden

Interior view of club

View of west façade with north interior stair

Interior view of club

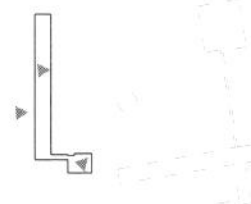

Narkomfin second floor hallway, photo by V. Griuntal. 1930

Bridge connecting main building to club, south end

View under the bridge, photos taken immediately after completion of building

The black pilotis at north entrance, photo taken immediately after completion

Apartment type K with mezzanine, photo by V. Griuntal, 1930

Interior mezzanine of the type K apartment Ginzburg used as studio

Lower type K level with mezzanine above

Internal stairs of Miljutin's penthouse

Miljutin's penthouse in the 1970s

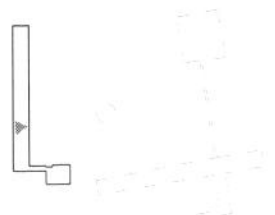

Dining room in Miljutin's penthouse in the 1970s

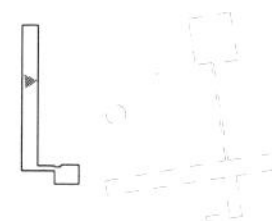

Interior of Miljutin's penthouse

The north façade of the club, photo by V. Griuntal, 1930

The club and connecting bridge, photo by V. Griuntal, 1930

East façade with view of open gallery on second floor taken from *Žilišče*

Perspective view of the northern facade of the communal wing of the Narkomfin House. Negative 13 ×18. Glass, B&W, re-filmed from the photo in the 1930s. Inventory # TH-18507

Main interior view of club, photo taken immediately after completion

Interior view of club, photo taken immediately after completion

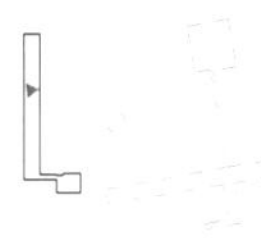

Sister building on Gogolevskij Bulevar, Moscow, seen from courtyard

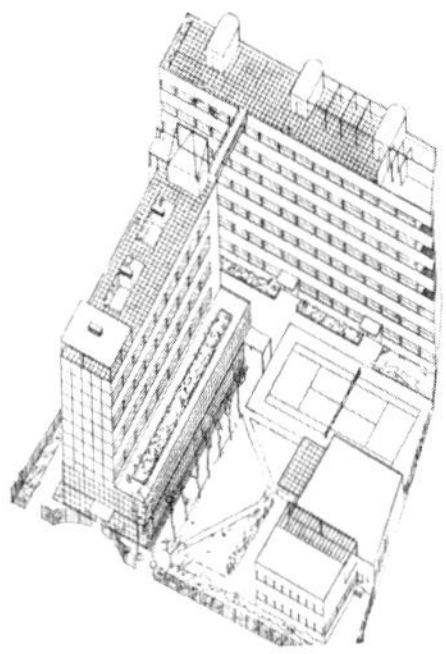

Sister building on Gogolevskij Bulevar, Moscow, seen from street

Lisagor's F-type apartment seen from upper level in the building of Gogolevskij boulevar 8, Moscow. Photo before his arrest in 1937. Source: Lisagor's memorabilia saved by a friend

Lisagor's F-type apartment in the Gogolevskij boulevar building. Photo before his arrest in 1937. Source: Lisagor's memorabilia saved by a friend

Lisagor's F-type apartment upper level with kitchen and an added bed. Photo before his arrest. Source: Lisagor's memorabilia saved by a friend

Lisagor's Gogolevskij boulevard F-type apartment upper level with desk

Lisagor's Gogolevskij boulevard F type apartment upper level with bathroom

Photographs 2002–2011

Eastern façade seen through the park after pilotis space was filled with additional, conventional apartments after the war, photo 2005. Photo: Udovički

View of the east side façade looking north, photo 2008. Photo: Udovički

View of the north end of the building with a Stalinian apartment skyscraper built in the 1940s, photo 2005. Photo: Udovički

The Narkomfin building next to the skyscraper built in the 1940s. Photo: Udovički

East façade 2008. Photo: Udovički

East façade, 2008 condition. Photo: Udovički

North-east façade 2011. Photo: Udovički

Fragments of east façade, 2011. Photos: Udovički

East façade, 2002 condition. Photo: Udovički

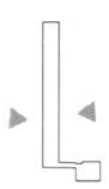

East façade, 2011 condition. Photo: Udovički

2011 condition. Photo: Udovički

2011 condition. Photos: Udovički

Connecting bridge between the apatment building and the club, 2002 condition.
Photo: Udovički

2008 condition

Bridge and apartment building, seen from the south, 2008 condition

Decaying of the Building

South façade, 2002 condition. Photo: Udovički

Photo: Udovički

2011 progression of decay of the south façade. Photos: Udovički

2011 south-east corner. Photos: Udovički

2011 window sill

2011 semi-circular balcony

2011 condition, immured pilotis, left. Right, second floor balcony along the inner hallway. Photos: Udovički

2008 condition. Photos: Udovički

2011 condition. Photos: Udovički

2011, connection between club and apartment building. Photo: Udovički

2011 condition, north façade with single balcony. Photo: Udovički

2011 condition. Photo: Udovički

2011, north façade with single balcony. Photo: Udovički

2011 condition, second floor hallway. Photo: Udovički

2011 condition, south wall. Photo: Udovički

Type F, internal stair leading to upper level and door open to the hallway. Photo: Udovički

Main stairway at south end of building. Photo: Udovički

2008 Miljutin's apartment. Photo: Udovički

2008 Miljutin's apartment. Photo: Udovički

2008 interior of the club. Photo: Udovički

Epilogue

The narrow swimming pool next to the American Embassy will be replaced with a 4-level underground parking garage for the use by the residents and business tenants and, possibly, by visitors to the nearby shopping center Novinskij. A large park with a four-lane swimming pool is planned in front of the building with an underground pedestrian tunnel to the shopping center. How realistic these proposals are remains to be seen. Possible obstacles include ineffective and corrupt bureaucracy as well as preservationists' objections based on Narkomfin's "architectural monument" status.

2015

The current state of the building provides a glimpse of hope. The roof of the building is now called Health Space with a café offering regular yoga sessions. A few successful businesses occupy the units on the top level: OOO Biletov, Med-Media, Soft Culture, Fuzzy Cheese and others. Anton Nossik has a renovated apartment in the building. "This is the first place in Moscow," he says, "where I enjoy coming to work and returning home. Ginzburg's crazy socialist utopia failed but the space he created is really magical. There is some irony in the fact that the communal lifestyle dreamed up by Constructivists was realized by capitalist Senatorov. We, residents and business tenants, actually form a vital community."

V. P.

Cafe "Holynoot" interior. Photo: Paperny

Cafe "Sinitsa" on the roof. Photo: Paperny

Yoga on the roof. Photo: Paperny

"Healthy Space" on the roof. Photo: Paperny

Yoga on the roof. Photo: Paperny

Yoga on the roof. Photo: Paperny

Med-Media office. Photo: Paperny

Selected Bibliography
Manuscripts

Agarov, P., *Vesma Poleznij Sputnik Každoj Hozjaik v Domašem Obihode*, 1909 č n.

Agienko, A., *Za Novyj Byt* Moscow: OGIZ-Moskovskij Rabočij, 1931.

Aleksandrov, E. A.(ed.), *Byt i Kultura*, Moscow: Moskovskij Rabočij, 1968.

Andreev, P., *Domovedenie*, Pantelevyh, 1893.

Anikst, Mikhail, *Stalinist Architecture: Alexeji Tarkhanov and Sergeji Kavtaradze*, London: King, 1992.

Architecture: The Search for New Solutions in the 1920s and 1930s, New York: Rizzoli, 1987.

Bahterev, M. & Razumovskij, *A., Kulturno-Bytovoe Tovariščestvo*, Moscow/Leningrad: Molodaja Gvardia, 1930.

Bann, Stephen, *The Tradition of Constructivism*, New York: Viking Press, 1974.

Barhin, G. B., *Sovremmenoe Rabočie Žilišče*, Moscow: NKT, "Voprosy Truda," 1925.

Boudon, Philippe, *Le Corbusier's Pessac Revisited*, Cambridge, MA, MIT Press, 1979.

Boym, Svetlana, *Common Places: Mythologies of Everyday Life in Russia*, Cambridge, MA: Harvard University Press, 1995.

Buchli, Victor, *The Material Culture Reader*, Oxford & New York: Berg, 2002.

Buchli, Victor, *The Narkomfin Communal House, Moscow : The Material Culture of Accommodation and Resistance,1930–1991*, Cambridge, UK: University of Cambridge, 1996.

Buck-Morss, Susan, *Dreamworld and Catastrophe*, Cambridge, MA: MIT Press, 2002.

Central Committee of the Communist Party (Bolsheviks) of Ukraine, *Kulturno Bytovaja Rabota Sredi Robotničii Krest'ianok*, Harkov: Knigospilka, 1929.

Čeredina, I.S., *Moskovskoe Žil'e Konca XIX–Srediny XX Veka*, Moscow: Arhitektura-S, 2004.

Conference Proceedings *Stalinistische Architektur Unter Denkmalschutz?*: Eine Tagung des Deutschen Nationalkomitees von ICOMOS und der Senatsverwaltung fur Stadtentwicklung und Umweltschutz in der Architektenkammer, Berlin: I COMOS, 1996.

Conquest, Robert, *The Great Terror: Stalin's Purge of the Thirties—A Reassessment*, Oxford: Oxford University Press 40th Anniversary edition, 2008. [First published 1968.]

Cooke, Catherine, *Russian Avant-Garde Theories of Art, Architecture and the City*, London: Academy Editions, 1995.

Cooke, Catherine, "The Town of Socialism," Ph.D. Thesis, University of Cambridge, 1974.

Das Narkomfin-Kommunehaus in Moskau (1928-2012), Petersberg: Imhof, 2013.

Dubniak, V. "Za Zdorovoe Žilišče" in *Za Zdorovyj Kul'turnyj: Zbornik Statei*, Moscow: Gosudarstvenoe Učebno-Pedagogičeskoe Izdatel'stvo, 1931. Cambridge, MA: MIT Press, 2002.

Dunham, Vera, *In Stalin's Time: Middle Class Values in Soviet Fiction*, (Introduction Richard Sheldon). First published Cambridge University

Press 1976. [Revised and expanded: Duke University Press, 1990].

Engels, Friedrich, *The Origin of the Family, private Property and the State*, New York: Pathfinder Press, 1972.

Fitzpatrick, Sheila,"The Civil War as a Formative Experience" in Abbot Gleason & Peter Kenez (eds.) *Boshevik Culture*, Bloomington: Indiana University Press., 1985.

Fitzpatrick, Sheila, *The Russian Revolution: 1917–1932*, Oxford: Oxford University Press, 1982.

Ginzburg, M., "Revolutsia i Kultura," quoted in Anatole Kopp, *Architecture et Mode de Vie*, Grenoble: Presses Universitaires, 1979.

Ginzburg, M. Ja, *Arhitektura Sanatorija NKTP V Kislovodske*, Moscow: Izd. Akademii Arhitektury SSSR, 1940.

Ginzburg, Moisei, *Style and Epoch*, Cambridge, MA: MIT Press, 1982 [First Published in Moscow 1924.]

Ginzburg, Moisej, *Žilišče: Opyt pjatiletnej raboty nad problemoj žilišča*, Moscow: Gosstroizdat,1934

Goldman, Wendy, *Women, the State and Revolution*, Cambridge: Cambridge University Press, 1993.

Gradov, G. A. *Gorod i Byt,* Moscow: Literatury po Stroitel'stvu, 1930.

Groys, Boris, *The Total Art of Stalinism: Avant-garde, Aesthetic Dictatorship, and Beyond* [translated by Charles Rougle], Princeton, N.J.: Princeton University Press, 1992.

Han-Magomedov, S. O., *M. Ja. Ginzburg*, Moscow: Literaturi po Stroitel'stvu, 1972.

Han-Magomedov, S. O., "Mihail Ohitovič–Tvorcy Avangarda, Moscow: Fond "Ruskij Avangard," 2009.

Han-Magomedov, S.O., *Moisej Ginzburg*, [Prefazione di Vieri Quilici], Second edition, Milano: Franco Angeli, 1983.

Han-Magomedov, S.O., *Nikolaj Ladovskij—Tvorcy Avangarda*, Moscow: Arhitektura, 2004.

Hazard, Jonathan, *Soviet Housing Law*, New Haven: Yale University Press, 1993.

Heller, Mikhail, & Nekrich, Aleksandr H., *Utopia in Power*, New York: Summit Books, 1986.

Henderson, Susan R., "A revolution in the Women's Sphere: Grete Lihotzky and the Frankfurt Kitchen" in D. Colman, Elizabeth Danze and Carol Henderson (eds), *Architecture and Feminism*, Princeton, NJ: Princeton University Press, 1996.

Higer, R. Ja, *Proektovanie Žilišče*, Moscow: OKTI 1935.

Hillier, W & Hanson, J., *The Social Logic of Space*, Cambridge: Cambridge University Press, 1984.

Holmgren, Beth, *Women's Work in Stalin's Time*, Bloomington: Indiana University Press, 1994.

Hudson, Hugh D., *Blueprints and Blood: The Stalinization of Soviet Architecture 1917–1937*, Princeton, N.J. :Princeton University Press, 1994.

Khan-Magomedov, S.O., *Pioneers of Soviet ARchitecture*, London: Academy Editions, 1983.

Khazanova, Vidgaria, *Sovetska Arhitektura Pervoji Piatiletki: Problemi Goroda Buduščego*, Moscow: Nauka 1980.

Kiaer, Christina, *Imagine No Possessions: The Socialist Objects of Russian Constructivism*, Cambridge, MA: MIT Press, 2005.

Kisel'nikova, N.V., "'Suščnost' i Istoričeskie Osobenosti Meščanskoj Morali," Kandidat' Nauky [PhD] Moscow: Lomonosov State University, Faculty of Philosophy, 1985.

Kostov, T. *Kultura i Meščanstvo* Moscow: Molodaja Gvardija, 1930.

Kotkin, Stephen, "Shelter and Subjectivity in the Stalin Period" in William Brumfield & Blair Ruble (eds), *Russian Housing in the Modern Age*, Cambridge: Cambridge University Press and Woodrow Wilson Center Press, 1995.

Kožanyj, P. *Rabočoe, Žilišče i Byt*, Moscow: Izdatel'stvo V.C.S.P.S., 1924.

Kožanyj, P. and Pyžova, N. eds. *Kak Stroit' Novyj Byt*, Moscow: Voprosy Truda, 1925.

Krugljakov, Ju. *Rekonstrukcija Žilnyh Kvartalov*, Leningrad & Moscow: Gos. Izd. Standardizacija i Racionalizacija, 1933.

Krupskaja, Nadežda, *O Bytovyh Voprosah* Moscow: & Leningrad: Gosudarstvennoe Izdatel'stvo, 1930.

Kurella, A. *Krasivaja Žizn'*, Moscow: Molodaja Gvardija, 1930.

Larin, Ju. and Belusov, B."Perspektivy Razvitija Žiliščnoj Kooperacii" in Ju. Larin & Belousov, *Za Novoe Žilišče*, Moscow: Izdanie Centrožilsojuza, 1930.

Le Corbusier, *La Ville Radieuse*, Paris: Editions de a Ville, 1935.

Lodder, Christina, *Russian Constructivism*, New Haven: Yale University Press, 1983.

Meissner, T., Schäfer, B., Straße, C., *Zusammenfassung der Ergebnisse zur Bauaufnahme am Narkomfin-Haus*, August 2009.

Miliutin, Nikolai, *Sotsgorod*, Cambridge, MA: MIT Press, 1972.

Miliutin, Nikolai, *Sotsgorod*, Cambridge USA, 1974, Basel 1992.

Miljutin, N. A., *Problema Stroitel'stva Socialističeskyh Gorodov. Osnovnye Voprosy racional'noj Planirovki i Stroitel'stva*. Moscow, 1930.

Milutina, Katja, Moja Žizn' v "NARKOM FIN-e" Unpublished Manuscript, 2012.

Miljutina, Katja, "My Naš, My Novij Mir Postroim" Unpublished Manuscript, 2011.

Miller, Daniel, *Modernity: An Ethnographic Approach*, Oxford: Berg, 1994.

Moore, Henrietta, *Space, Text and Gender*, Cambridge: Cambridge University Press., 1986.

Nikiforov, N. *Protiv Starogo Byta*, Moscow: Moskovskij Rabočij, 1929.

Organovič, M. *Za Novyj Byt*, Moscow: & Leningrad: Molodaia Gvardija, 1928.

Osipovič, M. *Za Socialističeskuju Perestrojku Byta*, Moscow: Sovetskoe Zakonodatel'stvo, 1929.

Osipovič, M., *Za Socialističeskuju Perestrojku Byta*, Moscow: Sovetskoe Zakonodatel'stvo, 1931.

Parker-Pearson, Michael & Richards, *An Architecture and Order: Approaches to Social Space*, London: Rutledge, 1994.

Pasini, Ernesto, *La "Casa-comune" e il Narkomfin di Ginzburg*, Rome: Officina, 1980.

Powel, Kenneth, Catherine Cooke and Justin Ageros, *The Avant-garde: Russian Architecture in the Twenties*, London: Academy Editions, 1991.

Rappaport, Amos, *House Form and Culture*, Englewood Cliffs, NJ: Prentice-Hall, 1982.

Ricœur, Paul, *A Ricœur Reader: Reflection and Imagination.* Mario J. Valdes, New York: Harvester Wheatsheaf, 1991.

Rodčenko, A. *Domovodstvo, Vypusk 1, Kak Pravil'no Vesti Svoi Dom* Moscow: Glavpolitprosvet, 1928.

Rykvert, Joseph, *On Adam's House in Paradise,* Cambridge, MA: MIT Press, 1989.

Samson, Ross, "Introduction" in Ross Samson (ed.) *The Social Archeology of Houses*, Edinburgh: Edinburgh University Press, 1990.

Schapiro, L. *The Communist Party of the Soviet Union*, New York: Vintage Books, 1971.

Sedov, Vladimir, *Dom NARKOMFIN-a:Esej o Značenii odnoj Postrojki* [V., The House of Narkomfin: An Essay on the Importance of a Building], Mu-Ar, Moscow, 2008.

Semško, N.A. *O Svetlom i Temnom v Rabočem Bytu*, Moscow: Central'nij Institut Sanitarnogo Prosveščenija Narkomzdrava SSSR, 1929.

Senkevitch, Anatole, "Trends in Soviet Architectural Thought: The Growth and Decline of the Constructivist and Rationalist Movements," Ph.D. Thesis—Cornell University, June 1974.

Shanks, Michael and Tilley, Christopher, *Social Theory and Archeology*, Oxford: Polity Press, 1987.

Sheftel', S. *V Bytovoj Pohod*, Moscow: Izdatel'stvo 'Vlast' Sovetov' Pri Prezidiume VCIK, 1931.

Shtein, Viktor, *Za Novyj Byt!* Leningrad: Izdatel'stvo Krasnaja Gazeta, 1929.

Smidovič, S. *Rabotnica i Novyj Byt*, Moscow & Leningrad: Gosudarstvennoe Izdatel'stvo, 1927.

Sorokin, A. & Markovič, I. *Socialističeskaja Perestroika Byta i Zadači Rabočej Bytovoj Kommuny*, Moscow & Leningrad: Molodaja Gvardija, 1931.

Stites, Richard, *Revolutionary Dreams: Experimental Life in the Russian Revlution*, Oxford University Press, 1989.

STROJKOM, RSFSR, *Tipovye Proekty i Konstrukcii Žiliščnogo Stroitel'stva*, Moscow, 1930.

Tovariščestva, Moscow/Leningrad: Molodaja Gvardjia, 1934.

Travin, I., *Material'no-Veščnaja Sreda i Socialističeskij Obraz Žizni*, Leningrad: Nauka, 1979.

USSR 1917–1933: Architektuur, Stedebouw. Catalogue of an exhibition on Soviet architecture and town planning held at the Delft Technical High School, 1969–1970. [Delft, 1969].

Vernin, Brigade E. et al., *Doma-Kommuny: Materialy Konkursov*, Leningrad: N. T. O.

Viola, Lynn, *The Best Sons of the Fatherland: The Workers in the Vanguard of Soviet Collectivisation*, Oxford, 1987.

Vladimirskij, A. & Šeftel', C. *Kulturno-Bytovaja Rabota v Domah*, ed N. Semaško, Moscow: Mosoblispolkom, 1931.

Woof, Elizabeth, *The Baba and the Comrade: Gender and Politics in Revolutionary Russia*, Bloomington & Indianapolis: Indiana University Press, 1997.

Zalivako, Anke & Cramer Johannes, *Das Narkomfin/ kommune-Haus in Moskau (1928–2012)*, Petersberg: Imhof, 2013.

Zarina, M.M. *Domovodstvo*, Moscow & Lenigrad: Gsudarstvenoe Izdatel'stvo, 1928.

Žižek, Slavoj, *In Defense of Lost Causes*, London: Verso, 2008.

Žižek, Slavoj & Costas Douzinas (eds.), *The Idea of Communism*, London: Verso, 2010.

Selected Bibliography
Essays

Abelsky, Paul "Moscow May Breathe New Life into the Crumbling Narkomfin Landmark," in *Architectural Record*, 195. 4 (Apr 2007): 36.

Bliznakov, Milka, "Soviet 'Housing During the Experimental Years : 1918-1933 '' in *Russian Housing in the Modern Age*, ed. William Brumefield et al., Cambridge University Press & Woodrow Wilson, 1993.

Buchli, Victor, "Moisei Ginzburg's Narkomfin Communal House in Moscow: Contesting the Social and Material World," in *Journal of the Society of Architectural Historians*, 57, 2 (Jun 1998): 160–181, 241.

Cecil, Clementine, "Modern History: Stalinist Zeal and Post-communist Corruption Have Left Some of Moscow's Finest Architecture in a State of Ruin," in *Blueprint* (London, England) 230 (May 2005): 76–77, 79–82.

Gregory, Rob, "Outrage: State Modern?," in *Architectural Review*, 217. 1299 (May 2005): 34.

V. G. Gruntal, "Russia, 1929, Edificio d'appartamenti del commissariato del popolo per la finanza (Narkomfin) (1928-30), Mosca, Russia. Architetti: M Ginzburg, I. Milinis. Dopo il 1930," in *Casabella* vol. 66, no. 703, Sep 2002: 95.

Kokkinaki, Irina, Rezvin, Vladimir, "Campaign for Narkomfin: 1928–1930, Prototype of Communal Housing in Moscow Threatened by Total Deterioration," in *Newsletter (International Working-Party for Documentation and Conservation of Buildings, Sites and Neighborhoods of the Modern Movement)* 6 (Nov 1991): 60–67.

"NARKOMFIN: Un logement social 'experimental' à l'heure du Sovitétisme," Martel Labrecque, Francis, in *Architecture Québec* 149 (Nov 2009): 6–9.

Sainz, Jorge "Moiséi Ginzburg: Edifición Narkomfin, Moscú, 1928–1930" *AV Monographs*, 56 (Nov 1995): 36–37.

Sainz, Koktin, Stephen, ''Shelter and Subjectivity in the Stalin Period,'' in *Russian Housing in the Modern Age*, ed. William Brumefield et al., Cambridge University Press & Woodrow Wilson, 1993.

Viola, Lynne, "The Second Coming: Class Enemies in the Soviet Countryside, 1927–1935." in J. Arch Getty & Roberta Manning, (eds.) *PurgeStalinist Terror: New Perspectives*, Cambridge University Press, 1993.

Biographies

Dmitrij Chmelnizki

Dmitrij Chmelnizki, born in 1953 in Moscow, studied architecture at the Polytechnic Institute in Duschanbe and the Academy of Fine Arts in Leningrad. from 1979 to 1987 he was a practicing architect at various places in the Soviet Union before moving to Berlin in 1988, where he kept working as an architect. In 2003 he completed his Ph.D. at the Technical University in Berlin on the architecture of Stalin, "Ideology and Style." His research focuses on Soviet architecture, and as an artist he exhibits his paintings in Russia and Germany.

Danilo Udovički-Selb

Danilo Udovički-Selb is Associate Professor at the University of Texas at Austin School of Architecture, and holds a Ph.D. from MIT (History, Theory and Criticism of Architecture). In 2004 he was a Senior Fellow at CASVA (National Gallery of Art), and is currently Faculty Member of the Center for Russian, East-European and Eurasian Studies at UT Austin. In 2009 he was invited to join the Moscow Committee for the Defense of the VHUTEMAS Legacy. His most recent work on Soviet and French topics of the 1930s includes a monograph by the University of Norway at Trondheim; a contribution to the Fondation Le Corbusier; a contribution to the book dedicated to the Voyage en Orient Centenary; the first scholarly study on Charlotte Perriand, edited by Mary McLeod (Abrams); a contribution to a monograph dedicated to O. S. Han-Magomedov (Moscow: NIITAG); and numerous essays in international journals and exhibition catalogues (including the *London Journal of Contemporary History*; the *Journal of Architectural Historians*; the George Pompidou Center; DOCOMOMO publications; and the Canadian *Urban History Review*). He writes regular architectural criticism for the *Giornale dell'Architettura* in Torino, Italy.

Alla G. Vronskaya

Alla G. Vronskaya is a postdoctoral fellow at the Swiss Federal Institute of Technology (ETH) in Zurich, and was a research fellow at the Department of Classical Western Art at the State Institute of Art Studies in Moscow. Currently she holds a three-year teaching appointment at the ETH, Switzerland. She holds a Ph.D. in the history and theory of architecture from Massachusetts Institute of Technology and a Candidate of Sciences degree in art history from the State Institute of Art Studies. She has been a recipient of the Getty Research Institute pre-doctoral fellowship, Dumbarton Oaks junior fellowship, and the Swiss Government excellence scholarship, among other awards.

Tijana Vujošević

Born in Belgrade, Tijana Vujošević graduated as an architect from Yale University in 2002 and in 2010 completed her Ph.D. in history and theory of architecture at the Massachusetts Institute of Technology under the supervision of Mark Jarzombek. She is currently Assistant Professor of architecture at the University of Western Australia in Perth. Vujoševićć has written on contemporary Russian art, the Moscow Metro, 1930s Russian bathhouses, absurd aspects of sustainable design, and the role of French philosopher Jacques Rancière in architectural pedagogy. Her main interest is how architects of real and fictional environments imagine the protagonist of modern life. She is currently finishing the manuscript of her first book, *Utopia and Banality: Designing the Communist Self.*

Yury Volchok

Yury Volchok graduated at the Moscow Engineering and Construction Institute in1966 and at the Lomonosov Moscow State University in 1974, where he later earned his Doctorate in Architecture in 1978.

He is Professor at the MARHI (Moscow School of Architecture) in the History and Theory of Contemporary Architecture and Urban Planning Department. He is Head of the Science and Research Institute for the History and Theory of Contemporary Architecture, and the author and collector of over 150 studies on various topics of the 20th century and contemporary architecture issues. His areas of concentration include:

- Twentieth century architectural and urban planning history
- Architectonics of form making
- Preservation of the twentieth century's architectural heritage and identification of prospective urban improvement and form making trends. He is Supervisor and Curator of exhibitions, including scientific prototyping, and the work of Russian Avant-garde masters (K.S. Mel'nikov, I.I. Leonidov, M.Ja. Ginzburg, et al.) and their involvement in the everlasting dialogue between the architect and the city.

Vladimir Paperny

Vladimir Paperny received his MA in design from the Stroganov Art Academy in Moscow, and his Ph.D. in Cultural Studies from the Russian State University for the Humanities. His Ph.D. thesis "Architecture in the age of Stalin: Culture Two" was published in Russian (Moscow, 1996, 2006) and in English (Cambridge University Press, 2003, 2011). Since moving to the US in 1981, Dr. Paperny was visiting professor at USC, the Woodrow Wilson Center, and Bristol University, UK. He also worked as Art Director (*Orange Coast Magazine, The Workbook*). He is currently a visiting professor at UCLA. He also continues working at his design studio in Los Angeles. His articles, essays, and columns (in both English and Russian) appear in many such publications, including *Snob, Architectural Digest, Project Russia*, and *Speach*. His collections of essays include *Mos Angleles, Mos Angeles-2* (NLO, 2004, 2009) and "Fuck Context?" (TATLIN, 2011).

Photo and Drawing Credits

Danilo Udovički-Selb
Front cover, Pages 157, 158, 159, 160 (right), 161, 162, 163, 164 (left), 165, 167, 168, 169, 170, 171, 172, 173, 174

Courtesy Ščusev (Shchusev) State museum of Architecture, Moscow
Pages 18, 27 (bottom right) 48, 53, 54, 55, 56, 57 (upper), 59, 63, 65, 67, 68 (left), 69, 72, 117, 118, 119, 120, 121, 122, 123, 124, 125, 126, 127, 128, 129, 131, 132, 133, 134, 135, 136, 137, 140, 141, 142 (left), 148, 149 (right), 150, 151, 152 (top), 174

Vladimir Paperny
Pages 20, 23, 25 (right), 26, 30, 179, 180, 181, 182, 183

Ellena Ovsianikova, courtesy Katia Miljutina
Page 94 (left)

Aleksandr Senatorov
Pages 25 (center and right), 27 (upper left),

Courtesy Getty Research Institute
Pages 42, 44, 45, 46, 55, 99, 96, 97, 98

Cheng Jia
Cover design,
Pages 33, 34, 36

Guangji Liu
Pages 38, 39

Aleksej Narodskij
Pages 94 (right), 138 (right), 160 (left). 165 (right), 175, 176, 177

Wiki Architecture
Page 46

Sovremenaja Arhitektura
Pages 51, 59, 60, 63, 65, 66 (right), 71 (center and right top), 89

Stroitel'stvo Moskvy
Page 57 (lower)

Moisej Ginzburg, *Arhitektura Sanatorija: NKPTV v Kislovodske*, 1940
Pages 81, 90

Nikolaj Miljutin, *Socgorod*, 1931
Page 85

A. E. Levinson and I. I. Fomin, in *Arhitektura i Stroitel'stvo Leningradskogo Soveta*, Moscow: Gosizdat', 1940
Page 87

Courtesy Aleksej Ginzburg
Page 100

Courtesy Centre Canadien d'Architecture / Canadian Center for Architecture
Photos of Solomon Lisagor's apartment on Gogol'evskij Bulevar, probably taken by the architect himself.
Pages 153, 154, 155

M. Ginzburg *Žilišče*, 1934
Pages (upper) 85, 114, 115, 139, 143, 149 (left), 152 (drawing), bottom (right)

Courtesy Central Archive for the Scientific-Technical Documentation of the City of Moscow, fond 2, op, 1, t. 11, delo 10024

Aleksandr Rodčenko
Page 26 (first left), 143

Courtesy Ekaterina (Katia) Miljutina
Pages 28 (upper right), 144, 145, 146, 147

Vladimir Gruntal
Pages 140, 142 (right), 143, 148

A. Studenkin, A. D. Chegodaev and M. Ju. Merkulov
Pages 117 to 127

Nikolaj Miljutin, courtesy Katia Miljutina
Page 129

N. A. Junusov
Page 128

Unknown photographer
Pages 82, 83, 86

Courtesy Pavel Kuznetsov
Page 171 (bottom right)